J. F. A. de Le Roi

Die evangelische Christenheit und die Juden

Unter dem Gesichtspunkte der Mission geschichtlich betrachtet

J. F. A. de Le Roi

Die evangelische Christenheit und die Juden
Unter dem Gesichtspunkte der Mission geschichtlich betrachtet

ISBN/EAN: 9783743653771

Hergestellt in Europa, USA, Kanada, Australien, Japan

Cover: Foto ©Lupo / pixelio.de

Weitere Bücher finden Sie auf **www.hansebooks.com**

CONTENTS

OF THE SECOND VOLUME.

CHAPTER I.

BRIGHTON — 1851.

PAGE

Interest of Mr. Robertson in Social Questions. — Sermon preached in Mr. Drew's Church to Workingmen. — He is accused with Mr. Maurice and Professor Kingsley of Socialistic Opinions. — His Answer. — The "Record" Newspaper reasserts the Charge after his Death. — Letters of Mr. Maurice on the Subject. — Letters of Mr. Robertson on Professor Kingsley's Sermon. — Letter from Mr. Drew containing Extracts from Mr. Robertson's Letters on the same Subject. — Declining Health. — Lectures on the Epistles to the Corinthians. — Lecture to Workingmen at Hurstpierpoint. — Close of the year 1851 1

Letters from March 14, 1851, to December 5, 1851.

I. Ruskin's "Stones of Venice." — A clear Conception, or an infinite Feeling of Truths, which is best? 20
II. Changes in the Representation of the Virgin in Art. — The Virgin as Intercessor with the Father. — Analogous Idea in "Evangelicalism." — Truth at the Root of these Ideas. — Truth at the Root of Mariolatry. — Wrongs done to Women . 22
III. Ruskin. — The way to read much and well. — The System of Louis Blanc 24
IV. Warning to one entering London Life 26
V. To the same. — Excitement and its Correctives . . . 27
VI. Edwardes's "Punjaub." — "Why was John the most beloved?" — Desire for humbler, simpler Life . . . 29
VII. Fear of Imbecility. — Description of strange Symptoms . 31
VIII. Apologue à la Menenius on the essential difference between the Nature of Man and that of Woman 31
IX. Opening of the Great Exhibition 35
X. "Non-spirituality of the yearning for Death" . . . 36
XI. The Rest of the Future 37

XII.	Estimate of his own Ministry in the Pulpit	38
XIII.	Mode of looking at Dogmas. — The Opposition to his Teaching, and his Consolation	39
XIV.	Answer to the Question, "Is it wise to read both Sides of the Questions of Religious Truth?"	41
XV.	"The Progress of Society?"	44
XVI.	Visit from Mr. Maurice	45
XVII.	What Science, in its mode of viewing things, can and can not do	46
XVIII.	On the Book "The Law of Man's Nature"	48
XIX.	On the same	48
XX.	On an article on Carlyle	49
XXI.	"The Necessarian Scheme." — The Measure of the Spirituality of "Material Manifestations"	50
XXII.	Leigh Hunt. — Covent Garden Market. — Influence of Beauty on Love	52
XXIII.	Co-operative System	54
XXIV.	What am I, an Eclectic in Theology or not?	55
XXV.	Visits to the Poor. — Professor Kingsley's Sermon. — How to read the Bible	58
XXVI.	The Pulpit. — Political Preaching. — Preaching for Show	59
XXVII.	The possible work of Womanhood in the Future. — Tennyson's Vision of Sin. — Clerical Backbiting	61
XXVIII.	Justification by Faith	64
XXIX.	The Baptismal Controversy	66
XXX.	Luke xviii. 8. — Reading. — Kossuth	70
XXXI.	Daily Life and Reading. — Speculation and Faith	72
XXXII.	Love to Christ. — "If a man love not his brother whom he hath seen," &c.— Kossuth	73
XXXIII.	Attack by the "Record"	76
XXXIV.	Kossuth. — Transient Enthusiasm. — Policy of Non-intervention	76
XXXV.	Eternity and Time. — Review of "In Memoriam"	78
XXXVI.	Devout Feeling and Morality. — Socrates. — Hartley Coleridge. — " Binding and loosing Sin."	81

CHAPTER II.

1852.

Feelings and Interests of Mr. Robertson in January, 1852. — His Pleasure in Ornithology. — His resolute Work. — Character of his Sermons. — His Humility, Gentleness. — His proud Sternness and Indignation. — Two Anecdotes in Illustration. — His Efforts in behalf of the Mechanics' Institute. — The two Lectures on the "Influence of Poetry on the Working Classes." — Their Results upon the Workingmen. — Letters of Mr. Drummond and Lord Carlisle upon the Lectures and the Replies. — Criticism by the "South Church Union." — Reply on the Points, "that Severance from all Parties and Maxims is a *first* Principle in seeking after Truth"; that "Poetry is always most cultivated in effeminate Ages." — Visit to Cheltenham. — Sermons preached at Lewes Assizes. — Address presented by the Young Men of his Congregation. — His Speech on the Occasion. — His Confirmation Class. — The Elections at Brighton in 1852. — Proposition to open the Crystal Palace on Sunday. — Sermon and Letters on the Subject. — Orthodox Attacks. — Close of the Year 83

Letters from January 24, 1852, to December, 1852.

XXXVII. The Peace Party 119
XXXVIII. Was God's Plan for Humanity thwarted by the Fall? . 119
XXXIX. The Assizes at Lewes. — A Trial for Murder. — Importance of Forms 120
XL. "Feeling" as Critic of Capital Punishment. — The French and the English Watchwords. — Death of a Friend's Wife 123
XLI. Religion is Poetry. — Antagonism of Aristocratic Sympathies and Democratic Principles 124
XLII. Depression. — Extract from Sermon ; Loss of the *Birkenhead* 126
XLIII. The Belief in a Future Life 127
XLIV. Contrast of the Exhaustion consequent on London Gayety, and that consequent on Laborious Work . . 128
XLV. Prefatory Observations to M. Zaba's Lecture on Mnemonics 129
XLVI. Margaret Fuller Ossoli 135
XLVII. Condition of teaching well — Necessity of some Diffuseness 136
XLVIII. Delight in Intense Heat. — Margaret Fuller Ossoli. — Reply to a Lady who had resolved to quit Trinity Chapel. — Pain at this Desertion 137
XLIX. Margaret Fuller Ossoli. 139
L. Ireland. — Absenteeism. — Emancipation Bill . . 139
LI. Lewes Assizes 141
LII. Inspiration 143
LIII. Effect of the Apostolic Anticipation of the End of the World. — The main Doctrine of Christ. — Romans ix. 20, 21. — Inspiration of the Bible. — Truth is judged by the Spirit, not by the Understanding. — "Who is my Neighbor?" 145

LIV. America. — Anticipation of War. — How People loved him 150
LV. Self-sacrifice and the Sentimentalisms which degrade it . 151
LVI. State of Ireland. — Thoughts on the Case of One who had labored but failed to Remedy the Evils on his Irish Estate. — Antagonism to Evil. — David's Denunciation of his Enemies. — Gorgeous Sunset 152
LVII. Funeral of the Duke of Wellington. — England recognizes her Great Men at last 156

CHAPTER III.

1853.

Friendship of Mr. Robertson with Lady Byron. — State of his Health. — Advance of Disease. — Sermons of this Year. — The Principles which underlie his Teaching. — Adoration of the Virgin. — Sacrament of the Mass. — Purgatory. — Apostolical Succession. — The Seven Sacraments. — Suggestive, not dogmatic Teaching. — The Peacemaker. — Foundation of his Teaching. — His Position with regard to Unitarianism. — Lecture on Wordsworth. — Letter in answer to a Criticism, in which he discloses the Loneliness of his Heart. — Wordsworth and High Churchism. — Letter replying to one of the High-Church Party who urged him to unite himself to them. — Increasing Weakness. — Visit to Cheltenham. — His Congregation offers him a Curate. — The Vicar puts a Veto on his Choice. — Last Sermons preached in Trinity Chapel, May 29, 1853 158

Letters from January 5, 1853, to May 18, 1853.

LVIII. Benvenuto Cellini's Life 189
LIX. Mr. Maurice's Sermons on the Crystal Palace Sunday Question 190
LX. Failure of originating Power of Thought. — Cellini's Life . 190
LXI. Religious Sentimentalism. — Solemn Sense of the Responsibility of the Preacher 192
LXII. Life of mere Amusement fatal to a Christian Life. — Austerity of Youth and Age contrasted 194
LXIII. Two possible Sides to Religion 195
LXIV. Visit to Lady Byron. — Pleasure in Peaceful Life. — Legends of the Madonna. — Sermons on Roman Catholic Doctrines 196
LXV. Belief in "a Proposition dependent on Comprehension of the Terms of the Proposition." — Visit to a Farmer. — Deep Depression caused by his Illness. — False Familiarity of " Evangelicalism." — Fatal Evil of Facility in devotional Expression 198

CONTENTS.

LXVI. Effort to harmonize and strengthen the Mind. — Health of Towns Act. — Wordsworth. — Value of the Prestige of Rank 202
LXVII. Laws of Health; God's Laws 205
LXVIII. Advice as to reading the History of England. — Manner of Reading 206
LXIX. Life and Illness. — No High Goodness without Strength. — Accident at the Railway Station 209
LXX. Powerlessness except as Working from Life. — Influence of Sacred Pictures. — Humboldt's Letters. — The "Genius Loci" 212
LXXI. Visit to Cheltenham. — The Novels of Scott. — Modern French and English Novels, and the Question they open 213
LXXII. Return to Work, and Return of Pain. — " My Novel " . 216
LXXIII. Symptoms of Coming Death 217
LXXIV. 1 Cor. ix. 27. — "If there be any Virtue," &c. . . . 220
LXXV. "Not as I will." — Contrast between the Past and Present 221
LXXVI. The Beauty of Good Health. — " Wordsworth's Life." — Increasing Weakness 222

CHAPTER IV.

JUNE, JULY, AUGUST, 1853.

Mr. Robertson leaves Trinity Chapel forever. — The Controversy with the Vicar of Brighton. — The last sad Months. — His Death and Burial 225

CHAPTER V.

Robertson's personal Appearance. — Is he to be judged from his Letters or his Sermons? — His passionate Heart and inquiring Intellect. — Necessity of Self-expression. — The Work of his Life. — Results of his Preaching; of his Labor among the Workingmen. — Results of his Life and Teaching; as a Clergyman; as the Uniter of Parties; the fearless Speaker; the prudent Christian; the individual Thinker. — Accused of Latitudinarianism and Faithlessness to the Church of England. — The unexampled Circulation of his Sermons. — Recognition of the Value of his Work since his Death. — Subscription at his Funeral. — Bust erected in the Pavilion; in the Bodleian. — Memorial Window at Brazenose. — Farewell 240

APPENDIX I.

Letters from Mr. Robertson to Mrs. Robertson, written during a Tour in the Tyrol and a short Sojourn at Heidelberg 257

APPENDIX II.

Letters written by personal Friends of Mr. Robertson in Illustration of his Life and Character 283

APPENDIX III.

Notes of two Sunday Afternoon Lectures on Genesis xviii.— Genesis xxii. 325

APPENDIX IV.

A few of the Questions and Answers on the Catechism compiled by Mr. Robertson for his Confirmation Class, and a Letter to a Candidate 341

APPENDIX V.

The Inscriptions on Mr. Robertson's Tomb; on the Window in Brasenose Chapel; on the Bust in the Bodleian. — List of Subscribers to the Window 355

LIFE AND LETTERS

OF

THE REV. F. W. ROBERTSON.

CHAPTER I.

BRIGHTON — 1851.

Interest of Mr. Robertson in Social Questions. — Sermon preached in Mr. Drew's Church to Workingmen. — He is accused with Mr. Maurice and Professor Kingsley of Socialistic Opinions. — His Answer. — The "Record" Newspaper reasserts the Charge after his Death. — Letters of Mr. Maurice on the Subject. — Letters of Mr. Robertson on Professor Kingsley's Sermon. — Letter from Mr. Drew containing Extracts from Mr. Robertson's Letters on the same Subject. — Declining Health. — Lectures on the Epistles to the Corinthians. — Lecture to Workingmen at Hurstpierpoint. — Close of the year 1851.

Letters from March 14, 1851, to December 5, 1851.

DURING the first six months of this year, 1851, no external occurrences of any importance broke the monotony of the life of Mr. Robertson. There are, however, a number of letters which exhibit some of the phases of thought and feeling through which he passed from January to June.

His interest in social questions continued to increase. His correspondence proves that he studied and endeavored to refute the views of Louis Blanc. In March he spoke at a meeting held to provide lodging-houses for the poor. On Whit Sunday he preached a sermon on the social and religious aspects of the Great Exhibition.

In June he was asked by Mr. Drew, of St. John's Church, Charlotte Street, Fitzroy Square, to preach one of a series of sermons addressed to workingmen. He consented, and chose as his subject the story of Nabal and David. The sermon, which is published under the title of "The Message of the Church to Men of Wealth," vol. i. "Sermons," is an embodiment of his views on the subject of the rights of property and the rights of labor.* It brought him into an undesired notoriety. The public protest of Mr. Drew, after Mr. Kingsley's sermon, in which the former repudiated before his congregation the teaching of the latter, naturally attracted the attention of the press; and Mr. Robertson was involved with Mr. Maurice, Mr. Kingsley, and Mr. Drew in a general accusation of socialistic opinions. The cause of the accusation is an amusing instance of the danger of propinquity. It happened at that time that Mr. Maurice and Mr. Kingsley were prominent persons in a movement called Christian Socialism, and the office where their business was transacted chanced to be opposite to St. John's Church. The series of sermons in the church, and the work in the office, were at once connected by some wiseacres of the press, and the report arose that both Mr. Robertson and Mr. Drew were involved in a movement "with which," to use Mr. Drew's words, "they were never at any time, directly or indirectly, connected." Mr. Robertson was attacked by one of the papers, and accused of preaching democratic principles. He answered that the expression, "democratic principles," was too vague to deal with; that the only expression in

* He continued the subject afterwards at Brighton. Vol. ii., Ser. 1.

his sermon which bore upon the subject of democracy was a distinction drawn between the reverence to authority which is declared in Scripture to be a duty, and the slavish reverence to wealth and rank which is confounded with that duty, and in Scripture nowhere declared a duty: that if by democratic principles was meant Socialism, — Socialism was not only not advocated, but distinctly opposed in his sermon.

Immediately after his death, the "Record" newspaper reasserted the charge of socialistic opinions; and a correspondence, of which the following letters from Mr. Maurice form a part, was published in its columns:—

No. 1.

June 26, 1851.

My dear Mr. Robertson,— I fear very much that I have allowed myself to forget the painful position into which I have been the means of bringing you. It has disturbed me much, since I saw you last night, to reflect that we may have weakened your influence, and added to some people's hard thoughts of you, by bringing you into connection with us and our unpopularity. I felt much ashamed of the vanity and injustice of any proposition about printing our sermons together, which only occurred to me at the moment, and which I perceived afterwards would be doing injustice to you. I can only ask you to forgive me for having tempted you to engage in the work, which I certainly never supposed would end as it has done. I think, if you do not object, that I will write a quiet letter to the "Daily News," fully admitting their right to say anything they please of Christian Socialists; but begging them, in common justice, not to confound you with us, as you never called yourself by any such name, and as your sermon was neither Socialist nor High Church in any ordinary view of either epithet, but what they themselves would confess to be a liberal and manly utterance. If you can suggest any better way in which I can act, or if you wish me to abstain from that way, I will do as you like; at all events, will you let me express how much the great pleasure of having seen you and made your acquaintance is mixed with pain at the thought of having made you feel more than ever the divisions and confusion of the Church?

Yours very truly,
F. D. MAURICE.

No. 2.

TO CAPTAIN ROBERTSON.

January 8, 1854.

MY DEAR SIR,—I very much regret that my absence from London has delayed my answer to your note of the 31st December. It must have made me appear neglectful of your wishes. I trust that you will believe that my reverence and affection for the memory of your son would render any suspicion of indifference to his character, or to his relatives, especially painful to me.

The inference which you draw from your son's own statement, and which was confirmed by my letter, is altogether correct. He never, even for a moment, identified himself with the Christian Socialists, or entered into any of their plans. I never had the pleasure of seeing him till the spring of 1851, when I called upon him at Brighton, at the request of Mr. Drew, who was in no way connected with our proceedings. It happened that Mr. Kingsley and I were asked to preach sermons in the same course with him, and that Mr. Kingsley very reluctantly accepted the invitation. But other persons were also asked, who would entirely have disclaimed his views and mine; and the character of the Church in which we were successively to appear showed that our only bond was a common feeling that the Church was to labor for all classes, but particularly for the working-classes. When I found that the circumstances connected with Mr. Kingsley's sermon had led the newspapers to confound the different preachers in Mr. Drew's church together, I proposed, as you have seen, entirely to exculpate Mr. Robertson — the only person, beside Mr. Kingsley and me, who had yet delivered a lecture — from the charge. He very generously declined my offer in a note (the only one, I believe, I ever received from him, certainly the only one which was not of a merely formal character), which I was looking at the other day, and which I shall hope to send you when I return to London. But I am certain he declined only from his characteristic chivalry and unwillingness to shrink from us while we were in disgrace, not because he in the least adopted our name or was disposed to take part in our plans. From the time of our meeting in London, in the summer of 1851, to the time of his death, I never saw him or had any intercourse with him by letters. I sent him one of my books, and preached once in his church (when he was absent and without his knowledge); but I never had the slightest reason to imagine that he sympathized in any opinion of mine, theological, moral, or economical. I always felt that he was doing a great and noble work, amidst much misrepresentation and obloquy, and I was anxious not to give him more to bear than fell naturally and necessarily to his lot. The exceeding delight which it would have given me to learn from him, and to have received his hints and corrections of my views, would have been purchased too dearly if I had led his enemies or his friends to suppose that he was responsible for any words or acts which they might be disposed to condemn in me.

There are two obvious verbal inaccuracies in the copy of my note which you have sent me, but I will not say they are owing to you or me. If you should find that the original does not warrant my alterations, pray publish it according to your reading. But make any use of that letter, as well as of this, which you may think desirable.

Believe me, my dear sir, faithfully yours,

F. D. MAURICE.

P. S.—If you wish it, I will write to the "Record" or any other paper; but the chance of my letter being inserted is, I should think, small (at least in the "Record").

The two following letters agree with the expressions in the letter of Mr. Maurice, and prove that Mr. Robertson, while wishing Mr. Maurice and Mr. Kingsley God-speed in their work, and refusing to shrink from their side, neither adopted the views they then held, nor gave his personal sanction to the means they employed:—

July, 1851.

MY LORD,—I feel sure that I shall be excused for taking up a few minutes of your lordship's time in making an observation on the remarks which you have kindly sent me on Kingsley's sermon, which I do, because I think him a man worth putting in a true point of view, though I scarcely know him.

I quite admit the politico-economical errors in the sermon. It is false to attribute solely to the selfishness of the moneyed classes that which arises partly out of the tendency, and encouragement of the tendency, to multiply like rabbits in a warren, and the degrading admission by philanthropists of the impossibility of checking that instinct. It seems to me a great mistake to lead the working-classes to suppose that by any means independent of their own energy, moral improvement, and self-restraint, their condition can be permanently altered. And what he says of the accumulation of capital is vague and declamatory. All this I have said to him. Nor does it seem to me (I speak ignorantly) that co-operation can long replace competition without becoming competition itself, between bodies instead of individuals; or that the good of it can be other than that education which it may give to the working-classes, *in transitu*, in the points of foresight, self-control, and providence. But disagreeing with the views which Kingsley *does* hold, I still think it only fair to say that I believe that sermon misrepresents them. In an address published, or soon to be published, I am told he has very strongly stated the opposite and corrective truths, even offending the men by the energy with which he has vindicated the necessity of unequal and even large accumulations of capital.

All I am anxious for is that sympathy should be felt, or rather candor extended, towards the exaggerations of generous and unselfish men like Kingsley, whose warmth, even when wrong, is a higher thing than the correctness of cold hearts. It is so rare to find a clergyman who can forget the drill and pipeclay of the profession, and speak with a living heart for the suffering classes, not as a policeman established to lecture them into proprieties, but as one of the same flesh and blood vindicating a common humanity. And therefore Mr. Drew's protest, and the Bishop of London's cold condemnation, and almost equally cold retractation, appear to me so sad, as representations of Church-of-Englandism. Besides, is it not in the nature of things almost to be wished, and certainly inevitable, that exaggerated statements on the one side should be balanced by even over-warm declarations of the opposite truth? We have been drilling the poor into loyalty and submission for 300 years. Is it not to be expected that at last, men looking with their own eyes into the "glorious law of liberty," should express in rather indignant terms what is a surprising discovery to them, " You have left one great half of the Gospel untaught, its bearing, namely, upon man's civil freedom, and its constant siding with the degraded." And the accumulation of capital, an abstract right, requires to be checked by a deeper right. *Summum jus summa injuria.* Christianity must come in to balance and modify political economy.

I do not know whether I am justified in sending this long dissertation to your lordship, especially knowing from your public career how entirely you sympathize with all that is generous, and, in the true sense of the word, free. I suppose I was incited to it by delight at finding that your lordship had so fairly and candidly judged Kingsley's discourse, and by a desire to modify the impression on some points which his own words have produced.

November 25, 1851.

MY DEAR MR. HUTTON,— I must, in the midst of many small engagements, find one minute to reply to your letter.

In the co-operative plan I have a very limited hope. Eternal laws seem to me against them, and were they to succeed, it appears to me that it would only be competition in another form, — of association against association, instead of that of individual against individual. And if this were to be prevented by legislative enactment, I think evils far worse than those of competition would result. The fatal objection to the Louis Blanc scheme is, in my mind, that it makes no provision for an original instinct in our own nature, that of individuality and property. However, that the principle of rivalry is to be our only law, and left to work with pedantic cold-blooded adherence to maxim, — let who will be crushed, — I can never believe to be the intention of God. All goes on here by the antagonism of opposites, and I doubt not we shall find how to reconcile at last the two equally true and Christian positions :

1. Shall I not do what I will with mine own?
2. No man said that aught which he had was his own.

If we were all Christians in fact as well as by right, the difficulty would be at an end; but I do not think that the attempts which begin with the society instead of the individual, will any of them solve the question. The latter, the

Christian way, some day or other will. Meanwhile I rejoice at all efforts from the world side; even failures teach us something:—

And for some true result of good
All parties work together.

Consequently, I wish God-speed to Mr. Maurice and his plans. I had a long conversation lately with Lord Carlisle about it, and he seemed much of the same opinion.

I sympathize deeply with Mr. Maurice. I do not agree with him entirely, either theologically or economically. But he is quite after my own heart in this, that he loves to find out the ground of truth on which an error rests, and to interpret what it blindly means, instead of damning it. He loves to see the soul of good, as Shakespeare says, in things evil. I desire to see the same; therefore I love him, and so far I am at one with him. I do not pledge myself to one of his opinions, and disagree with many. But he is every inch a man, and a right noble one.

Mr. Drew, who was brought by all these circumstances into close contact with Mr. Robertson, has kindly communicated to me his impressions in the following letter:—

MY DEAR SIR,—I will comply with your request that I would contribute a few pages to your forthcoming "Life" of my much-beloved and honored friend from some of my correspondence with him, and from my recollections of our intercourse.

That many have been sorely impatient on account of the delay of the long-promised "Life" is not at all surprising, and yet I am sure you have acted wisely in postponing it: for indeed Robertson is only now becoming adequately known, even to those who were most intimate with him: any image of his strong and lofty spirit which might have been presented before this time must have entirely failed in expressing the greatness by which we now know he was distinguished, even amongst the greatest of our generation. If the most inconsiderable men cannot be understood until they have been freed from their earthly environment of trouble and strife and toil, and death has cast its softening, purifying light around our memories of them, how truly may it be said that this transfiguration was needful in his case! Apart from ordinary causes of misconception, we remember his patient silence, his dignified reserve. Then, moreover, the seclusion in which much of his work — the mere amount of which has so much astonished us — must have been done, could only allow him to be seen, by even his nearest friends, in fragmentary disclosures. They had, consequently, but the most inadequate conception of his power and depth and self-devotedness: only now is he rising before them in the nobleness of a character which far transcends even the highest estimate they could have formed of him. And when I remember how marvellously — if I may not use a stronger word — much of the material for our present knowledge of him has been preserved, I feel it is indeed the duty of all who can add any contribution to it, to furnish this at once, even though it be at the painful cost of acknowledging that they were separated from him by strong differences of feeling and opinion. You are aware that this was my own case, though I most thankfully remember that these differences never interfered with the cordiality — I may say the affectionateness — of the intercourse between us. Gladly would I forget the circumstances to which I am referring, but in anything like a complete account of him they must be brought forward: nor will I withhold any *characteristic* sentence of his concerning them, though some of those sentences were uttered as strong, sometimes indignant, condemnation of proceedings which I believed I had rightly as well as conscientiously adopted.

It was in connection with the circumstances I am alluding to, and which are detailed with sufficient fulness in another page of this volume, that a large portion of our correspondence was carried forward. He afterwards continued it, though it was at length abruptly terminated, in consequence, I fear, of somewhat vehement expressions on my part of dissent from his views on an entirely distinct subject. The closely-written pages in his firm, clear handwriting which now lie before me, seem to bring out, even more strikingly than anything of his I have elsewhere seen, some marked features in his character, which are so admirably described in one of those noble pages which picture the ideal minister of "The Kingdom of Christ," that I might almost think my friend was in the view of its gifted writer. Spiritual forms, which the majority have need to see reflected in sensible mirrors, rose up before him in their naked substance and majesty; good and evil were to him present, not as means to some result, but as themselves the great ends and results to which all is tending. . . . . He had a certain habit of measuring acts and events, not by their outward magnitude, but according to their spiritual proportions and effects. . . . . So he reverenced poverty and helplessness; he understood that that truth is the highest, not which is the most exclusive, but which is the most universal; and the immediate vision of God, and entire subjection of heart and spirit to His loving will, seemed to him the great gifts intended for man, after which every one, for himself and his fellows, may aspire. Robertson embodied this description; and he did so, I believe, in virtue of that purity and humbleness of spirit to which this vision of God and of His truth, and this entire submission to it, have been promised. His judgment was thus deep, just, and comprehensive, because he, too, had learned to seek his Heavenly Father's will, and not his own. His willingness to do that will gave him his profound insight into his Lord's teaching, and the strong conviction, which has passed into so many other spirits from his own, that it is of God.

Here, in his singular purity and truthfulness, and in his constant devoutness, we have the secret of what we need not scruple to designate his prophetic insight into truth, and habitual consciousness of its invisible and deep harmonies, and, along with this, his prophetic sympathy also with the weak and perplexed and overborne. Beneath all conventional, and, indeed, all outward expressions of the mind of God, and through all the means and institutions through which His grace is working for our recovery, he ever looked to the realities and purposes to which they were subservient, and strove with all his concentrated energy, always doing with all his might the task of the present hour, to set forth what he then looked on in closest adaption to the exigencies of his place and time. This often led him, after the manner of the ancient prophets, to speak as if he were disparaging other truths and ordinances, which, in fact, no one reverenced more deeply than himself. Nor was he unconscious of his liability to be misunderstood in consequence, and of the odium it might bring on him. Yet he deliberately maintained his purpose, and earnestly claimed for others the same "liberty of prophesying" which, on this ground, he used himself. Thus he says:—

"We knew Kingsley's heart, his zeal and earnestness; and if any of his sentences were liable to misconstruction, we ought patiently to have waited till time and our own explanations could have supplied what was wanting..... The Son of God said many things *very* liable to be misunderstood; and sober people thought them very dangerous; protested against them, 'lest the Romans should come and take away their place and nation.' I admit the rashness of Kingsley's verbiage; but rashness is a thing to be loved, not rebuked. My brother, or another officer of his name, by the last 'Gazette,' was rather too forward in the action with the Kaffirs, and fought them with a few men nearly alone. The commanding officer said it was rash, for he lost several men, but praised his gallantry warmly. I wish to God we had a little soldier's spirit in our Church! ....

"No! the Church of England will endure no chivalry, no *dash*, no effervescing enthusiasm. She cannot turn it to account, as Rome turns that of her Loyolas and Xaviers. We bear nothing but sober prosaic routine; and the moment any one with heart and nerve fit to be leader of a forlorn hope appears, we call him a dangerous man, and exasperate him by cold unsympathizing reproofs, till he becomes a dissenter and a demagogue..... Well, I suppose God will punish us, if in no other way, by banishing from us all noble spirits, like Newman and Manning, in one direction, and men like Kingsley, in another, leaving us to flounder in the mud of

commonplace, unable to rise or sink above the dead level.
Day by day my hopes are sinking. We dare not say the
things we feel. Who can? Who possibly may, when 'Records,' 'Guardians,' brother ministers, and lay hearers, are
ready at every turn to call out heterodoxy? It is bondage
more than Roman. And if a man sets his face like a flint,
and desperately runs a-muck with his eyes shut, caring not
who is offended, then he injures his own spirit, becomes, like
noble Carlyle, ferocious, and loses the stream of living waters in dry desert sand, fructifying nothing, but only festering
into swamp shallows. ..... Imprudence, half-truths, rash cries
of sympathetic torture. Yes! But through all these I would
hold fast by a man if I were sure he was sound at heart, and
meant differently from what he seemed to mean..... I hold
to heart, to manhood and nobleness, not correct expression.
I try to judge words and actions by the man, not the man by
his words and actions..... What I have said in behalf of
Kingsley I have said quite as strongly from my own pulpit
in behalf of Tractarians. By standing by a man I mean not
adopting his views, if they are not our own, but tolerating
them, and that to an almost unlimited extent,— unlimited, at
least, in comparison with the limits which the most liberal I
know propose. And if I were convinced he meant rightly,
then by standing by him I should include defending and explaining. ..... I am afraid my illustrations are somewhat too
military, but I was rocked and cradled to the roar of artillery, and I began life with a preparation for, and appointment
to, the 3d Dragoons. *Dis aliter visum.*"

You may here see how deliberately he used much of
that language which, in some instances, might be condemned as marking vehement one-sidedness on his
part; how perfectly he was conscious of those complementary balancing truths which were apparently forgotten by him when he urgently insisted on others

which he looked on as neglected. This is also further seen when he writes:—

Kingsley assumes, perhaps, more than I should, that human selfishness lies at the bottom of our social evils. I believe that the contravention of laws which will avenge themselves, as, for instance, improvidence and foolish marriages, have had their share in the production of our present embarrassment; and that it is one thing to cry woe to those who have kept back the hire of the laborers who have reaped down their fields, and another to denounce it against those whose fault has been partly ignorance, partly supineness. But then (he adds) "this is my opinion, mine only," he having a right to his. Moreover, he may be more right than I think. Our foolish sentiment in promoting marriages, and declaring submission to a brute instinct a Christian duty; our non-education of the people through party squabbles; our suffering a vast population to grow up while Church extension meant only more churches and more salaries; and while bishops in Parliament defending the Church meant only bishops rising whenever the stipends of the Church were in danger, and sitting still when corn-laws, or any other great measure affecting the numbers and food of the people, came into question. All these things, when I think of them, make me doubt whether Kingsley's theory has not a deep, deep, awful truth at bottom. Besides, for 3,000 years it was the theory and tone of God's best and truest, of His prophets, His brave ones; and I shrink from saying, very authoritatively, that his view is wrong, though at present I do think it imperfect.

It is quite true that Kingsley took no notice of the blessings of constituted order, &c. But they were no very particular blessings to the wretches who were rising by thousands before his tortured imagination. Blessings to you and to me, and to nobles, and well-to-do tradesmen, and to all Belgravia; but Kingsley felt he had something else to do besides lauding our incomparable constitution, — viz. to declare the truth that there is an emancipation yet unaccomplished, which will be woe to Belgravia, and to hock-drinking tradesmen, and to us, the ministers of the Church, if we do not accomplish.

If, for many reasons besides the sorrow of even seeming to have needed such words of expostulation and rebuke, one might be painfully reluctant to copy out these passages, yet surely no one, revering my friend's character, and desiring to have it fully represented, would have one of them suppressed. I think he would not, for the very reason which might at first seem to require this suppression. For not only are they plainly distinguished from that railing fanaticism of the mere demagogue with which, on a superficial glance, they might be confounded; but they are, in fact, essentially, nay antithetically, opposed to it. This is seen in the consciousness that may be discerned, in even the most vehement of my friend's utterances, of all the force belonging to every view of the question in debate that was urged by his correspondent. He could also sympathize with the motives and feelings of those who were sincerely resisting him. "Nevertheless," he says, in the same letter from which the above extracts are taken:—

I repeat I do you warmly justice. If I did not, I assure you I should not have taken the trouble to write as warmly and strongly as I have done; I should have let my sad and indignant feelings remain pent up. I have poured them out to you, because I do think it is worth it, and that there is a much greater chance of union by so doing. I am sure of you, as of myself, that you are not on the side of the Pharisaisms and Respectabilities in the sense in which I spoke of them. Respectabilities, in a now familiar Carlylian sense, is a word implying, at least to me, persons like Balaam, or persons who are respectable, and nothing more; persons who are simply and selfishly conservative, — not Conservatives, because I honor many of them, but persons who hate stir and reformation, because these get down to facts, and disturb cobwebs.

One more extract may be given from his letters on this subject. It is the last which I received from him relating to it. Some of his words here are worth copying, for the sake of showing the intense hatred — and surely it was the hatred of him who said, "Do not I hate them, O Lord, that hate thee?" — with which he regarded some of the malignant forms which sectarianism assumes amongst us : —

I have just had sent me the "Record," in which your letter appears, and thank you heartily for the generous defence of me which it contains. The "Record" has done me the honor to abuse me for some time past, for which I thank them gratefully. God forbid they should ever praise me! One number alone contained four unscrupulous lies about me, on no better evidence than that some one had told them, who had been told by somebody else. They shall have no disclaimer from me. If the "Record" can put a man down, the sooner he is put down the better. The only time I have ever said anything about Socialism in the pulpit has been to preach against it. The Evangelicalism (so called) of the "Record" is an emasculated cur, snarling at all that is better than itself, cowardly, lying, and slanderous. It is not worth while to stop your horse and castigate it; for it will be off yelping, and come back to snarl. An evangelical clergyman admitted some proofs I had given him of the "Record's" cowardice and dishonesty, but said, "Well, in spite of that I like it, because it upholds the truth, and is a great witness for religion." "So," said I, "is that the creed of evangelicalism? A man may be a liar, a coward, and slanderous, and still uphold the truth!"———

Vehement! some may say; but surely in such vehemence there was heavenly wisdom! Are not these words of his in profound concord with the divinest that have been addressed to us? Did he not speak thus because, in closest personal communion, he had deeply inbreathed the spirit of Him who, of all, spake sometimes most severely, as well as most lovingly and tolerantly? Was not this intense feeling, that so flowed out from him on all sides, part of the "reasonable, holy, and living sacrifice," which could not — should we, in love for him, desire that it might — have been prolonged? When I think of the consuming pain this broadly intense sympathy must have cost him, I recall as selfish and inconsiderate the wish that he were still here to help us in the great conflict of our generation. Robertson would have helped us all, by his deep insight and large open-heartedness, on whichever side of the strife we are contending. Of his genius and his energy we are bereaved, but all may endeavor to maintain his sympathy and tolerance; and I shall be glad that I have overcome the reluctance to send you some of the words he addressed to me, if any shall be helped in that endeavor by reading them.

Sincerely yours,
G. S. Drew.

All through this year Mr. Robertson's health continued to decline. In June a strong memorial was presented to him from Drs. Allen and Whitehouse, "urging me," he wrote, "to give up my work for some months, and prognosticating unpleasant consequences if I refuse." In January he had already written to a friend excusing himself for remissness in sending the usual notes of his sermons.

The lassitude he suffered from prevented his enjoying the Exhibition; the crowd and noise irritated and wearied him. But his work did not suffer, nor his energy decrease. In June he began to lecture in the afternoons of Sundays on the Epistles to the Corinthians. He introduced the course by a masterly account of the state of Corinth and its parties at the time of the Apostle Paul. He continued these lectures till his death, and the last he ever preached was on the last chapter of the second epistle. They have now been published; though from notes so meagre and unfinished that no idea of them, as delivered, can be formed. All the color and glow have perished; the thoughts alone remain. They are valuable, however, for their insight into St. Paul's character; for the way in which the principles applied by St. Paul to Corinthian parties and Corinthian society are brought to bear upon the parties and society of this age; and especially valuable for their *method* of exposition. They form almost a manual of the mode in which the Epistles should be treated in the pulpit. For this reason they were likely to be more acceptable to clergymen and teachers of the Bible than to the generality of readers. And so it has proved. From ministers of all sections of the Church and of Dissent, even from those who differ most widely from Mr. Robertson's opinions, testimonies to the value of these Lectures have been received.

As to these opinions themselves, an interesting letter, written to a Roman Catholic friend, will be found,— No. xxiv.,— in which he states his position in the Church, and the principles on which he taught during the year 1851.

In October he crossed to Ireland for his usual rest,

and returned to Brighton in November. It will be seen, from his letters, how strong an interest he took in the movements of Kossuth, and with what wise calmness, despite of all his enthusiasm for liberty and against oppression, he endeavored to penetrate to the root of the question of Hungary.

He crowned the year and his exertions in the cause of social reform by a lecture to workingmen at Hurstpierpoint, — notes of which have been published. The main ideas were borrowed from Channing's Essay on the Elevation of the Working-classes; but he clothed them with such new thought that he made them altogether his own. So closed for him the year 1851. It was a year during which his work, ever arduous and wearing, was rendered doubly so by misconception and attack, and by the pressure and pain of advancing disease. But he bore up nobly and endured, as seeing Him who is invisible. From this time forth till his death his life and energy were those of a race-horse, the spirit of which needs no spur, but which dies exhausted with victory at the winning-post.

LETTERS FROM MARCH 14 TO DECEMBER 5, 1851.

I.

To a Friend.

March 14, 1851.

Thank you most gratefully for the "Stones of Venice!" There are no writings which, at the present moment, offer such interest to me as Ruskin's. They give a truth to repose on which is real, whatever else is unreal; and as a relief from the *dim* religious light of theology, in which one seems to make out the outline of a truth and the next moment lose it in hopeless mystery and shadows, they are very precious, — more precious than even works which treat of scientific truth, such as chemistry, for *they* do not feed the heart, and that is the thing that aches and craves in us just now to a degree that makes the resentment against such people as Miss Martineau on the one side, and the evangelicals on the other, almost *savage*. I have been and am reading the "Modern Painters" again, with renewed enjoyment and sense of soothing.

You do not "get a clearer conception of truths." You are "less able wholly to understand." Could it be otherwise? If, instead of a clearer conception, you are getting a grander idea, even though it should give a bewildering sense of indefiniteness and infinitude, is not this gain rather than loss? Who can "understand?" If a man understands spiritual truth, I should think he *knows*, because he feels little about it. If you are exchanging measurable maxims for immeasurable principles, surely you are rising from the mason to the architect. "Seven times?" No, — no, — no, — seventy times seven. No maxim, — a heart principle. I wonder whether St. Peter *wholly understood* that, or got a very clear *conception* from it. A sublime idea he did, no doubt, which would forever and forever outgrow the outline of any dogmatic definition; but just so far as St. Peter could define less what he believed on that point, he would know more. And yet I dare say there were respectable Pharisees in that day who would gravely shake their heads and say, that it was a dangerous thing to do away with old-established rules and throw a man upon the feelings of a vague unlimited principle.

It seems to me that this feeling of vagueness is inevitable when we dare to launch out upon the sea of truth. I remember that half-painful, half-sublime sensation in the first voyage I took out of sight of land when I was a boy; when the old landmarks and horizon were gone, and I felt as if I had no home. It was a pain to find the world so large. By degrees the mind got familiarized to that feeling, and a joyful sense of freedom came. So I think it is with spiritual truth. It is a strangely desolate feeling to perceive that the "Truth," and the "Gospel," that we have known, were but a small home-farm in the great universe, but at last I think we begin to see sun, moon, and stars as before, and to discover that we are not lost, but free, with a latitude and longitude as certain, and far grander than before.

II.

I spent last evening with Mrs. Jameson and Lady Byron. The conversation turned at first chiefly on the gradual changes in the feeling towards the Virgin, which are marked by the forms of representation of her. It seems that the earliest appearance of the Virgin and Child dates in the fifth century; before that, the Virgin was alone. The first representations of this change bore a striking resemblance to the heathen statues and *relievos* of Juno nursing the infant Mars. Then came pictures in which the Virgin is represented as crowned by her son, — at first kneeling before Him, then sitting a little lower than He, then on a level with him. For many ages she appears as intercessor between Christ the Judge and the guilty earth; in this respect personifying the idea which, among many modern Christians, is personified by Christ as the Lord of compassion : while He represented that conception which they now assign to the Father, — offended wrath, needing intercession, and scarcely appeased. This shows, however, I think, the radical truth of the idea. Love and justice are really one, — different sides of each other; love to that which is like God is alienation from that which opposes Him. In this light, too, the heart realizes Him as an unity, when the intellect is subordinated, and does not dialectically divide, that is, in our highest moral state; but when the understanding begins to busy itself with these conceptions, they are necessarily conceived of as two, not one, and the beings in whom they inhere are necessarily conceived of as distinct.

I look upon that Middle-Age statement, and the more modern one, only as forms, and perhaps necessary forms, of thought, which are false in the higher regions of belief in which the heart, loving, lives. She showed me some exquisite forms of the Virgin by the elder painters, when feeling was religious, — Perugino, Fra Angelico, Raphael. Afterwards the form became coarse, as the religious feeling died off from art. I asked her how it is that the Romish feeling now is developing itself so much in the direction of Mariolatry; and she said that the purer and severer conceptions of the Virgin are coming back again, and visibly marking Romish art.

Briefly, I will tell you what I said in answer to her inquiries. I think Mariolatry was inevitable. The idea most strongly seized in Christianity of the sanctification of humanity attached itself to Christ as the man; but the idea naturally developed contained something more, — the sanctification of womanhood. Until, therefore, the great truth that in Christ is neither male nor female, — that His was the double nature, all that was most manly and all that was most womanly, — could take hold of men, it was inevitable that Christianity should seem imperfect without an immaculate woman. Swedenborgianism has therefore, it seems, a similar dream, and so has even atheism. I am told that Comte, the French philosopher, has broached a somewhat corresponding *rêve* in his "Anticipations of the Future." We only want, he thinks, and shall have, the glory of woman to worship. He is an atheist. Alas! if he be right, we shall have to search elsewhere than in the ball-going polkaing frivolities in female form which offer themselves as the modern goddesses.

From this the conversation turned on capital punishment. I declared for it, wishing that it should be abolished for murder, and inflicted only on those who are guilty of wrongs to women. For murder is a trifle, — life is not of so much value, — and the tenderness for human life is not one of the noblest signs of our times, for it is not commensurable with a hatred of wrong; whereas in the other case society is worse than unchristian; that which is wrong in a woman is doubly so in a man, because she does with personal risk what he does with risk to another, in personal security and damnable selfishness.

III.

I rejoice that you have taken up Ruskin; only let me ask you to read it very slowly, to resolve not to finish more than a few pages each day. One or two of the smaller chapters are quite enough, — a long chapter is enough for two days, except where it is chiefly made up of illustration from pictures; those can only be read with minute attention when you have the print or picture to which he refers before you; and those which you can so see, in the National Gallery, Dulwich, &c., you should study, with the book, one or two at a time. The book is worth reading in this way: study it, — think over each chapter and examine yourself mentally, with shut eyes, upon its principles, putting down briefly on paper the heads, and getting up each day the principles that you gained the day before. This is not the way to read many books, but it is the way to read much; and one read in this way, carefully, would do you more good, and remain longer fructifying, than twenty skimmed. Do not read it, however, with slavish acquiescence; with deference, for it deserves it, but not more. And when you have got its principles woven into the memory, hereafter, by comparison and consideration, you will be able to correct and modify for yourself. Together with this, I would read carefully some other book of a totally different character; some narrative of human action and character, — if stirring and noble so much the better. I have just finished the first volume of Major Edwardes's "Punjaub," a history of wonderful adventures, but too long. I could not recommend it to you, but some day I will give you a very brief epitome of it.

I am endeavoring to do my work more regularly, simply, and humbly, — trying as it is, and against the grain, and deeply as I feel the need of some physical enterprise.

Tell ——, with my kind regards, that Louis Blanc's theory requires something besides a warm heart and a quick perception to fairly judge. There are certain laws of society, as certain as the laws of matter, which cannot be reached intuitively, or by feeling, but require study, — very hard study; and the misfortune of his theory is, that, appealing to those whose feelings are quick, and sense of the wrongs of things as they are, acute, it is very fascinating; but whether it is true or not, demands a far calmer study of the laws of the universe than his superficial theory generally gets. Feeling says, "Relieve the beggar, and you cannot be wrong"; Fact says, "The relief of beggary can be proved the worst injury to the community." Socialism and Fourierism will draw in many generous spirits, but it must bring about, at last, evils tenfold greater than those it would relieve. I never read anything more pitiably self-destructive than the digest of Louis Blanc's doctrine, in a catechism by himself. Succeed it cannot, but it will probably be tried some day, perhaps on a large scale; and if so, the social disorganization which must ensue, and the agonies and convulsions in which society will reel to and fro, and the reaction from it, will be, perhaps, the most terrible lesson which the world has ever learnt.

This is the invariable result of protection, — the forcible compression and hindrance of the laws of nature until they burst. Louis Blanc thinks God has made very bad laws, and he would make better. So thought a wiser than Louis Blanc, or fifty Louis Blancs, — Plato. He considered the partialities of maternal love very pernicious, and would have prevented a woman knowing her own child, making her the mother of all the children of the state. Of course maternal partialities are full of evil, but on the whole, that being God's system, will work better than the universalism and state education of Plato, however sublime the conception may seem. The only difficulty is to create the feeling which is to be the motive, that is all. Mr. —— the other day was very learnedly descanting before some ladies upon the modern invention of throwing red-hot shot and red-hot shells. Red-hot shot I had heard of at Gibraltar. But I humbly ventured to ask respecting the red-hot shells, — how they got the powder in? That is the difficulty in Louis Blanc's system. Nevertheless, it will be tried; and, like the red-hot shell system, the result will be, — an explosion.

IV.

To one entering London Life.

MY DEAR ——, — Gavazzi's Exeter Hall orations and this electro-biology are of the exciting class of stimuli which I reckon dangerous and useless. The first leaves nothing behind, morally or intellectually; the second belongs as yet to the witchcraft and mesmerism class, which may hereafter be reduced to calm rules and become scientific; but at present, except to scientific and classifying minds, I think useful for nothing but to kill the disease of *ennui* by exciting the Athenian desire of *loving* "some new thing."

Do let me earnestly entreat you to use force to overcome this craving after stimuli of this class; it is time and money lost. One tenth part of the time and attention given regularly to the acquisition of some of the branches of information for which London affords so many opportunities would relieve you from *ennui*, and will leave something behind. Suppose you try the mental discipline of giving all the hours which you would fritter on such things to one pursuit, — say an interesting attendance on some course of not abstruse lectures. I pray you to grasp my principles, not my rules; for to say *this*, *that*, and *that* are exciting, and leave nothing behind, is to give dead rules. Remember the spirit and philosophy of that which I say.

V.

To the Same.

Last night I wrote so rapidly to save the post that possibly my meaning may have been obscure. What I intended to say was this: the life you are now about to enter will be one of an exciting character; diminish it as you will, yet balls, theatres, late hours, varied society, must necessarily make the atmosphere you breathe highly stimulating. What you want in your other life is a corrective and emollient.

It matters little that you avoid the theatre and music, if in their stead you substitute Gavazzi, with his theatrical *pose* and voice, and his exciting orations. I do not say that under no circumstances it would be desirable to hear him. Were you for months in a dull country town, I should say it might be well to vary its monotony by such an excitement, and its exaggeration might be even wholesome as the counteractive of an extreme; but under present circumstances, if you are really in earnest in your desire to discipline your spirit and get the peace which can alone come from watchfulness, I should say it is one of those indulgences which must be pernicious, though one which, of course, the worn, jaded London ladies must find most delightful, varying their excitement with a fresh stimulus, and giving them horseradish when they are tired of mustard, cayenne when wearied of horseradish. This, I believe, Mr. ——, too, has done for them, and probably this is what sermons generally accomplish. One spoonful of cayenne to six of mustard, and Soyer himself could not then give such piquancy to their week,—would to God I were not a mere pepper-cruet to give a relish to the palates of the Brightonians!

Well, to proceed: I think natural facts most valuable for your mind to repose upon; but the class which you select are precisely those which, instead of giving the repose of philosophic certainty, leave the mind in a whirl of wonder and perplexity; the disputed facts, which are not recognized as facts, which produce controversy and excitement,—mesmerism, electro-biology, odology. Half the time—nay, one tenth of the time—wasted upon the charlatans who invent these, or mystify the real facts contained in them, would put many in possession of truths quite as marvellous, infinitely more beautiful, because their connection with life and usefulness is known, and far more capable of disciplining the mind towards peace, and rest, and God. I can see no effect produced by the others except bewilderment, dogmatism, or scepticism. Let philosophers examine them, separate the error from the facts, and then we can look at them; but at present, entirely untrained in such studies, we are as little able to distinguish the laws of the universe from jugglery as a ploughman is to separate vaccination from the charm system; and the appeal to judgment in these matters seems to me always a great presumptive proof of something false.

Besides which, the popular mind, always craving belief, takes up implicitly these crude *phenomena* with a reverence which is so much abstracted from rightful objects; and then the vacillation and perpetual uncertainty in which the mind is left produces a glow of excitement which betrays what is in fact the real attractiveness in these pursuits,—the power they have to give excitement with no mental trouble. Excitement is the natural reward of toil; but that is a healthy excitement. Felt by the philosopher it is delicious, calm, and productive of valuable exertion; but felt without mental or physical effort, ending in itself, and existing only for the sake of itself, it is, by a just law, self-destructive; just as spirits may be safely taken during hard exercise, but at the peril of him who takes them in a sedentary life.

O that I could make every one feel this principle as I feel it, — and as a principle! I give many rules, " but the letter killeth, the spirit of the law giveth life." If men could but get a living insight into the principle, which is to me as clear as noonday, the application of it would be easy; and, as in religious matters, the irksome, irritating restriction, "Touch not, taste not, handle not," *this, that*, and the *other*, — would be dispensed with.

VI.

I have finished Edwardes's "Punjaub," and am about to begin it again, though it is in two thick volumes. I turn to the history of military adventures and to science with a sense of refreshment and home, which intensifies as life goes on. Edwardes was a very fine fellow. He went as political agent with a Sikh army to the valley of Bunnoo, which Runjeet Singh had subdued and made tributary, but the tribute of which had never been collected, except once in three or four years, with great bloodshed and war. In three months Edwardes subdued one of the four tribes which inhabit it by negotiation; forced the others to raze with their own hands four hundred forts which might have stood a year's siege; knowing nothing of engineering, built a fortress for the Sikh army, and compelled the refractory Sikhs, who had never done anything of the kind before, to build it; collected the tribute; shot a fanatic, who rushed into his tent, after having slain the sentry, to murder him; disbanded a mutinous regiment; tried hundreds of causes in a country where justice had never been heard of before.

To turn to a different question: "Why was John the

most beloved?" I suppose we learn from the fact the rightness of personal preferences,—certain minds being more akin to other human minds than certain others,—but also that in the highest hearts this affinity will be determined by spiritual resemblances, not mere accidental agreeabilities, accomplishments, or politenesses, or pleasant manners. Again, I imagine that the union was one which had nothing to do with mental superiority; that might have been more admirable: John was lovable. Not talent, as in St. Paul's case, nor eloquence, nor amiability drew Christ's spirit to him, but that large heart, which enabled him to believe because he felt, and hence to reveal that "God is Love." It is very remarkable, however, that his love was a trained love. Once John was more zealous than affectionate. But he began by loving the human friend, by tending the mother as a son, by attachment to his brother James; and so, through particular personal attachments, he was trained to take in and comprehend the larger Divine Love. I should say, then, that he was most lovable, because, having loved in their various relationships "men whom he had seen, he was able to love God whom he had not seen." He is most dear to the heart of Christ, of course, who loves most, because he has most of God in him, and that love comes through missing none of the preparatory steps of affection, given us here as Primer lessons. . . . .

Upon me there is a growing conviction, deepening into a feeling that is at times very solemn and very mournful, that my path lies in a different direction,—in humble work done more humbly than I have done it,— more in the valley: in simple life, more severe and more solitary. I must mete out what of existence remains to me. Like Hamlet, "I have had dreams,"* and therefore, like him, am unable to "count myself king of infinite space."

* Robertson was aware that the other reading —"bad dreams"— was the more correct one, but he always preferred the reading in the text of his letter.

VII.

The only shade of uneasiness that ever crosses my mind is the perhaps that it will not end *so*. What I have reason to fear is imbecility. They all admit that. Last night, till dawn to day, suffering kept me awake, gnashing the teeth, or rather setting them, like poor Prometheus, in defiance of the vulture's beak. Only my vulture was feeding on my cerebellum, and digging its talons in a most uncivil and ferocious way into the organs of emotionness, philoprogenitiveness, obstinacy, &c., &c., leaving the nobler organs free. Now, what is to be said for phrenology after this? Does it not refute the whole system? Had the said bird been pulling at the organs really in use by me, — that is, all that is most sublime in humanity, — it had been intelligible. But what business on earth has he to stick his claws into a part of my nature which from the cradle has been protested against, disowned, defied, conquered? Is it revenge being now taken for the victory, and am I to be, like the Princess in the "Arabian Nights," consumed by the flames of the genie she had reduced to a cinder? Bad image apart, there is something in the whole matter which perplexes me as a philosophical question and a question of justice; for I know, as well as the organs indicate, that it is not the overstrained intellect that is wearing life out, but the emotional part of nature, which all life long has been breathing flames which kindled none and only burned itself.

VIII.

On reaching home yesterday evening I took down Liebig's "Chemistry," and found that the ultimate elements of organic bodies are principally four, — viz: carbon, oxygen, hydrogen, and nitrogen. That is, the difference between hair, flesh, bone, and between skin, bark, wood, &c., is caused not so much by their being composed of different elements as by the different proportions in which these four chief ones are mixed up.

In the visons of the night a dream presented itself, mingling this information with the subjects of our conversation, and the question whether woman is merely an unemancipated negro, as you say, her powers and qualities in all respects like those of men, only uncultivated, or, as I say, a being spiritually as well as physically different, — having, if you will, all the elements, moral and intellectual, the same in number as man has, only differing in the proportions in which they are mixed up; that difference, however, constituting a difference of nature as real as the difference between leaf and flower, wood and fruit. As *you* say, Woman is to Man what the gristle of a child is to the hard skull of an adult; as *I* say, what the brain is to the skull, or the flesh to the ribs.

Methought I overheard the muscular fibre, i. e. the flesh, of the human body, enviously grumbling against the bones. The flesh averred that it was essentially identical with bone, wanting only a different position and a harder education. That great muscle in the centre of the body, the heart, took upon herself the office of champion of the rights of oppressed flesh, and spoke, — " Feeble and degraded muscles! after six thousand years of abject inferiority, I summon you in the sacred name of abstract principles. Are we not identically the same as the bones? What are the bones? — Carbon, oxygen, hydrogen, nitrogen. What are we? — The same, minus a few pinches of phosphate of lime. The elements of our nature are identically those of bone. And yet for these long centuries we have been treated as if we were of a softer and feebler nature, — condescendingly, insultingly protected from outward injury, as if we could not protect ourselves; looked upon as the ornament and living beauty of the bones; treated — I blush with shame to say it — as the cushions on which the bones repose, as if we were merely existing for their solace and relaxation. Even I, of bonier texture than you, poor slaves! I am bone-locked and hemmed in on every side, unable to expand, cabined, cribbed, confined, forbidden from the development of my noble nature by the coercion of a horrid jealous rib!

(For it may be remarked that the heart, albeit proud of being less soft and less sensitive than other muscles, was yet unable to restrain the use of certain spasmodic *dashed* words, like "horrid," which betrayed the existence of more nervous substance and sensibility than she would willingly have admitted. And the occurrence of these, in the midst of slang-like and bonier expressions, produced sometimes an odd confusion.)

Some very tender muscles, situated at the extremity of the fingers, spoke in reply to the swelling heart thus:—

"Wondrous sister! Thy words are full of awe; and we have been thrilled with the mighty conception which thou hast suggested to us of being as the bones! But let us take sweet counsel together. Dost not thou sit in the centre of the body, determining the quality of every atom of carbon, hydrogen, and nitrogen, before it passes into the bones? Are not we, then, through thee, our great mother, arbiters of the destiny of those bones, whom thou, with divine indignation, callest horrid? We know that thou art less feebly sensitive than many of us, for we recollect how, in the days of Charles II., thou wast handled alive by a surgeon, and didst not flinch any more than if thou hadst been bone. But we pray thee to consider what would be our fate were we to change our nature. Should we not *wear* out by our friction, instead of elastically rebounding? Does not our very shrinking save us? Nay, would not the bones be harder still than we, and instead of, as now, loving forbearing pressure, *come through us*, if we did not feel? Besides, some of us have a secret liking for those bones, feel their support, and cling with great affection to our ribs. Thou speakest of great principles, which we do not understand,— oxygen and hydrogen. Thou art very wise, and we are very foolish, — we only know that flesh is flesh and bone is bone. Thou sayest flesh is bone: but we cannot help thinking that we are as nature made us, and better so. Thou meditatest, mighty philosopheress! on nitrogen and carbon. To us bones are dear. We think that all the discipline which thou recommendest would make us only firmer and healthier flesh, but flesh still, and that only by destruction of our nature could we become bone. We do not wish the bones ever to forget that we are flesh, or to treat us as bone treats bone. We should as soon expect a gentleman in the course of conversation to forget the difference of sex, — to consider only mind *versus* mind, and, smiting the feminine possessor of the mind upon the shoulder, to say, " Come, hold your jaw, old fellow." Most magnanimous heart! We are very tender, and do not like to have it forgotten that we are made of flesh and blood."

Methought the heart heaved with scorn, and replied: —

" Ye concrete feeblenesses! I am then, not as ye are. The abstract principles of my nature are identical with those of the tyrants. I will alter the proportions; I will appropriate a little of the lime which the heartless bones monopolize. I, too, will be a bone." (" *Heartless* bones." N. B. — This was the last touching inconsistency of the flesh of which the heart was ever guilty.)

She persisted in her resolve. By degrees her eloquent and throbbing utterances became stilled in silence. She got harder and harder, and knocked against the ribs, blow for blow, giving knocks, and receiving them with interest. The last wish she expressed was to be made acquainted with Anatomy practically, being certain that she should be as callous to the knife as any bone.

She got her wish; but it was not until she had become ossified.

Upon the *post-mortem* examination I could not, however,

but remark that, even denaturalized as her discipline had made her, she did not look like genuine healthy bone, but a sort of gristle, neither red nor white, neither hard nor soft, but tough,—altogether an unnatural, morbid, amorphous mass, like unprepared caoutchouc when you cut it through, only not so elastic.

The surgeon shrugged his shoulders, and dropped her into a jar of spirits of wine, to take her place among the monstrosities of an anatomical museum, observing that she was too hard for a feminine pin-cushion, and too soft for a masculine cannon-ball.

Glenara, Glenara, now read me my dream.

IX.

May 7.

—— was very enthusiastic about Louis Blanc, his philanthropy, his *beaux yeux noirs* and *pensées*, his aristocratic bearing, and *bien gantées* hands. It is very difficult, in a woman's enthusiasm for a system, to climinate the adventitious and personal influences and get at the real amount of intelligent and genuine admiration of the *belles idées* which remains as a residuum behind. Ravignan and socialism—nay, perhaps I may add, with a little sly malice, Mazzinianism, mesmerism, to say nothing of homœopathy—would contend against us, dull, careworn expositors of threadbare truths, with fearful odds on their side, if *beaux yeux noirs* and white gloves are to be unconsciously accepted as legitimate weapons.

I am sorry I could not go with you to the Exhibition opening, but as circumstances then were it would have been impossible. I was in a very small humor for any enjoyment whatever. For myself I do not feel the smallest regret. Gala days and processions never, even as a boy, gave me any pleasure, and I always feel inclined to moralize in the Hamlet vein when I see grown men and women playing at theatricals off the stage. For instance, the pageant which I saw on the opening of Parliament suggested no thoughts but those which belong to a sense of the ridiculous. A review, suggesting the conception of a real battle, is a different thing, and impresses me to tears. I cannot see a regiment manœuvre, nor artillery in motion without a choking sensation, but pomps with feathers and jewels and fine carriages always make me sad or else contemptuous. Pageants never leave a sense of grandeur, but always of meanness and paltriness, on my mind. It is not so with a mountain or a picture. I would far, far rather go through the Exhibition without a crowd, and quietly get a few ideas, as I trust I shall do.

I am delighted to find that you enjoy the Exhibition. When did I despise it as a frivolous thing? The pomp of the procession I cannot care for, — the Exhibition itself is improving and intellectual.

X.

Ralph King, Lady Lovelace's son, who has taken a strange fancy to venerate me, came down from town with his tutor to be at church on Sunday, by his own wish. He came to breakfast with me on Monday, and with great *naïveté* and originality expressed his interest in the view I had taken on Sunday of the non-spirituality of the yearning for death, and remarked "that it was suicide without the courage of suicide." An evangelical lady came into the vestry to express her bewilderment at the doctrine. I replied that I thought it was best to set a standard that was real, actual, and human, not one either insincerely or morbidly professed; that many an evangelical clergyman, after an ultra-spiritual discourse, in which desire for heaven and God at once was taught as the only Christian feeling, would go home and sit over his glass of port very comfortably, satisfied with it as before, until heaven comes, — which I considered a sure way of making all unreal. "Well," said she, "I thought you, of all people, were like St. Paul, and that you would wish for a heavenlier life as much as he did." "First of all," said I, "you thought wrong; next, if I do wish to die, it is when I am in pain, or out of conceit with life, which happens pretty often, but which I do not consider spirituality." It is only an ungracious way of saying, "I am dissatisfied with what Thou hast given me, and do not like the duties that are mine at all. I am in pain, and want to be out of pain; and I suppose a great many very commonplace people could say the same piece of sublime discontent. Could not you?"

The fair saint was silenced.

XI.

To a Member of his Congregation.

Brighton: May 9, 1851.

My Dear ——: — I thank you much for the interesting letter you sent me, which I enclose. I did not know Mr. —— beyond the acquaintance of a single evening, but was extremely pleased with his son-in-law. He is at rest, I doubt not, now, — in that deep awful rest which is the most endearing of all the attributes of the life that shall be, — the rest which is order instead of disorder, — harmony instead of chaotic passions in jar and discord, and duty instead of the conflict of self-will with His loving will. It is a noble thought, and I never hear of any one who has probably attained it without a feeling of congratulation rising to the lips. You sign yourself "gratefully." If that is in reference to any good in instruction you may think you have derived from my ministry, — and I can conceive no other, — there is in the kind feeling far more to humble me than to give me joy. May God bless you!

XII.

To the Same.

Brighton: May 16, 1851.

My Dear —— : — I am deeply grateful for your note, but, I can only say again, more surprised and humbled by it than even gladdened. Yet I can rejoice, if not for my own sake, yet for yours. That a ministry full of imperfection and blind darkness should do *any* good is a source to me of even new wonder. That one in which words and truth, if truth come, wrung out of mental pain and inward struggle, should now and then touch a corresponding chord in minds with which, from invincible and almost incredible shyness, I rarely come in personal contact, is not so surprising, for I suppose the grand principle is the universal one. We can only heal one another with blood, — whether it comes from the agony itself, or the feeble and meaner pains of common minds and hearts. If it were not for such rewards and consolations, unexpectedly presenting themselves at times, the Christian Ministry would be, at least to some minds, and in the present day, insupportable. Once more, thank you. I do trust, with all my heart, that your estimate of the effects of what you hear on your own heart may not be delusive. I know that spoken words impress, and that impression has its danger as well as its good. Hence I cannot even rejoice without fear, for I confess that at best pulpit instruction seems to me to be as pernicious as it is efficacious. And Carlyle's view of stump oratory is only too mournfully true. To spend life and waste all strength of nerve and heart upon it, seems like a duty of sowing the sea-sand.

Still, some good is done, but much less than people think; and the drawback, which you correctly state, is one which must always be allowed for as a very large deduction from its apparent effects, — I mean the absence of any immediate opportunity of carrying transient impressions into action, and the exhaustion of the feelings which are perpetually stimulated for no definite result.

At the highest, all I count on is the probability that in many minds a thought here and there may strike root and grow, mixing with life and ordinary trains of feeling a somewhat higher tone than otherwise might have been, and bringing forth results which will be unconscious and utterly untraceable to the mind that originated them, just as it would be impossible to say whence the thistledown came, that is resulting now in a plentiful crop of weeds, alas! — the simile is an ominous one, — on the downs above.

XIII.

To the Same.

Brighton : May 17, 1851.

My dear ——: — I send you back Carlyle's letter. I have read Bushnell; there are some good things in him, but on the whole I think him most shadowy and unsatisfactory. He does not sufficiently show that dogmas express eternal verities and facts; that they are what a mathematician might call approximative formulas to truth. In this spirit I always ask, what does that dogma mean? Not what did it mean in the lips of those who spoke it? How, in my language, can I put into form the underlying truth, in correcter form if possible, but in only approximative form after all? In this way purgatory, absolution, Mariolatry, become to me fossils, not lies.

Of course people speak bitterly against my teaching, and of course I feel it keenly. But I cannot help it, and I cannot go out of my way to conciliate opposition and dislike. Misapprehension will account for part. Partly the divergence is real. But to place the spirit above the letter, and the principle above the rule, was the aim of His Life, and the cause of the dislike He met with: therefore I am content.

And this, by the way, affords an answer to one part of your perplexity, viz., whether it be not dangerous to draw so exact a parallel between His office and ours? I only reply that, except in feeling a fellowship and oneness with that Life, and recognizing parallel feelings and parallel struggles, triumphantly sometimes, I do not see how life could be tolerable at all. He was Humanity, and in Him alone my humanity becomes intelligible. Do not tremble at difficulties and shoreless expanses of truth, if you feel drifting into them. God's truth must be boundless. Tractarians and Evangelicals suppose that it is a pond which you can walk round and say, "I hold the truth." What, all? "Yes, all; there it is, circumscribed, defined, proved, and you are an infidel if you do not think this pond of mine, that the great Mr. Scott, and Mr. Newton, and Mr. Cecil dug, quite large enough to be the immeasurable Gospel of the Lord of the universe."

Dare to be alone with God, my dear ——, trust Him, and do not fear that He will leave you in darkness long, though his light may dazzle. Was not He alone in this world?—unfelt, uncomprehended, suspected, spoken against? And before Him was the cross. Before us, a little tea-table gossip, and hands uplifted in holy horror. Alas! and we call that a cross to bear. Shame! yet still I do admit, that for a loving heart to lack sympathy is worse than pain. Do not hesitate to ask me about anything I say, if it seem difficult. I would gladly explain to any of my congregation anything I meant to say, if I said it obscurely, or if it seemed to conflict with their conceptions. But to you, at any time, I will with true enjoyment give such explanation, so never doubt about asking me.

XIV.

To the Same.

Brighton : May 21, 1851.

MY DEAR —— : — The question you put is by no means an easy one to answer; whether, namely, it be right and wise for you to read on both sides of the question, — or rather, I should say, questions? for on this subject they are endless, and grow up like Hydra's heads.

I could not reply, No: for that is the very advice given by the Romish Church, which we so much blame; and it is very inconsistent in us to condemn their prohibitions of heretical or Protestant books to the laity, if we, tractarian or evangelical clergy, forbid, as is constantly done, the perusal of books which we judge heretical. We say they are afraid of the truth, else, they would not forbid inquiry; and I do not see why unitarians, rationalists, or sceptics, might not retort the same charge on us. The fact, however, that they who so condemn the Romish Church find themselves compelled to very inconsistently imitate their conduct, is a proof, I think, that even in that most anti-Protestant proceeding there is a truth, inevitably acted on by every one in his own way, if we could only disengage it.

Now, first of all, the questions of religious truth are interminable, and a lifetime would scarcely suffice to even pass the outworks of them all. Next, very few minds are in possession of the means or of the severe mental training which qualifies to set out as an original discoverer of the truth; so that if we cannot begin with a large number of truths, which must be considered as first principles and settled, life must be one perpetual state of Pyrrhonism and uncertainty.

On the other hand, to refuse to examine when doubts arise is spiritual suicide; and I do not see how, on this principle, any progress in truth could ever have been made. Why should the Pharisees have been blamed for the views so long stereotyped on the Jews for remaining in Judaism?

One consolation, however, at once suggests itself. The condition of arriving at truth is not severe habits of investigation, but innocence of life and humbleness of heart. Truth is felt, not reasoned, out; and if there be any truths which are only appreciable by the acute understanding, we may be sure at once that these do not constitute the soul's life, nor error in these the soul's death. For instance, the metaphysics of God's Being, the "*plan*," as they call it, "of salvation," the exact distinction between the divine and human in Christ's Person. On all these subjects you may read and read till the brain is dizzy and the heart's action is stopped; so that of course the mind is bewildered. But on subjects of Right and Wrong, Divine and Diabolic, Noble and Base, I believe sophistry cannot puzzle so long as the life is right.

I should say, therefore: —

1. Remember how much is certain. Is there any doubt about the Sermon on the Mount? Whether, for instance, the Beatitudes are true to fact? Whether the pure in heart shall see God? Any doubt, whether to have the mind of Christ be salvation and rest? Well, if so, you may be content to leave much, if God will, to unfold itself slowly; if not, you can quietly wait for Eternity to settle it.

2. I think the only thing that can be said is broadly this: I would not read controversially. In this bewildered age of "Yeast" (by the by, the author of "Yeast" ought not to cry out about fermentation, unless he can show how it can be made bread, nor ought any one, duty now being rather to be silent), — in this age of "Yeast," an age in which, like Diana's worshippers, all are crying out loudly, the greater part not knowing why, or what the questions really are, it seems to me that the more we confine ourselves to simple duties the better. Be assured that there

is little to be known here: much to be borne: something to be done. What you are, and what your life means, you do not know. God only knows. You must be content with twilight, except when contrast with darkness makes the twilight seem, as it really is in comparison, a blaze of light.

Specially, in your own case, would not this be your duty? You have regular appointed teaching with which you are not dissatisfied. I should be the last to urge you to blind yourself by it, or refuse to receive light from any other quarter which, *presenting itself*, might make that teaching seem wrong; but so long as it appears to you not darkness, but light, surely it would be wisest, for your own peace and the harmony of your life, not to go *out of the way* to investigate and seek for views which may make that little light questionable. Try, rather, to live upon the truths you have for certain, and let them become firmer and firmer. How can you expect to fathom questions in which the wisest of the age have been sounding in vain? This conviction once settled, I think we shall become content to wait,—a great lesson; and let God teach us by degrees, instead of fancying we can find it all out by effort. Do you remember Wordsworth's—

> Think you 'mid all this mighty sum
> Of things for ever speaking,
> That nothing of itself will come,
> But we must still be seeking?

We do not trust God; we trust ourselves. We do not believe that He seeks us; we fancy we have to seek Him. We are anxious to know *all about* God, and meanwhile we never think of knowing *God*. God, instead of religion, and much more, God, instead of theology, is what we need to believe in.

I would avoid all controversy, written or spoken, if I were you. Controversy with acquaintances mystifies, renders you suspected, and embitters your own heart. Besides, how can you explain what you think or feel with no endorsed words which will be honored, as the bankers say? Then the controversial books of the day are so merely "Yeast," that they will leave your mind bewildered. I myself follow this plan as much as possible. I mix little with the religious world, and so avoid discussion. I read little of divinity, much more of literature, though that, from mental prostration, is now next to nothing. And I try to trust in God,—God and our souls; there is nothing else to trust to. And I am sure I should be giving you dreary advice were I to say, read on all sides of the question. No, I rather say: trust in God,—live in Him,—do his will,—and rest.

XV.

—— is a very sensible, good, and, I should think, wise man. I like what he says about the impossibility of any man being comprehensive, and not French, German, English, &c. There has been but one Son of *Man*.

Poor Comte! I recollect that there is in his work the usual amount of French vanity and nationality, which mars everything great. They have not a world-wide man: with all our egotism, we have. And, indeed, I think all our greatest men are more universal, more submissive to eternal and not merely conventional laws. Compare the Duke and Napoleon, though the talent of the latter was probably far greater.

Well, I care very little for the progress of society, if that only means that, some centuries hence, individuals will eat, drink, and sleep more abundantly and more cleanly than the masses now, those individuals being mortal, perishable, and dying out forever. They take away all that makes humanity grand, and then ask you to care for it and its progress. I care for religion,—for the hope of *a church;* that is, a society more united in each other, because more united in God. But separate from that, and the possibilities of nobleness which that involves, the destinies of the race appear to me little more interesting than the contemplation of the prospects of a tray of silkworms, — obscene and crawling reptiles, which may hereafter become moths, and die, when the eggs are only laid. The whole universe, in this aspect, is to me a hideous phantasm, — the cruel practising-shop of some demon experimentalist, who creates Frankensteins to be wretched and accursed, and makes them better every new attempt. Pleasant consolation for us, — no! me, the Frankenstein, to know that some centuries hence there will be no more anomalous, semi-noble, semi-banned, and blighted Frankensteins.

No, no, no! There is some better thing than that; and French atheism must get a human, humble, loving heart before it can even guess what.

XVI.

May, 1851.

I send you a letter which I received from Mr. Drew, pressing me into the service. This morning I had a long visit from Mr. Maurice, which kept me from writing to you at length. His countenance is benign, full of thought, marked with sorrow, — but conquered sorrow. Probably, from knowing his mind beforehand, I read large powers of sympathy with Humanity. He told me, simply and strongly, that he had seen and been pleased with my published addresses. I ought not to have said a long visit; it was under an hour, as he had to go off by the eleven o'clock train. I again declined joining in the course of lectures, — this time chiefly on the ground of health, for, indeed, I feel shattered, mentally unfit for such an effort, nor have I any desire left for prominence; the valley of existence is most fit for me. I am young enough in years, but too gray in heart, to buffet with the mountain tempests which blow on more lofty situations. Maurice, gentlemanly and calm, about fifty years of age, spoke less than I did. I was ashamed to feel that I had the talking to myself, and learned nothing except a lesson of humility. He thinks that the clergy of the Church of England may be now the leaders of the nation, if they will only give up the phantom of power for its reality, and sympathize with the working classes heartily and truly.

I have to be at the lecture to-night, so I must conclude.

XVII.

May 24.

Your account of your conversation with Brewster and Ashburner is very interesting. Some time ago I know that Faraday said he considered that they were just in sight of the discovery of the principle of life, "the distant discovery was already felt trembling along the line." It is enough to make one's brain reel, indeed, to think on these things.

It appears to me, however, that great mistakes are made in the expectations entertained with respect to what science can do. The scientific mode of viewing things is simply human: it is not God's way. Creation is one thing, — dissection is another. Dissection separates into organic parts, shows the flesh laid on the skeleton, &c.; but God did not make first a skeleton and then flesh. Life organized to itself its own body. And so too, according to Science, the final cause of the sensibility of the skin, and the insensibility of the parts below the skin, is the protection of the parts most exposed from injury. The extremities of the fingers are most sensitive; the heart and bones have few nerves. Had this been reversed, had the skin been apathetic and the interior parts sensitive, great pain would have been the result, to no purpose, and the parts exposed might have been destroyed, burnt, or broken without giving warning of danger; whereas, as it is, the most delicate parts, like the eyelid, are protected by an acute sensibility, which defends them at the most distant approach of injury.

Well, the anatomist says the final cause of this arrangement, that is, the end which was the cause of its being so arranged, was the protection of the structure. Of course the anatomist can go no further; but there are ends, which the anatomist's science does not even touch, subserved by these sensibilities,—the education, for instance, of the character and heart through pain; a much higher end, properly speaking, more truly the final cause of pain, than the preservation of the organic framework from harm. In all such departments Science must forever be at fault. She has not the organ nor the intuitive sense whereby their truths are discovered. It is like attempting to explain the ecstasies of music by mathematics. Mathematics have to do with music, because music coincides with mathematical truths and principles; but there is something in music which no mere mathematician can pronounce upon or discover,—a something which the very child who has an ear knows by intuition. He can tell the child, and Jenny Lind herself, the laws on which her science rests, much better than Jenny Lind knows, or with the deepest study could know; but then the spirit and life of it,—he is a miserable *charlatan* if he pretends to to say a word about them as discovered, or even discoverable, by mathematical science.

So with electricity, phrenology, &c.; they can tell us phenomena, but what lies beyond those phenomena they cannot tell forever. And the pretence to do it is the great absurdity of these *charlatans*, like Mr. Atkinson and Co. Christ told us, but by the intuitions of the soul, not by science.

I wonder whether this is intelligible, for I am so really worn in mind, far rather than in body, that I can scarcely get my mind to work at the simplest thought, without a sensation of restlessness. I wish it were not so, but this will all come round with time and rest.

XVIII.

Thanks for the information respecting Mrs. ——. I am afraid to go, lest my conception of the characters should be again linked with inferior associations. I do not think any woman could understand Macbeth or Macduff, only because both their good and bad are essentially masculine. And Lady Macbeth must be either sublime or ludicrous. Twenty to one on the latter. I wish I had heard "Midsummer Night's Dream," but I was otherwise engaged.

I return Sterling, &c. You must take the consequences of reading "The Law of Man's Nature." It is a book thoroughly worthless, but it also leaves a mental degradation which I would not accept as the price of the highest intellectual banquet. The author has done with Humanity what a certain lady did with a bone of a brother's skeleton, — made a whistle of it, and with equal good taste and good feeling. Luckily, the concord of sweet sounds was not very bewitching in either case, and if you persevere in hearing the whole concert you will have more patience and less inclination to wince from the discords of a heart out of tune from vanity than I had. I felicitate you upon your prospect of drinking for two days the music of the charnel-house. By the by, there is one inference worth drawing from the book. Whoever dethrones God, and sneers at Christ, must end in some such worship as — the idolatry of Mr. Mesmerist Atkinson.

XIX.

June, 1851.

In a letter I have just read of H. Martineau's, she says that her life was a series of abject discipleships till now, when she is "independent." I am glad you dislike the book. It is the most offensive I have read for a long time, — not because of its atheism, naked as that is, but because of the impertinent assumption of superiority which characterizes the letters of these inspired two. I can conceive a severe science compelling a mind step by step to the atheistic conclusions; and that mind, loyal to truth, refusing to ignore the conclusions or to hide them. But then I can only conceive this done in a noble sadness, and a kind of divine infinite pity towards the race which are so bereft of their best hopes; and have no patience with a self-complacent smirk which says, "Shut up the prophets; read Martineau and Atkinson. Friendship, Patriotism, are mesmerized brain; Faith, a mistake of the stomach; Love, a titillatory movement occurring in the upper part of the nape of the neck; Immortality, the craving of dyspepsia; God, a fancy produced by a certain pressure upon the gray parts of the hasty-pudding within the skull; Shakespeare, Plato, Hannibal, and all they did and wrote, weighed by an extra ounce or two of said pudding."

It is the flippant tone in which the most solemn hopes of the noblest humanity are disposed of that disgusts me. Besides, the angelic pair have deduced from their premises a conclusion of disproved, instead of not proven, which is all that science can ever pretend to show. She is inexcusable for saying that her limited capacities are to be the measure of all that is knowable. If there be a cause in this universe the effect of which she cannot perceive, that cause may be God, which simple possibility is quite sufficient to upset all she advances.

XX.

June, 1851:

I send you the article on Carlyle. Pray read it. It contains *some* truth and much falsehood,—the truth itself so torn from coherence with other parts of Carlyle's meaning as to be false. For instance, in column 2 he says that Carlyle reckons Christianity the most palpable sham and cobweb that ever superstition and hypocrisy invented; which is simply a slander and a lie, as he might have seen by a quotation he makes himself in column 3: "Sterling read a great deal; earnest books, — the Bible, *most earnest* of books, and his chief favorite."

Lie the second may be found where he says that the only persons for whom Carlyle's heart seemed to beat with congenial sympathy are the anarchists of Europe, &c. And this after reading Carlyle's "French Revolution" (if he did).

Of course the critique contains truth. Carlyle does cry out too much, in a way that has now become cant, against cant and shams, never even hinting a remedy; but this reviewer has never got into the atmosphere which he breathes, nor attempted to master his meaning and objects, without which thorough comprehension no one has a right to criticise.

XXI.

June, 1851.

Thanks for "Owen." I fear I shall have no time to read him, but I will try.

The necessarian scheme is intellectually impregnable; practically, an enormous falsehood; and in matters practical popular ideas are right, just as they are in metaphysical. There can be no Matter, metaphysics say, and say, it seems to me, irrefragably; but the popular conception is practically the true one, and the very highest philosophy, when it has completed the circle, gets back to that again.

So of the necessarian scheme. It is a half-truth, and we shall flounder away into fearful self-correction if we take the "Constitution of Man" instead of the prophets, economic well-being instead of the Gospel, and pet vice and crime as amiable diseases. I am still, in *many cases*, for the Christian virtue of an English oak-stick, with an English hand to lay it on, and show mercy when you have done justice.

Nevertheless, even this one-sided scheme contains a truth. It is quite true that poverty comes from crime; but it is also true that crime is often the result of poverty. Craniology, education, circumstances, &c., are causes, and must not be ignored. But they are not the only causes, and there is a something which can rise above them all nobly. Else I think the defence of the prisoner to his judge, when tried for stealing, was unanswerable: *Mais, mon Dieu, monsieur, il faut vivre.* In my humble opinion the judge's reply, however, on necessarian principles, was quite as philosophical when he said, *Je ne vois pas la nécessité,* and sentenced the thief to death.

I was well aware of the fact about the invisibility of the sunbeam till it impinges on earthly particles. Therefore I hold this visible universe to be the word or expression of God, who is visible thereby. I do not hold "material manifestations insufficient for spirituality," and only interrogate each such manifestation, "Of *what* art thou a manifestation?" For instance, a Lord Mayor's feast is a manifestation, and a very material one, of large resources, great contrivance, and vast aldermanic intellect. I acknowledge that I find it insufficient to prove great spirituality, though it is to a Greenlander's train-oil feast what the Exhibition is to his canoe. Multiply the alderman's paradise by the accumulated science of a thousand years, and I do not think it proves us a bit nearer the conversion of this earth into a kingdom of God. I will accept, however, a dish of *un*-crimped cod on a Christian's table, if you can find it, as such an evidence; or a soup-kitchen, or a ducal suggestion of curry-powder for starving people, provided it comes off his own plate. But the invention of piquant sauces, luxurious furniture, tasteful jewelry, &c., &c., &c., I humbly decline to accept as proofs of anything beyond the fact that man is a very sagacious and surprising beaver. A spirit? *Non, mille fois non,* unless he can show something more than this. Poor Robert Owen's book, right or wrong, raises Humanity, in my eyes, above a thousand Exhibitions. Cheops and Cephrenes built great pyramids; so did Rhamsinitus, a brick one, very marvellous in its day,—a new era in building, they say, as when glass superseded brick. The spirituality of those "material manifestations?" Mummy of the sacred cat! whose dry carcass has rested there these three thousand years at the expense of the life and breath of the myriad wretches who toiled for their pay of a few onions, — say how we shall unswathe the spirituality of that most manifest materialism out of thy most holy cerements. And yet I fancy the progress of the race was made thereby " patent to the masses," by a very royal patent! I grant the grandeur of understanding and "beaverism." I only say that I measure the spirituality of the grandest undertaking by the degrees of its unselfishness.

> Worth makes the man, and want of it the fellow:
> The rest is all but leather and prunella.

XXII.

June, 1851.

I have been reading some of Leigh Hunt's works lately, — the "Indicator," " A Jar of Honey from Mount Hybla," — and am surprised at the freshness, and sweetness, and Christian, not lax, spirit of human benevolence and toleration which existed in the heart of one who was the contemporary, and even colleague, of Byron. The "Indicator," a series of papers like the " Spectator," &c., is a most refreshing collection of ancient stories, and kind-hearted literary gossip. The " Jar of Honey," is, in fact, nothing more than a collection of all the sweet things that poetry has hived up for centuries in the literature of Sicily, from the times of Polyphemus, &c., &c., down to those of Theocritus, and even to the present day. There is no very transcendent talent anywhere, but good taste, refinement, tolerably extensive reading, and the springiness of a kind heart, imparting a life and newness to all he says.

You were unfortunate about Covent Garden Market; but it is not always so. Sometimes the brightness of that hour in London is very remarkable. Your description of the fog, dirt, smoke, bustle, &c., made me feel how little, how very, very little, we know and think of the suffering life of our fellow-creatures. To get a dish of green peas, or young potatoes, on a West-End table, how much toil and unknown deprivation must be gone through by human beings! It seems to me a great and good lesson to go through these crowded places to see what life is, — the life of the millions, not the few, — and then to think of our æsthetics, as Kingsley said, — and our life one long pursuit of enjoyment, and disappointment if we do not get it. When life to us, from mere heat, is simply endurance, what must it be to those who have only the shady side of a burning house to shelter them, and that only for a few minutes? — for if they stop, there will be no supper that day at home.

About Pascal's opinion that, as beauty perishes, attachment for the sake of beauty is not attachment, — well, I do not know. Mind gets weak; therefore to be attached to a person for mental qualification is not, &c., &c.; and character changes, therefore he who was attached to that which did not last was not attached at all. I do not think this is true. Beauty may be a lower cause of attachment, but I suppose persons may be really attached *for* that, not merely *to* that; and quite true that in a low nature that will be a low attachment. I do not think that in a high one it must. In some it kindles high and self-devoted feelings, just as in a degraded and sensual nature it produces selfish ones. Besides, it is untrue to say that *la petite vérole* will extinguish it necessarily; it may have begun on account of beauty, and then gone on to something higher. Chivalry, gratitude, habits of tenderness, I believe, would retain affection, provided it had not been quenched already. No, it would not be *la petite vérole* that would undermine it, but moral deformity which had been discovered uncorresponding to outward beauty. I am quite certain that beauty attracts an unvitiated heart only because it seems, by a law of our thought, the type of mental and moral beauty: and where these are not, disgust and reaction would come sooner and more surely than from small-pox. Further, I think that where qualities are loved and appreciated by habit, the beauty of feature is no longer observed, nor its absence missed. Expression reminds of what we know of the person, and the shape and color are actually forgotten. The ugliest man I ever knew, I actually at last thought handsome, and I do not believe that any beauty would seem surpassingly beautiful after it had once reminded of folly or evil.

XXIII.

Thank you for your account of the "Associations Ouvriéres." The time is coming, no doubt, when in some form or other, this principle will be tried. I do not expect that it can be the final form of human co-operation. It is too artificial, and, at present, only another shape of protection; for which reason I cannot feel very enthusiastic about the "self-sacrifice" which you think it implies. However, I am willing to accept it as a step to better things. That inalienable capital which your friends are forming, to belong only to the association, will after a time, become the capital of a wealthy corporation; and if many such corporations should arise, the struggle of the next generation will be to break them down: they will be bloated aristocracies of the year 2000, and the chivalry of that age will be exhibited in a crusade against them.

The elective affinities cannot hold five men together for a month. I wonder where we shall find a principle of cohesion to bind men together really, except interest; for chartisms and socialisms are only this.

I saw a family of love at the Zoological Gardens,—five leopards together, kissing and playing with one another. By and by a keeper came with sundry joints of a murdered sheep. The brothers began to growl and bite, each seized a bone and went off to his corner, snarling, and unable to enjoy for fear.

XXIV.
To a Roman Catholic Friend.
July 1, 1851.

MY DEAR MRS. ——: — I will briefly answer your question. What am I?

Not an eclectic, certainly.

An eclectic is one who pieces together fragmentary opinions culled out of different systems on some one or other principle of selection.

I endeavor to seize and hold the spirit of every truth which is held by all systems under diverse, and often in appearance contradictory, forms.

I will give you an instance.

A very short time ago, Mrs. Jameson was showing me the sketches she had made for her new work on Christian Art, exhibiting the gradual progress in the worship of the Virgin.

At first the sculptures were actual copies of known heathen goddesses with a child in arms; then the woman kneeling before the Son, — next the woman crowned, on a throne with the Son, but lower; after that, on the same throne on a *higher* level; lastly, the Son in wrath, about to destroy the universe, and the mother interposing her woman's bosom in intercession. These were distinctly different in date.

Well, I remembered at once, this is what the evangelicals do in another way. They make two Gods, a loving one and an angry one, — the former saving from the latter. Both, then, agree in this, that the anger and the love are expressed as resident in different personalities.

Now here I get a truth. Not by eclecticism, taking as much of each as I like, but that which both assert; and then I dispense with the formal expression of the thought. The Son and the Virgin, the Father and the Son, opposed to each other; this is the form of thought, in both false; the human mind's necessity of expressing objectively the opposition of two truths by referring them to different personalities, leaving them thus distinct, real, and undestroyed by a namby-pamby blending of the two into one, I recognize as the truth of both.

The evangelical "scheme" of reconciling justice with mercy I consider the poorest effort ever made by false metaphysics. They simply misquote a text. That he might be just [and yet] the justifier. Whereas St. Paul says, the just and the justifier: i. e. just *because* the justifier. The Romish view is as usual materialistic, but both express the same felt necessity. And, in fact, truth is always the union of two contradictory propositions, both remaining undiluted, — not the *viâ media* between them.

The Romish view, however coarsely and materially, expresses another truth. In Christ is "neither male nor female." Now the common view of His incarnation had only exhibited the fact that man, meaning the masculine sex, had become in Him divine. Soon, however, the world began to feel, — womanly qualities are divine too. Not the courage and the wisdom, which used to be deified, but the graces which Christianity has emphatically pronounced blessed. Now they did not perceive that this truth is contained in the incarnation of Him in whom met all that was most womanly and all that was most manly: that divine manhood means not divine masculineness, but divine humanity, containing both sexes as the mutual supplement of each other. Accordingly, what was left for them but to have a queen of heaven as well as a Son of God?

It is very curious that M. Comte, the French infidel, has, in his way, felt the same necessity. In his last work, I am told, he speaks of woman-worship as that which the age wants.

Thus, then, out of Evangelicalism and Romanism, I get one and the same truth. And out of Romanism and Atheism I get another truth, — not eclectically, but just as I should get oxygen out of rust, carbonic acid, mould, and then hold oxygen as one of the principles of the universe, because I found it in almost everything.

My system, no doubt, is vague; but it saves me from dogmatism, for I know that my mode of expressing the truth so eliminated, is just as much a form as the mode of Romanism, Evangelicalism, or Atheism, and may become just as bigoted and narrow; only I am quite saved, I believe, from gazing upon anything but the invisible and the eternal as reality. Meanwhile I try to feel with all, not as a latitudinarian, but so far as all or any hold, even formally and bigotedly, truths. And I feel that to them in that stage, *that* form may be necessary. It also keeps me humble; for I feel how almost impossible it is for a human mind to gaze on realities, essences, truths, except in the concrete, — just as oxygen can only be seen in combination with iron, for instance, when it becomes rust; with sulphur, when it becomes sulphuric acid, &c., &c.

Humanly speaking, therefore, it is impossible that I could ever become an Evangelical, a Romanist, or an Infidel. Neither of the two first, because I feel that they have only poor forms of truth, materialistic and metaphysical: not the last, because I feel too deeply, even in his negations, truth; in his "It is not," how much more truly "Something *is*."

I am blind and ignorant; but I can see this at least, that the blue, red, yellow, &c., reflected from sky and bush and sea, are not the light itself, but only reflected fragments of the light; the "elements of the world" on which the light is broken, but yet made visible. Some day you will feel this. *I think you feel it now*, and suspect that Romanism is not finality, but only uncouth stammerings of truth, and very, very coarse.

XXV.

I have had a long correspondence with Maurice and Mr. Drew. I asked Mr. Tower's brother to dinner a day or two ago. He is a sincere, earnest-minded man, very High Church I should think, but, like many of that school, generous and liberal. My visits among the poor to-day included two very sad cases. One, that of a poor family, the father of which is just dead, and the mother a hard-working worthy woman overwhelmed with grief, and crushed by inability to pay the funeral expenses. Only 4*l*.! And to think that 4*l*., lavished like pence by tens of thousands of the wealthy people in this country, can make eight or nine human beings free, and the want of it reduce them nearly to starvation. I was able to promise to defray the bill, — not all out of my own pocket; the gratitude and relief were touching indeed.

The other case was that of a poor creature, whom I left with what appeared an abscess in the cheek-bone. It is now pronounced cancer. The pain amounts to agony, incessant and intolerable. Morphine stupefies for a short time, and chloride of lime partly purifies the horrors of the mouth; but in that state now for months she must remain, and no earthly power can save her, scarcely any even assuage her torture. Since then I have — not laughed, — no, for my laugh is now a ghastly, hollow, false lie of a thing, — but I have dined, forgotten, talked, read, written, with no physical pain now to endure. How passing strange that misery of suffering is; and how questionable the right which two thirds of the world assume to themselves of filling their ears with cotton, that the moans may not break in upon their silken repose, and that the cry of the toiling thousands may float by on the blast unheard! But suppose that cry goes up to the ears of God, and He asks, "Whom did you relieve? whom did you clothe? whom did you feed, with your tens, hundreds, or thousands?" Assuredly, protest against Kingsley who will, he stood on a deep awful truth, "God will yet take account of the selfishness of wealth: and His quarrel has yet to be fought out." I have been thinking lately much, sadly, self-condemningly.

Had any one preached that all the evils of anarchy and insubordination proceeded from the selfish vanities of the poorer classes, forgetting that a revolution may be goaded on, it would have been one-sided and dangerous; but as soon as ever a man is found to state somewhat too strongly the case of the weak against the strong, the Churchman cries "Danger!" Danger to comfort and property, I suppose, which is the only danger that wakes up a protest.

Do not be dismayed or discouraged if the reading of Scripture does not suggest as yet. Receive, imbibe, and then your mind will create; but our mistake lies in thinking that we can give out until we have taken in. In all things this is the order. Poets are creators, because recipients; they open their hearts wide to Nature instead of going to her with views of her ready-made and second-hand. They come from her and give out what they have felt and what she said to them; so with Scripture, — patient, quiet, long revering, listening to it; then suggestiveness.

XXVI.

July, 1851.

I wish I did not hate preaching so much, but the degradation of being a Brighton preacher is almost intolerable. "I cannot dig, to beg I am ashamed"; but I think there is not a hard-working artizan whose work does not seem to me a worthier and higher being than myself. I do not depreciate spiritual work, — I hold it higher than secular; all I say and feel is, that by the change of times the pulpit has lost its place. It does only part of that whole which used to be done by it alone. Once it was newspaper, schoolmaster, theological treatise, a stimulant to good works, historical lecture, metaphysics, &c., all in one. Now these are partitioned out to different officers, and the pulpit is no more the pulpit of three centuries back, than the authority of a master of a household is that of Abraham, who was soldier, butcher, sacrificer, shepherd, and emir in one person. Nor am I speaking of the ministerial office; but only the "stump orator" portion of it, — and that I cannot but hold to be thoroughly despicable.

I had an hour's baiting from Mrs. —— yesterday, in reference, no doubt, to what the papers have been saying, and to reports of my last sermons. She talked very hotly of the practice of laying all faults at the door of the aristocracy, whereas it was the rich city people, on whom she lavished all her (supposed) aristocratic scorn, who were in fault, because they would live like nobles. Besides, did not the nobles spend their money, and was not that support of the poor? I wasted my time in trying to explain to her that expenditure is not production; that £50,000 a year spent is not £50,000 worth of commodities produced, and adds nothing to the real wealth of the country. I tried to show her that twenty servants are not supported by their master, but by the laborers who raise their corn and make their clothes; and that twenty beings taken off the productive classes throws so much more labor upon those classes. Of course such things are necessary; only employment does not create anything. Men engaged in carrying dishes or in making useless roads are employed, no doubt. But this labor does the country no good; and the paying of them for their labor, or the mere giving in charity, may make a fairer distribution of the wealth there is, but does not go one step towards altering the real burden of the country or producing new wealth. Extravagant expenditure impoverishes the country. This simple fact I could not make her comprehend. Then she got upon political preaching, — abused it very heartily, — acknowledged that religion had to do with man's political life, but said a clergyman's duty is to preach obedience to the powers that be, — was rather puzzled when I asked her whether it were legitimate to preach from James v. 1: "Go to now, ye rich men, weep and howl," &c., — asked whether it was possible for old women and orphans to understand such subjects; to which I replied, "No; and if a clergyman refuse to touch on such subjects, which belong to real actual life, the men will leave his church; and, as is the case in the Church of England, he will only have charity orphans, who are compelled to go, and old women to preach to."

On Monday I had a long visit from ———. He wanted me to preach in Percy Chapel for some schools. I refused. The system of "starring" it through the country is a contemptible one. If there is a feeble light in any man, the glow worm is the type which nature has given for his conduct, to shine or glimmer quietly in his own place, and let the winged insects come to the light if they like. Whereas the fireflies which fly in the West Indies, obtruding themselves about in people's faces, are caught and put under a watch-glass by the inhabitants, to show them what o'clock it is by night. When they have been used up they are thrown aside, and no one stops to see whether they live or die. The quiet little glowworm is seen only by those that love it. Birds of prey are asleep. What a pretty little fable might be made of this! For men and women it is true. She who will be admired, flashing her full-dressed radiance in the foolish or rather wise world's face, will be treated like the firefly, used to light up a party or to flirt with, and then, &c., &c.

XXVII.

"A firm belief that at some brighter period, when the world should have grown ripe for it, in heaven's own time, a new truth would be revealed in order to establish the whole relation between man and woman on a surer ground of mutual happiness. The angel and apostle of the coming revelation must be a woman indeed, but lofty, pure, and beautiful and wise: moreover, not through dusky grief, but through the ethereal medium of joy, and showing how sacred love should make us happy by the truest test of a love successful to that end." — *Helps.*

That is to me remarkable, as a coincidence with a favorite thought of mine concerning the origin of Mariolatry, which I have sometimes worked out, and also with an unmistakable tendency in the present day to revive Mariolatry; as if the truth in it were not yet got out.

It coincides, too, with the (sometimes frantic) efforts made for female emancipation, and outcries, especially in America, about their slavery; it coincides, moreover, with a philosophic speculation of M. Comte's upon this subject, who looks for the hope of the future in not hero-worship, but woman-worship.

I think it would shed a kind of setting light and glory upon the deathbeds of those whose aspirations have been high, and whose work is done in this world, if, as they go out of it, they could see some such hope for the race coming in, — as at the dawn of a former salvation, hearts old and worn with hopeless expectation, cried, "Lord, now lettest thou thy servant depart in peace." A work written by the author quoted above contains some interesting and valuable thoughts on this head, — not quixotic. Meanwhile, the hope of a flash of illuminating light, coming suddenly, yet by degrees, like the lightning from the electricity which has gathered through the summer months, slowly, and from a woman's heart, is a very precious thought, and one which so harmonizes with my own dim anticipations, that I mean to let my mind dwell on it much; for it is well to occupy one's self with a noble hope.

Tennyson's "Vision of Sin," too mystical for most people, has long been to me the shadowing of an awful truth: and the way in which high feelings subside into the despair of self, or scorn of others, is one of the most terrible facts of our humanity. I have seen how moral wreck and ruin here and hereafter may tremble upon the destiny of a single individual heart, and how, if such a one heart should fall into callousness or sin or recklessness, personal goodness would cease to be a matter of care; nay, dreadful to say, might become loathsome, as implying superiority to that other, and then there would be nothing left but plunge after plunge into degradation and vileness. So it is that feelings in themselves not ungenerous may become the very ministers and railroads which smooth the way for evil. At least, this is the utterance of the deepest thought on and result of what I have seen in life. It is expressed, perhaps, mystically, as it were, afar off, in indefinite and abstract terms, but it is no abstraction or vague dream.

I have caught Mr. —— in some impertinent condemnations of me behind my back. I have written to him straight, to ask him whether he said it or not. If he has, I will bring the matter to a point, and stop some of these smooth gentlemen, Mr. —— and Mr. —— included, who are all smiles and friendliness to my face, and treat me like a heretic or an infidel behind my back. I will put a stop to this backstairs clerical gossip and bigotry for a little time.

I have read no new book, except Leigh Hunt's "Autobiography." Leigh Hunt is interesting; he is full of little literary light gossip of Shelley, Byron, Hazlitt, Godwin, &c., and many other names I am familiar with. He has a very charitable and cheerful view of men and life; indeed, too much so; for men who do great things, who are made of sterner stuff, and do not take the rose-water way of making all sweet by making the surface odoriferous and pleasant, while all below is full of misery.

XXVIII.

My dear ——, — Your mamma showed me your questions to her, and I offered to answer them as well as I can, though it would be easier to do so *de vive voix* than on paper. That respecting the personality of the Devil I have already answered in a letter to your sister, though I am not sure that it was sufficiently detailed to be quite satisfactory or intelligible. Remember, however, that the main thing is to *believe in God*, which is the chief article of all the creeds. Our salvation does not depend upon our having right notions about the Devil, but right feelings about God. And if you hate evil, you are on God's side, whether there be a personal evil principle or not. I myself believe there is, but not so unquestioningly as to be able to say, I think it a matter of clear revelation. The Bible *does* reveal God, and except with a belief in God there will and can be no goodness. But I can conceive intense hatred of wrong with great uncertainty whether there be a Devil or not. Indeed many persons who believe in a Devil are worse instead of better for their belief, since they throw the responsibility of their acts off themselves on him. Do not torment yourself with such questions. The simpler ones are the deepest.

Next, as to St. James's assertion that "faith without works profiteth nothing"; which appears to contradict St. Paul's, who says that "a man is justified by faith without the deeds of the law."

Suppose I say, "A tree cannot be struck without thunder," that is true, for there is never destructive lightning without thunder. But, again, if I say, "The tree was struck by lightning without thunder," that is true, too, if I mean that the lightning alone struck it, without the thunder striking it. Yet read the two assertions together, and they seem contradictory. So, in the same way, St. Paul says, "Faith justifies without works," — that is, faith *only* is that which justifies us, not works. But St. James says, "Not a faith which is without works." There will be works with faith, as there is thunder with lightning; but just as it is not the thunder but the lightning, the lightning without the thunder, that strikes the tree, so it is not the works which justify. Put it in one sentence,—*Faith alone justifies: but not the Faith which is alone.* Lightning alone strikes, but not the lightning which is alone without thunder; for that is only summer lightning, and harmless. You will see that there is an ambiguity in the words "without and alone," and the two apostles use them in different senses, just as I have used them in the above simile about the lightning.

All this will be more plain if you consider what faith is. It is that strong buoyant confidence in God and in His love which gives energy and spirit to do right without doubt or despondency. Where God sees that, He sees the spring and fountain out of which all good springs: He sees, in short, the very life of Christ begun, and He reckons that to be righteousness; just as a small perennial fountain in Gloucestershire is the Thames, though it is not as yet scarcely large enough to float a schoolboy's boat; and just as you call a small seedling not bigger than a little almond peeping above the ground, an oak: for the word "justify" means not to be made righteous, but to reckon or account righteous.

Now observe, just as you count the seven springs to be the Thames *without* a flood of waters, and without the navy that rides on the Thames, and just as you call the sapling an oak, without the acorns, so God reckons the trust in Him as righteousness, because it is the fountain and the root of righteousness, being, indeed, the life divine in the soul. He reckons it as such (that is, He justifies the soul that has it) without works,—that is, before works are done, and not because of the works. But then that faith will not be without works; for the fountain *must* flow on, and the tree *must* grow, and the life of God in the soul, sanguine trust in

God, the loving and good One, *must* spring up with acts; for to say that it does not would be to say that it is dead, or that it is like summer lightning, or like the gutter, which is running past my house now, after a shower of rain, and which is no perennial spring. St. Paul says, Works — mere acts, — are not enough to justify us; because they are limited and imperfect. Ten thousand — a million — cannot, because even a million is a limited number. Nothing can justify but faith, for faith is infinite, and immeasurable like a fountain. True, replies St. James. But then do not think that St. Paul means to say that a living fount of faith will be barren, without works. The faith which saves, is not that kind which has no piety, but that kind which is ever prolific, — "a well of water springing up into everlasting life."

Tell me if this is plain, and tell me fairly and truly. I have great enjoyment in writing to you and your sisters, and I shall always have great enjoyment in answering all of your questions, or in assisting you in any way I can.

XXIX.

My dear Friend, — I will, in as short a space as I can, give you my notions on this baptismal controversy. I believe the Scripture doctrine to be this: —

Christ revealed the fact that all men are God's children. He proclaimed a new name of God, — the Father; and a new name of man, or Humanity, — the Son; a vital union, by a Spirit ever near, ever inward, — "a light lighting *every* man that cometh into the world." The grand distinctive truth contained in this, — I say distinctive, because, in a *way*, the Jews had acknowledged God as a Father, — was, that God was recognized as the Father of all; not Jews only, — there had lain the old falsehood, — but Gentiles too. This was the Gospel, so peculiarly the essential truth of the Gospel, that

St. Paul calls it "the mystery." "My gospel" is the thing hidden from ages and generations, viz. that the Gentiles should be fellow-heirs. This, then, is the message to the *world;* baptism is that message to the *individual.* You personally, especially, by name, A or B, are hereby informed of that truth, — you are God's child. You are henceforth to live as such, — not according to the old falsehood, as a child of the Devil, denying God your Father, living with no resemblance to him; but henceforth redeemed from that into privilege. There is a difference, however, between being God's child by right, and God's child in fact. All who are born into the world are God's children by right. They are not so, in fact, until they recognize it, and believe it, and live as such. To believe it, and live it, is to be regenerate. For instance, had the Dauphin of France been apprenticed to the cobbler Simon till twenty years of age, he was, by right, heir to the kingdom; but, in fact, ignorant of his right, with no royal character, but with base habits. Yet you could say, those were not his proper but his false nature. Now, a revelation made to him, even by a bad man, say by Simon, of the fact, would have altered all, put him in possession of new motives, and, supposing that accession had been possible, put him in possession of the kingdom. You would, rightly, then have said that the letter conveying that intimation, authoritatively, had made him a royal child and heir of the kingdom. Yet made only in a figurative sense, — made only as resting on a previous fact. That letter did not create him the first-born of France, but authoritatively revealed him as such. I believe that baptism does the same. I can, with all my heart, use the language of the catechism of the Church, and say, "In baptism I was *made* a child of God," &c.; just as a sovereign is made king by coronation, but only made so because he was *de jure* such before. And the act of a bad man or minister is just as valid as Simon's supposed intimation, because the fact is fact, — eternal fact, whether known or not, and quite independent of his character. A heathen is God's child if he only knew it. You send a missionary to him to tell him what he is, and to bid him realize his royal character; but being God's child *de jure* avails him nothing, unless he becomes such in fact, that is, changes his life and character, and becomes, like his Father, pure and holy. Then he is regenerate: God's child before unconsciously, God's child now by a second birth consciously. Nay, in fact, till now he was a child of wrath, in which again I entirely take the Church's words, "by nature a child of wrath." Yet that is not the proper real state, but the false one, unnatural and contradictory to our nature. I will only quote two or three texts: "*Because* ye are sons," &c. Sons before regeneration. Regenerated, that is, endued with a spirit of sonship, because sons. Here is the distinction *de jure* and *de facto*, the latter resting on the former. Again, "He came unto *his own*," &c. They were his own, observe, children *de jure*. "But as many as received Him, to them gave He power to *become* the Sons of God, even as many as believe on his name truly," — his name of Father. Once more "the like *figure* whereunto even baptism doth also now save us." It saves us *figuratively*, just as coronation *makes* a king; and therefore I love the language of the baptismal service. Baptism is, therefore, an authoritative symbol of an eternal fact; a truth of eternity realized in time, and brought down to the limits "then and there"; then and there made God's child; but it is only the realization of a fact true before baptism, and without baptism; the personal realization of a fact which belongs to all humanity, and was revealed by Christ; in other words, it is redemption applied. I disagree both with the Bishop of Exeter and Mr. Gorham. The Bishop, whose view is exactly that of the Council of Trent, holds that a miracle takes place in baptism; that one who not even by right is God's child, miraculously becomes such by the utterance of a form of words, and the sprinkling of water: the Eternal descends at the spell of a man. This is incantation, not Christianity; and I object to it, because it professes to create a fact instead of witnessing to it and being based upon it; I object to it, because it denies the great fact for which the Redeemer died, that all mankind are, *de jure*, God's sons, and that He bids them become such *de facto*. Mr. Gorham's view is to me still more offensive. The Bishop's, at least, has this advantage: it prevents sectarian narrowness, and attempts to decide who are and are not God's children, by the broad inclusion of all the baptized under that name. But Mr. Gorham holds that *sometimes* a special miracle takes place in baptism, and sometimes not; that when it does, it is in consequence of what he calls prevenient grace; consequently, he cannot call even all baptized persons God's children, to say nothing of the race. He opens the door to sectarian uncharitableness, judgment of one another, painful attempts to decide who are, and who are not the elect, and still more painful uncertainty to each individual whether *he* is presumptuous or not in believing himself God's son. It has all the evils of the Bishop's views and some of its own. A man is left to the uncertain and ever-varying play of his own emotions to judge this awful question: whereas baptism was given as a pledge to rest on. I know that I have a right to claim to be His child, to live as His child, and that if I do not, I am keeping myself out of a heritage which is my own. How do I know it? Because baptism has authoritatively declared it to me. But I cannot be vain, because it is a privilege not created by my feelings, but by eternal fact, and shared by the sweep who holds out his hat to me at the crossing of a street. He, too, is a child of God; my brother; and it is my shame if I treat him otherwise. God's image is in him, marred, it may be, or nearly invisible, but there. And so it was in the publicans and harlots whom Christ treated as human beings when the "religious people" of His day were very indignant at the idea. This is a grand and blessed truth taught by baptism, and not only taught but taught authoritatively, since it is not a *conventional* ordinance, but a divine command.

I do not know, my dear Mr. Trench, whether this rapid outline will be very intelligible; but every word I have written is capable of proofs and ramifications of thought which would fill quires, and I will not attempt to dilate. In reply to the question whether I think the Council have decided rightly, I should say I do. I do *not* think Mr. Gorham's view the view of the Church of England; but I think it is not irreconcilable with it, and I should be very sorry to see the Church pledged to any narrow form of thought which would exclude such shades of opinion. I have no doubt that the Bishop's view is more in letter reconcilable with the Church formularies, and I doubt not has been the view held by a large number of her leading divines; but I humbly trust that I would lose everything on earth rather than teach it or believe in it.

I envy you the society of the Eagles. I would give anything for leisure to think quietly, and get out of the jar of human life, and the perpetual necessity of talking, which consumes an amount of energy which should be thrown on action that few suspect or dream of. Count yourself happy that your life-calling is to do, and not to chatter. "Speech is of silver, silence of gold," says the German proverb; and the talker is to my mind, by necessity, the smallest of human souls. His soul must ever dwindle, dwindle, dwindle, for he utters great feelings in words instead of acts, and so satiates his need of utterance, the need of all.

XXX.

I shall reply at once to some of the questions in your letter. There is really a connection in the passage you refer to, Luke xviii. 8. He had already referred to the apparent slowness with which evil is redressed, — nevertheless, "God will avenge His own elect, though He bear long with them," that is, seem to delay; still, though this redress will come, when it comes, will they be expecting it? Will not hope and trust in it be worn out? "Shall the Son of Man, when He cometh, find faith upon the earth?" I do not, therefore, conceive that this passage even touches the question whether the human race will advance or deteriorate, whether religion will be spread universally or be extinct at Christ's coming; but another question altogether, for "faith" here means not faith generally, but faith with a special reference, — a reference to the redress spoken of: not to the Christian religion, but to the Christian tendency to despond when things look dark; and it seems to me that the sentiment is in spirit this, — that all those signal interferences which are called in Scripture "a coming of Christ" (particularly, of course, the final one), take place when all seems lost, when the most sanguine have ceased to hope. In Matthew xxiv. the same thought occurs perpetually. After enumerating the signs of dread, which seem to proclaim that all is over, *then*, He says, " Lift up your heads, for your redemption draweth nigh."

A bleak north wind has been blowing all day, and not improving the aspect in which people and life generally appear. I read a little of a German commentary, and visited some sick people, which is all that is useful done by me to-day. How worthless and meaningless most lives are!

Bright sunshine again. Certainly the contrast between this and Ireland, in respect to light and clear skies, is very striking. The heavens seem to me, since I came, brilliant, and wake up a feeling almost of surprise nearly every hour.

To-day I read, which seems a strange feeling, after so long a cessation, — German and reviews, the "Westminster" and "Fraser"; in the latter there is a historical article about Hungarian affairs, to be completed; but the present number is too general to be interesting. The "Westminster" is now, I am told, in the hands of Greg, whose talent is very great, and of Newman and that party. It is curious to read in a secular review articles on Immortality, Reason, and Faith, &c., — a striking sign of the times; for Religion must now be the question, so soon as sectarians shall have got rid of one another, like the Kilkenny cats: and, the field being clear, the real and awful questions that concern Humanity shall come to be debated by men emancipated from the fear of church-excommunications, and the shivering shrieks of the sectarians who have so long monopolized to themselves the title of religious.

I have begun Lange's "Life of Christ," — a masterly, erudite, deep work, written to meet Strauss and other sceptics.

Kossuth's speeches I mean to read; there is an account of them abbreviated in the "Examiner." "Fraser's" article says that he first rose into notice in 1833, as a reporter of parliamentary debates. His energy in learning English, so as to speak in the masterly way he does, and his independence in refusing all subscriptions made for him personally, tell highly in his favor, and compel interest; but whether he is a hero or not, I think the means of ascertaining — knowing all we can know from newspapers already biassed — are exceedingly slender. The "Examiner" speaks highly of him, and W. S. Landor writes enthusiastically. "The hardest thing in the world, sir, is to get possession of a fact"; so said Dr. Johnson, and that before mesmerism and homœopathy put in their claims to be fact.

XXXI.

I am very hard at work in teaching, visiting, and preparation for the pulpit. My reading has been long neglected and irregular. I am trying to get a little zest, and succeeding in it, — in the attempt to secure at least regularity.

A paper — one of Chambers's for the People — has just

been put into my hands on "Industrial Investments and Associations." The writer looks upon the workmen's associations as hopeless, and dispassionately endeavors to show that they conflict with irresistible laws. Nevertheless, he is desirous that they should be tried fully and fairly, in order that the question may be set at rest. I have not yet read it, but in just glancing over it, I am inclined to like the general tone, — that is good in all that Chambers publishes. To-day is sunny, but dim and autumnal, with that peculiar, watery shine cast on the yellowed leaves in my garden which makes them look so damp, limp, and autumnal. I have not yet been out of doors.

Mr. —— has much more definite and settled views than his brother, — a great advantage even when views are inadequate, for it saves from much uncertainty in action, much questioning *à quoi bon*, and much loss of time in speculation. In fact, I am more persuaded than I was, that speculation is, to the speculator himself, at least, an evil, whatever results it may give the world; and convinced — not more than ever, for that would be impossible — that to believe is a stronger thing, a greater source of strength, as well as evidence of it —than to doubt, always, of course excepting the cases of mesmerism and homœopathy, — no, not excepting them, for they are themselves scepticisms, not faiths, shaking trust in what has been received, and which did well enough, and not substituting any certainty in its place.

XXXII

I spoke to H—— about the worship of the Virgin, and he thought one reason for its prevalence is, that it puts before men the more affectionate side of truth; and he deplored the want of a more large appeal to the affections in Protestantism, saying that we worship Christ, but none of us love Him. I was silent, but the result of a scrutiny into my own mind

was that, with an exception, I scarcely love any one, or any
thing else, and that not because of any reference to His love
for me, which somehow or other never enters into my mind,
but solely in consequence of what he is and was, according,
at least, to my conception of Him and His mind and heart.
I do not know that this consciousness pleased me, because it
presented itself rather as a deficiency than as a power, — a
lack of human sympathy, the existence of a continually increasing number of repellant poles in my constitution, which
isolate me from my species, and make my antipathies more
marked than my sympathies. Whereas, St. John's conception of genuine love for Him, was that of an affection trained
in love for beings who exhibit the same Humanity which
was in Him, in weaker images, in the various relationships of
life. "If a man love not his brother whom he hath seen,"
how can he love God whom he hath not seen? Through
the visible as a school we rise up to the appreciation of the
invisible. Now my nature forces me to reverse the order, or
rather to skip the first steps, for I certainly have some sympathy — dreamy, perhaps useless — with the invisible, —
invisible personality, justice, right; but there they end, and
almost never go on, or go back, to the visible and human.
Those lines you have often quoted, of Burns, —

> I saw thee eye the general weal
> With boundless love, —

express a feeling which I can only imagine, not realize, except by a sort of analogy which is dreamy.

* * * * *

I suppose Kossuth is a man of very uncommon ability,
with much that is fine, and a good deal that is human about
him, but far higher in the scale of being than the scribes
who now, as of old, can believe in nothing greater than themselves, — it would be better if they could have a false worship with one generous emotion.

His speeches are wonderfully beautiful. There is a sincerity and fervor in them that cannot be altogether from sham; he must be a hero. That *esprit moqueur* of which "The Times" is the type does the heart no good.

* * * * *

I send you an extract from a letter about Kossuth, which will interest you. I have been patiently endeavoring to put myself in possession of his history, and to weigh the charges against him. I confess I incline strongly to the conviction that he is a true man, not without faults (who is?), but worthy of honor. After a century or two, liberators and heroes are received as demi-gods, and numbers who affect to pronounce the names of Tell, or Wallace, or Kosciusco with enthusiasm, sneer at Kossuth. Doubtless, in the worship of him there is a vast deal that is very ignorant. The mob throw up their caps, just as Shakespeare has so wonderfully described in "Coriolanus," because others shout. But by the mob I do not mean the working classes; they have read the whole subject of the Hungarian War long before this, and have a definite opinion upon the matter; but I mean the mob of the upper classes, who shout because others shout, and fancy themselves crazy with sublime enthusiasm, when they really know nothing of Kossuth, and are staggered when a contrary opinion is given. And I mean, on the other hand, the mob who follow "The Times" newspaper. I shall write seriously* to a friend of mine, who tells me that she is wild about Kossuth; and that, in reply to some rhapsodies of hers, her uncle has written her à letter of ridicule. Now, this is really dangerous. Enthusiasm being in fashion, she writes off noble sentiments about liberty, &c., and a hue and cry against Kossuth would still it all. This is not the enthusiasm nor the affection which will bide shocks; besides, it is a most dangerous habit to character to be able to cook up raptures whenever raptures are the rage. How is a woman ever to know what she feels or what she thinks?

* *Vide* letter xxxiv.

XXXIII.

You shall have in a day or two a copy of the "Record," containing an article in which I am attacked. I find it is only one out of several which I had never heard of until yesterday. They are beginning to think me of sufficient importance to be put down, and have discovered my fellow-conspirators in Archdeacon Hare, Maurice, and Donaldson, one of the first classical scholars in England, and Tennyson. Pretty good society; and to borrow an expression of poor Shelley, "I would rather be damned with such men than saved with the 'Record,'" at least, if the penalty of such a questionable salvation was being compelled to pollute my soul with lies and slander twice a week. But how very short-sighted to fly their blind buzzard at such small game as myself. Do they not see they bring my ministry into notice or notoriety, and give to it a prominence that it might never have gained by itself? It is like Mr. Kennaway preaching against the "Vestiges of Creation," and Folthorp's shop being besieged in consequence with purchasers of the book. Ridiculous and contemptible as the hostility of such a paper as the "Record" is, it chafes me, and deepens the feeling of defiant isolation, which is so undesirable.

XXXIV.

My dear ——: — Thanks many, for your letter. Do not write any more rhapsodies to your uncle about Kossuth. No enthusiasm will last long that is not deeply based, — a few sarcastic sneers will shake it; for if it comes from following the enthusiasm of others, it will go with the coldness of others. As to Kossuth, the truth is we know very little about him; and it is very hard to get at facts. He is a man of unquestionable genius, — unquestionably to a great extent sincere; but how far he has been a selfish man, or an ambitious man, or a rash, instead of a wise man, neither you nor I can determine, as the authentic history of the Hungarian struggle is not before us. Many of his own countrymen, equally zealous with himself for the liberty of Hungary, condemn him strongly; and I do not see how we can decide by mere feeling between them. I confess that I am not satisfied with the "all things to all men," which he has made his policy in his replies to Americans, French Red Republicans, people of Marseilles, and English Constitutionalists. I suspend my judgment because I can see a possibility of explanation; nevertheless, I am dissatisfied, and so I see is the "Examiner" of last week, — a stanch friend of the Hungarian cause. We shall see what ground he takes in America. I sent an interesting account of him to your mother, from an eye-witness; but I acknowledge I put little trust in speechifying; there was one, — only one trait which looks like claptrap in that letter, where he said, "Do you applaud that? To me it seems so natural not to be ambitious." I rejoice in the enthusiasm of the workingmen for him, for with them it is not a passion of three or four weeks' standing, but the result of a long-sustained interest in the Hungarian war, the details of which they read greedily while it was going on, and for which they subscribed their money. They may be wrong or right in the choice of a hero, but the enthusiasm which takes them out of themselves, and has cost them something, must do them good. I have been reading attentively such documents as I can procure respecting the Hungarian struggle and Kossuth's life. I am inclined on the whole to defend him, though by no means immaculate, and on the whole to admire him; but the less I am disposed to follow in the wake of "The Times," with its hue and cry against him, the less also do I feel inclined to follow in the wake of the mob, who cook up a nine-days' fever about him.

I do feel deep enthusiasm about Sir Charles Napier, because I have thoroughly studied his campaigns, know his motives, know how much he has sacrificed to principle, given up pensions, &c.; and at the same time see all his faults, after a due and fair balance of all which I conclude he is a right noble man; and all the sneers in the world could not shake this, nor the condemnation of the East India Company, nor the neglect of government, nor even his own eccentricities and vehemence.

In reply to your question, "Will Kossuth stir up England to support Hungary?" I reply, with all my heart, I hope not. If once the false principle of interference by one nation in another's quarrels were admitted in Europe, why should not France aid our socialists, or America aid the miserable Irish against their landlords? Each country must free itself within itself, and the freedom which comes from foreign intervention never can be real, because it cannot fit the people to use its freedom. One nation may aid another when oppressed by another; but the Hungarian question is one of their own internal constitution, and internal relations to the government. England may mediate and advise, if Austria will accept her advice; but if ever she interferes with Hungary, I think she will be guilty of a grave crime, — the very same crime into which France fell when she tried, by her propagandism, to revolutionize other nations, and which England so justly resented; which, too, neutralized the French Revolution, turned its glory into shame, and ended in a final failure.

XXXV.

Your questions about Eternity and a Future state puzzle me. Time is but (to us) the succession of ideas, long or short, as they are few or many; and Eternity, as we use the word, means nothing more than the endlessness of this succession. The distinction made by religious people between Eternity and Time, is an unthinking one. Eternity seems to me a word expressive of a negation; it does but deny a termination to that mental state which we call time, for time is a subjective thing; existing, that is, in us, not externally to us, — a mode of our being. Do you remember that little book, "The Stars and the Earth"? It made very comprehensible how time is merely dependent upon our limitations, and how to an unlimited being there must be no time, — how, in short, the annihilation of the sense of space would be the annihilation of the idea of time. As to what our being in a future state shall be, what its enjoyments, or whether the affections here shall be those there, and whether they shall be, as here, mutable or progressive, I confess myself utterly without a clew to decide. To my mind and heart, the most satisfactory things that have been ever said on the future state are contained in the "In Memoriam." By the by, "The Times" has attacked the Poem; allowed it much merit, but criticised severely. Part of the criticism is just, and part miserably small. The use of such antiquated words as "bourgeon," "gnarr," may be objectionable. Be it so. Well, two words in a poem are not quite fatal to a claim of genius. The charge of irreverence is utterly false, —

<blockquote>
And dear as sacramental wine *
To dying lips, is all he said, —
</blockquote>

that is, on things divine.

The reviewer is very severe on this. But does human friendship convey no grace of God to the soul? Do holiest remembrances of God's saintliest reveal nothing of God? If they do, how exquisite here the word "sacramental" is, as applied to them. O most foolish Thunderer! Then he is very merry about the shadow waiting for the keys " to cloke me from my proper scorn," talks of Hobbs and locks unpickable. Blind beetle! the shadow, death, has been identified in a previous page; the reader is in possession of the metaphor. Tennyson prays that he may be hidden in this

---

* The lines have been altered and not improved:
"And dear to me as sacred wine," &c. — ED.

shadow from his own scorn before he, — "forgets," I think, for I have not the passage before me. The reviewer objects to the word "cloke," because shadows do not cloke. Nor does light clothe; but if the poor man had read "robed in light," he would have thought it quite correct, because it is a common expression. Another: —

> That each who seems a separate whole
> Should move his rounds, and fusing all
> The skirts of self again, should fall,
> Remerging in the general soul.

"Of the two mysteries, the shadow with the cloke is probably the easier"; so says the reviewer, who, in this, as well as other places, evidently copies almost whole sentences from Macaulay's castigation of Robert Montgomery; but this critic is not a Macaulay. Now to the passage. The subject is the possibility of the loss of personal consciousness in the hereafter, and of being resolved into the consciousness of the universe. Possibly the unhappy wight did not know that this is a theory largely held by foreign metaphysicians. It is quite clear that he never read the deep, wondrous Hindoo mythology, at the very root of which this conception lies. The "skirts of self" are simply the outskirts of individuality, — that which marks off the conscious Entity from the All, — an expression which requires thought, no doubt; but, then, the theory which he is opposing is not quite as easy as the articles of the daily newspapers, with which this gentleman is familiar; and I do not see why Mr. Tennyson is to be expected to make the statement of it intelligible at first reading to a penny-a-liner. Then comes the criticism about the whole being exaggerated, and expressed sometimes in terms of amatory fondness. Exaggeration is, of course, to be tried by the affections of a paid *littérateur* or politician!

> A statist art thou, in the van
> Of public conflicts trained and bred?
> First learn to love one living man,
> Then mayst thou think upon the dead.

Of course it is exaggerated love to those who feel feebly. Then, as to the amatory tenderness: this, too, is ignorance of human nature; the friendship of a school-boy is as full of tenderness, and jealousy, and passionateness, as even love itself. I remember my own affection for G. R. M. How my heart beat at seeing him; how the consciousness of his listening while I was at reading or translating annihilated the presence of the master; how I fought for him; how, to rescue him at prisoners' base, turned the effect of mere play into a ferocious determination, as if the captivity were real; how my blood crept cold with delight when he came to rescue me, or when he praised me. And this miserable quill-driver, in the very spirit of flunkeyism, calls this poem exaggerated, because all the poetry of the affections is made ludicrous by remembering that this Amaryllis was a barrister at the Chancery bar. If the Chancery bar, or any other accident of a man's environment, destroys the real poetry of life, then the human soul has no worth but that which comes from its trappings,—an idea which I reckon about the most decisive proof of a vulgar soul which can be found. As to the tenderness, too, he is obliged to include Shakespeare in the accusation. Now, it may be a very presumptuous thing to say, but it is just conceivable that Shakespeare knew as much about what is human and true, and what is the true mode of expressing it in words, as this writer.

XXXVI.

That is a striking passage which you quote, about the Jews having believed and swindled since the days of Jacob. It shows how separable devotedness may be from morality; there being religious men who are immoral, and moral men who are unreligious, the former chiefly amongst southern temperaments, the latter amongst the northerns.

That, too, about Socrates: I am certain that most Englishmen would have hemlocked him, just as the Jews built the sepulchres of the old prophets, and in the spirit of their fathers stoned the prophets and crucified the prophet of their own day: thus allowing the deeds of their fathers.

I read Hartley Coleridge's life with pain and instruction. Something wrong in the blood, both father and son wanting will. "Coleridge," said some one of the father, "is a good man,— a very good man; but, somehow, as soon as a duty presents itself in a practical way he cannot do it."

On the subject of binding and loosing, I do not know how I can explain it better; but remember "loosing from sin" implies making a severance between it and the soul; "binding it," means identifying it with the character. You seem to look upon it as only relating to a forgiveness which is irrespective of character, and so the forgiveness of man is no doubt an uncertain pledge of God's forgiveness. Now I show a *fact:* that man does actually bind and loose,— does fix sin upon the character,— does by his treatment take the burden off and free from it henceforth. No one can deny that fact. It may be very dreadful, or very glorious, but here it is, and we cannot divest ourselves of our power, we can use it or abuse it. We may, representatively, show mercy when we ought to show God's wrath, and *vice versâ*, but effects follow whether we will or not. Of course there are counteracting circumstances mercifully interposed; otherwise, the unjust judgments of men, singly and collectively, would be, in every case final, which would be hideous indeed. A man unjustly condemned and shunned may be wise and strong enough not to accept it in any sense as mirroring God's award; but to a weak and ill-informed conscience, even when innocent, it does so far represent it as to make him an outcast, and at last degraded. "Give a dog an ill name," &c. Much more, then, does it carry this power when the guilt is real. The Church, which is Christian society, and every Christian individual, are to perceive this power instead of disclaiming it, and to use it for God, and truly, instead of untruly.

CHAPTER II.

1852.

Feelings and Interests of Mr. Robertson in January, 1852. — His Pleasure in Ornithology. — His resolute Work. — Character of his Sermons. — His Humility, Gentleness. — His proud Sternness and Indignation. — Two Anecdotes in Illustration. — His Efforts in behalf of the Mechanics' Institute. — The two Lectures on the "Influence of Poetry on the Working Classes." — Their Results upon the Workingmen. — Letters of Mr. Drummond and Lord Carlisle upon the Lectures and the Replies. — Criticism by the "South Church Union." — Reply on the Points, "that Severance from all Parties and Maxims is a *first* Principle in seeking after Truth"; that "Poetry is always most cultivated in effeminate Ages." — Visit to Cheltenham. — Sermons preached at Lewes Assizes. — Address presented by the Young Men of his Congregation. — His Speech on the Occasion. — His Confirmation Class. — The Elections at Brighton in 1852. — Proposition to open the Crystal Palace on Sunday. — Sermon and Letters on the Subject. — Orthodox Attacks. — Close of the Year.

Letters from January 24, 1852, to December, 1852.

THE only record of Mr. Robertson's life and pursuits during the first month of this year is the following letter to a friend in South America: —

60 Montpelier Road, Brighton : January, 1852.

.... What shall I say of your bitter loss? There is nothing to be said. God is Love. All is well and all is right. These are the old, simple, primary truths; but time alone can teach you and me *how* true. Do you know Tennyson's "In Memoriam"? It is the most precious work published this century, — written in memory of his friend Arthur Hallam, and exhibiting the manifold phases through which the spirit passes, of rebellion, darkness, doubt, through the awful questions about personal identity hereafter, reunion, and the uncertainty whether Love be indeed the law of the universe, on to placid trust, even cheerfulness, and the deep conviction, — all is well. Tell me if you have it or have seen it. To me it has been the richest treasure I have had. For, except in this conviction, the first and simplest, on which we have ever to fall back from more artificial and complicated theories, — God is, and God is Love, I can see nothing in this life but a hideous, waste, howling wilderness, with siroccos and sand-pillars, overwhelming everything, and scorching up everything. . . . .

All things go on here as usual. I have been doing all I can for the working classes, in whom I take much interest. . . . .

I wonder whether you could do anything for me in assisting a study I have taken up after long disuse, — that of ornithology? If you could get any one to shoot and make a collection of the Demerara birds, skinning them and filling the skins with tow or cotton, and preserving them from insects by the best means at hand, arsenical soap, corrosive sublimate, camphor or corn pepper, and packing them up carefully and dry, in tow or any such substance, it would be a great prize to me. Demerara has some beautiful birds, and some very important ones. Even the common birds would be uncommon here. Skill is required in skinning them, and care. No doubt there is some one more or less expert at this in your neighborhood. Charge me with all expenses: A trifling remuneration would induce some amateur sportsman to collect the rare birds, and the common ones are easily got. Hawks, owls, ducks, among others, would be welcome, not *stuffed*, only skinned and filled lightly with cotton, &c., the brains, and so on, being removed. . . . .

Farewell, may God bless you, comfort and strengthen you.

Affectionately and ever yours,
FRED. W. ROBERTSON.

It is interesting to mark in this letter the re-awakening of his early interest in ornithology. He had received this fresh impulse from the case of stuffed birds which Mr. Hancock, of Newcastle-on-Tyne, had sent to the Exhibition of 1851.

Mr. Hancock (he writes in March, '52) tells me that his engravings of the falcons are nearly ready for publication. I have urged him to preface them with a treatise on the art of taxidermy. If I were a man of wealth, I would as readily give him £150 for his case, as I would give £4,000 for a Raffaelle, and rather; for his works stand alone, with nothing second to or like them.

During the brief seasons of recreation which Mr. Robertson took, he pursued, while shooting, the study of the natural history of birds. One of his letters is full of his joy at finding a rare heron, and of the anxiety which he spent on stuffing it. A friend of his, who was much with him in his expeditions, said that every bird which crossed the path furnished him materials for conversation. He pictured in the happiest manner their habits, nests, eggs, and migrations. It was impossible to help catching the enthusiasm with which he spoke of his boyish adventures in the woods. He would have loved well the adventurous career of a wandering naturalist. Wilson's wild existence among the American forests haunted him like a dream of pleasure. It is impossible not to feel more and more, as his letters unfold his character, how intolerable the cabined and monotonous life in a fashionable town, with its over-civilized race of dull pleasure-hunters, must have been to such a spirit. Yet, chafing inly at every step, he bound himself by resolute will to do his duty to the last. Self-repression, — self-sacrifice, — these were not mere names to him. He never relaxed his effort. Though at times a complaint of his loneliness is, as it were, dragged out of him, the complaint did not shadow behind it idleness as its cause. No pain, mental or bodily, caused him to omit the smallest portion of his work. He says, in a sermon preached the first Sunday of 1852, and it was the expression of his inmost feeling: " The motto on every Christian banner is, — Forward ; there is no resting in the present, no satisfaction in the past." And his sermons in this year seem to have become more sorrowful in tone, and especially more earnest. They read like those of a man who felt that death was near. They are startling sometimes for their bold exposition of views distasteful to what is called the " Orthodox party." The opposition and impertinence he suffered from seem to have had the effect of driving him into stating, in broad and sometimes in harsh lines, his convictions. His manner became more repellant, even proud. Proud as he was, his humility was also great. Quite unaffected, it touched those who did not mistake the self-dependence of the man for self-conceit, with a sense of strange beauty, so much of the air of childhood seemed to float about it, so much receptiveness, willingness to listen, self-forgetfulness. But, when attacked unjustly, wilfully misrepresented, this very humility made his indignation greater. He strove to be gentle to all men; but, to his deep regret afterwards, the haughty soldier-spirit broke out sometimes. When the injury he resented was a personal one, he apologized frankly for his anger, if it had transgressed the bounds of Christian indignation; but when he was indignant with falsehood, injustice, or cowardly wrong done to another, it was terrible to see his whole face knit itself together with wrath; his mouth, generally soft with feeling and flexible with change, and habitually sad, grow to a fine line of concentrated force. The words he then used were startling from their power. He was never violent, never "in a passion" when he spoke, but each word fell like a sledge-hammer upon its point and on its victim. I have been told that once, when he found it necessary to denounce a man for a dastardly and wilful crime, that his words had all the awfulness of a judicial sentence; that the hardened sinner writhed under them as if under a whip. To this, I think, he alludes in a letter, when he says, " Once in my life I felt a terrible might. I knew, and rejoiced to know as I spoke, that I was inflicting the sentence of a coward and a liar's hell." For his was not that maudlin Christianity which dwells on the tenderness, and never on the indignation of Christ, which remembers only " I am come to seek and save that which was lost," and forgets, " Woe unto you, scribes and Pharisees, hypocrites!" This sternness was often shown unexpectedly. Slight acts, passing scenes, in which other men saw only folly; a word, a glance, a gesture, which others saw nothing in, he shuddered at, and spoke of indignantly. For he felt the base spirit which prompted the apparently trifling act and expression; he looked on them by the light of a pure heart, and by the experience of past history, and saw them in themselves and in their effects as Sin.

Two anecdotes sufficiently show, the first how proudly, and the second with what almost awful boldness, he could speak. They will also account for much of the virulence with which he was assailed. A man who answered his opponents so, could scarcely expect to be gently treated in return. One Monday morning an elderly gentleman introduced himself as having been of great service to young clergymen. He arraigned the sermon he had heard in Trinity Chapel the day before; spoke of dangerous views and the impetuosity of young men; offered himself as a weekly monitor, and enumerated in conclusion the perils and inconveniences to which popular preachers were subject. Mr. Robertson, who had remained silent, at last rose. "Really, sir," he said, sternly, "the only inconvenience I have experienced in being what you are pleased to call me, a popular preacher, is intrusion like the present"; and he bowed his censor out of the room.

Another day, a lady, with whom he was slightly acquainted, assailed him for "heterodox opinions," and menaced him with the consequences which in this world and the next would follow on the course of action he was pursuing. His only answer was, "I don't care." — "Do you know what don't care came to, sir?" — "Yes, madam," was the grave reply, "He was crucified on Calvary."

The Workingmen's Society, which in the earlier months of 1851 had been reformed under his auspices, was necessarily weakened by its schism, and was now struggling for existence. He was incessant in his endeavors to consolidate it. In November, 1851, he says, "I have been at workingmen's meetings and lectures every evening." It was suggested to him that an address on some subject of general interest would materially assist the Institution. To the formal request made by the secretary, he returned the following answer:—

In reply to your communication of the 21st, which I only had last night, after an absence from Brighton, I beg to say, that after much consideration I have come to the conclusion that it is my duty not to refuse the request made to me.

I am very unfit at present for the excitement of addressing numbers.; but knowing that the insufficiency will be pardoned, and feeling deep interest in the success of the workingmen, I shall not allow this to stand in the way.

I was not aware that the name of the Institution was to be changed. Is not this virtually acknowledging that the former attempt was a failure, instead of the society being, as I believe it is, the old one purified by experience? Not knowing the reasons for the change, which perhaps are valid, at first sight I am inclined to regret it. There is much in names, especially when they are associated with recollections which can be appealed to, and when they adhere to a society through many shocks and changes. Besides, "Workingman" is a noble title for any human being: a human being's right title. "Mechanic" is a poor class title, like Agriculturist, Botanist, Sailor, &c., &c. Besides, it is not true as a designation for your society; a schoolmaster is not a mechanic, nor a retail dealer of any kind, yet many such are in the society. Ought you not, like good soldiers in a great cause, *to stand to your colors?*

In pursuance of this promise, the two published lectures on "The Influence of Poetry on the Working Classes," were given in February, 1852. They were delivered extempore, and before an audience of more than a thousand in number. The wonderful fluency, wedded to impassioned feeling, which made them so telling in delivery, did not imperil their effect when printed, for they were as full of concentrated thought as if he had elaborately written them. He himself considered that some of his statements were too concise.

The lectures, however, are not the less, but the more valuable, from their conciseness of thought. Too well known to describe, they have some autobiographical interest. Scattered through them are anecdotes of his earlier life and feeling, and short sentences such as these: "The poetic temperament is one of singular irritability of brain and nerve"; "There are three things in this world which deserve no quarter, — Hypocrisy, Pharisaism, and Tyranny";— sentences which reveal the man in his constitution and his hatreds. Throughout them his rapturous delight in a military career breaks out. Nowhere is he so eloquent as in describing the glorious death of the heroes of Trukkee, the gathering of the bravest in battle round the torn colors, which symbolized courage and honor, and the chivalry of war in contrast with a selfish and ignoble peace. The closing sentence, spoken in anticipation of a French invasion, is full of his own spirit. Often, with most unclerical emphasis, did he express his wish to die, sword in hand, against a French invader.

Thus much I will dare to say. If a foreign foot be planted on our sacred soil, — if the ring of the rifle of the Chasseurs de Vincennes be heard upon these shores, terrible as the first reverses might be, when discipline could be met only by raw enthusiasm, — thanks to gentlemen who have taught us the sublime mysteries of capital in lieu of the old English superstitions of Honor and Religion, they may yet chance to learn that British chivalry did not breathe her last at Moodkee, or Ferozeshah, or Sobraon, or Goojerat, or Meeanee, or Hyderabad. They may yet be taught that there is something beyond the raw hysterics of a transient excitement in the spirit of self-sacrifice which we have learned from our Master's Cross. They may yet discover that amongst the artisans, and peasants, and workingmen of England, there are a thousand thousand worthy to be brothers of those heroic eleven who sleep beneath the rocks of Trukkee, with the red thread of Honor round their wrists.

These addresses were not resultless. The workingmen of Brighton, for the first time told that Poetry did not belong to one class alone, but to all who felt within them the common passions of Humanity, at once assumed their right. The works of many of the poets were added to their library. Their power of appreciating the highest poetry was believed in, and then they believed in it themselves. They became conscious of their powers. From the Life of Christ Mr. Robertson had learned this great principle of education; to make men recognize their own spiritual capabilities by throwing himself in trust upon those capabilities. In these lectures he carried that principle into secular things. And the men *were* roused. They read the poets eagerly; sharp discussions arose among them on the comparative merits of Pope, and Walter Scott, and Tennyson. One part of the lecturer's aim was thus attained. The men employed in a dull mechanic round, or in coarse hand-labor, were led into a refined and pure region both of intellect and feeling. They desired to find and to feel the beautiful. It was a step in their elevation.

A more tangible result of the lectures was, that they brought in sufficient money to make the fortune of the Institute. They were at once published from the corrected notes of the reporter. Two letters which their author received are worth publishing, for the remark and reply which were elicited from him.

The first was from Mr. Henry Drummond:—

DEAR SIR:—I have received your essay with many thanks. It appears to me that you are the only person who is grappling with the natural infidelity of minds educated in everything except religion. . . . .

On sending this letter to a friend, Mr. Robertson wrote:—

Mr. Drummond's letter is interesting, inasmuch as it exhibits a deeper perception of what I was aiming at than I have yet seen in any one. To produce a belief in the reality of the invisible Truth and Beauty, is the chief end of my insignificant work here.

The second was from Lord Carlisle:*—

I would not thank you for your most acceptable present, till I had enjoyed the pleasure of making myself acquainted with its contents. I have recognized in them all the high ability and the generous and delicate feeling which I could have expected.

Upon one or two points of mere taste we may not wholly agree, but there is no part of what you inculcate with which I agree more fully than that in which you commend universality of taste. I have some doubts, for instance, about this,— "The best poetry demands study as severe as mathematics require."

I take what appears to me to be the highest of human compositions,— the "Iliad" and "Macbeth,"— and I think they are both eminently intelligible without pain or effort. Perhaps I would give up "Hamlet" to you, not "Othello."

I think you rate Dr. Johnson's poetical powers too low.

> Rest undisturbed within thy peaceful shrine,
> Till angels wake thee with a note like thine.

* These letters have been already published in the preface to "Lectures and Addresses of the late F. W. Robertson."

I must not, however, indulge in mere prattle. Let me repay your kindness in the same coin, of however inferior value. I assure you, with all truth, that I look on some things I have said with more complacency, when I flatter myself that there is some identity of view between us.

Lord Carlisle sent with his letter a copy of his "Lectures on Pope," and Mr. Robertson replied:—

I will not allow a post to pass without thanking you for your kind present and kinder note, the approval of which I feel to be very invigorating. I was very glad to find that there was not a syllable of the "Lecture on Pope" which jarred with my estimate of him, which I a little feared. But the passage quoted from Warton, p. 10, and another of your own, p. 16, "'T was not so much the pomp and prodigality of heaven," &c., express, though with far more precision, exactly the reasons which I briefly alleged for ranking Pope in the second order, but, in that order, first. I congratulated myself much on perceiving so far this agreement, and in all the admiration which the lecture contains I heartily concur.

The passage, p. 105, "Heaven was made for those who had failed in this world," struck me very forcibly several years ago, when I read it in a newspaper, and became a rich vein of thought in which I often quarried; especially when the sentence was interpreted by the Cross, which was failure, apparently.

My sentence, "The best poetry demands study as severe as mathematics require," is very justly open to criticism; but more, I think, from the unfinished abruptness of the phraseology than from its real meaning. The best poetry has a sense which is level to the apprehension at once; not being obscure in expression, nor metaphysical or scholastic in thought; but then any one who had caught this meaning at the first glance would be greatly mistaken if he supposed that he had got all, or nearly all, it meant.

The dew-drop that glitters on the end of every leaf after a shower, is beautiful even to a child; but I suppose that to a Herschel, who knows that the lightning itself sleeps within it, and understands and feels all its mysterious connections with earth, and sky, and planets, it is suggestive of a far deeper beauty:. and the very instances you allege, "Macbeth" and the "Iliad," would substantiate what I *meant*, though not what I awkwardly perhaps seemed to say. "Macbeth," all action, swift and hurried in its progress towards *dénouement*, is intelligible at once. But I spent myself many weeks upon it, and only at last began to feel that it was simple, *because* deep. Some exquisite and fine remarks of Mrs. Jameson on certain characters in it, and profounder ones of Coleridge on others, have brought out a meaning that we feel at once was *in it*, and not forced *upon it*. In the sense I meant, I should say "Macbeth" could not be understood, especially as a whole, except with hard study.

I am very much tempted to accept the challenge of page 28, in the "Lecture on Pope,"—"I would beg any of the detractors of Pope to furnish me with another couple of lines from any author whatever, which encloses so much sublimity of meaning within such compressed limits and such precise terms."

If it were not that the cartel is addressed only to Pope's *detractors*, I think I should allege that wonderful couplet of the Erd Geist in "Faust":—

> So schaff' ich am sausenden Webstuhl der Zeit,
> Und wirke der Gottheit lebendiges Kleid;

at least, if I might interpret them by Psalm cii. 26, 27.

In the graceful courtesy with which your lordship acknowledges that there is "some identity of view between us," I receive the best and most cheering reward that my little pamphlet has obtained.

The criticism he received was not, however, altogether friendly. He was not left without the benefit of a little honest hostility. The "South Church Union," — the organ of the High Church party at Brighton, — gave him the benefit of its opposition. The points it attacked appear from the following letter: —

I send you the " South Church Union," containing a Tractarian review of my lectures on poetry, much fairer than an Evangelical would have written, and on the whole as discriminating as could be expected from the essential difference between his position and mine: only, as was naturally to be expected, mine is only half understood and caricatured, though not intentionally. For instance, he falls foul of my "first principle," "sever yourself from all parties and maxims." Now there is a double ambiguity which belongs to such a rule. It may be a merely negative one; in which case it is only latitudinarianism, being equivalent to "it does not matter what you think, provided you are not bigoted to one opinion above another." And this is the way in which he has chosen to understand it; but in the way I said it, it became a positive rule, as indeed the context showed, " Servant only to the truth"; in other words, " Surrender yourself to no maxims, because you must be servant to something much higher, namely, truth." Doubtless the way of attaining truth is not indicated in that sentence, nor could it be; it is a second lesson, — I was giving one at a time. The way of reaching truth is by obeying the truth you know. "If any man will do His will, he shall know," &c., but it was not my business to introduce that, in that connection. There is another ambiguity in an expression of which the reviewer has not failed to take the false alternative: I call it a "*first* principle." Now "first" may refer to time, or it may refer to importance. In reference to time the statement would be false, and in this sense in one part of his remarks he has understood it; but in reference to importance it is perfectly true.

To illustrate this: I put a loaded gun in the corner of a room, and tell my child not to touch it. There is a rule or maxim. Knowing nothing of the reason of my command, his plain duty as a child is implicit servile obedience to my order; his conscience should be grieved if, even to prevent its being broken by a fall, he is induced to touch it, because there is a harm in doing it which is to him mysterious and unknown. But suppose him older, and suppose him to understand, by natural intelligence, that the reason of my prohibition was to prevent the possibility of its exploding, and suppose him to see a sheet of paper fall from the table on fire close to it, what would his duty be, — to cleave to the maxim, or to cut himself adrift from it? Surely to snatch up the forbidden gun directly. His first duty, in point of time, is to obey the rule; his first in point of importance, is to break it. Indeed, this is the very essence, according to St. Paul, of the difference between the legal and the gospel state. In the legal state we are under tutors, governors, and must not go beyond rules; for rules are disciplining us to understand the principles of themselves. But in the gospel state we are redeemed from this bondage, serving in newness of spirit, and not in the oldness of the letter. We discern *principles*, and are loyal to them; we use rules or dispense with them, as they save or destroy the principle for which they exist. We are free from the law, that is, we are free from slavish obedience to the maxims; and this not because we are in a latitudinarian way free from the principles, but exactly because we have become devoted to them in true allegiance. And so far as a man is not devoted to them he is not free from the law, but still under it, that is, he must still be restrained by maxims, for he is not fit to be trusted with the guardianship of principles. A boy who had clearly understood his father's motive about the gun, but had a secret inclination to hear it go off, would be just as unfit to dispense with the strict letter even in the case of danger from fire, as if he was profoundly ignorant of the cause of the law's enactment.

And so in art and religion. First, in point of time, submit to rules; but first in point of importance,—the grand aim indeed of all rules,—rise through them to the spirit and meaning of them. Write that upon the heart and be free: then you can use the maxim, not like a pedant, but like an artist,—not like a Pharisee, but like a Christian.

The reviewer has made, in his zeal, another singularly wild statement, that poetry is always cultivated chiefly in those ages in which effeminacy prevails. He quotes Plato's "Republic" in profound ignorance of Plato's meaning, and infers that poetry vitiates.

Now it is an odd thing for a Tractarian to do this. What was the glorious symbolism of the Middle Ages, their majestic architecture, but poetry,—were those effeminate ages? Does *he* at all events count the age of Michael Angelo, Raphael, Fra Angelico, a feeble, irreligious age? Among the Greeks, Homer, Sophocles, Æschylus, stood foremost; classical scholars do not generally select their age as the one particularly remarkable for effeminacy. Dante was something of a man, and the Italian republics were in their glory in his day. Goethe, Schiller, may be very heterodox; but the age which witnessed the wars with France was not a soft one. Chaucer, Shakespeare, Spencer, Milton, poor, feeble, degenerate men! and in what an age of Sybarites they were nursed to voluptuous lullabies!

The good gentleman ought to have recollected that a Coryphæus of his party has ascribed a somewhat nobler office to the poet than that of enfeebling the soul. Do you remember that fine passage in the "Christian Year,"—

> Sovereign masters of all arts,
> Know ye who hath set your parts?

While writing, an idea has struck me that it would be almost worth while to send the substance of what I have said here as a reply; for some principles are involved and no personalities.

Almost immediately after the delivery of these lectures he revisited Cheltenham.

Cheltenham: Feb. 24, 1852.

It is nearly three years (he says) since I was here, and how much is altered! — most of my once large acquaintance are gone: only a few friends remain, but they have all met me warmly. I feel myself far more changed within. How beautiful this country is, though there is yet no foliage! I was never so struck with the beauty of the surrounding hills as to-day. I saw all the old spots on hill and valley, with innumerable stories of past days annexed to them.

I was at Christ Church, my old place, this morning, and felt old associations come over me as if four and a half years had not rolled between; but the changes in the congregation told the truth. Many of the places were empty, — some who had filled them gone, many dead; children came up to me as young men and young women, saying, "Don't you remember me?" and there was a visible increase in wrinkles and gray hairs. The music nearly overpowered me, for the old hymns and tunes, and the tones of the organ, went home. . . . .

This afternoon, instead of going to church, I walked into the country across the fields, and through some of the pretty neighboring villages, with my brother. The day was fresh but fine, and the Cotswold Hills, which surround Cheltenham, exhibiting a great variety of outline, and rich in woods, were in extreme beauty from the coloring. Among these hills are some of the loveliest valleys I know anywhere. The building, too, of Cheltenham is far better in style than that of Brighton, — greatly varied, and almost all the detached villas in good taste, some Italian, others Elizabethan; but there is an air of lightness and grace about it which is quite different from cockneyism. This is much assisted by the abundance of trees with which the town is filled; many of the streets like boulevards; one long walk of ancient elms, a noble avenue.

During the second visit, the revival of old associations, and the inevitable comparison of the past with the present, brought with them only unmingled pain. I have thrown together below the most interesting passages referring to his stay at Cheltenham.

March 8.

I had a walk with Struan and Mr. Munro. The day was lovely in the extreme. We went over the hills, one of my favorite walks. The more I see of this place and the environs, the more I am struck with its beauty, as if I had never seen it before; yet in all probability part of the beauty of scenery depends upon your knowing all the points far and near, so that imagination assists the eye very much, and you supply what you know to what you see, fancying all the time that you see it. Ruskin, I recollect, has some good remarks on this. In our walk we came to a pretty village churchyard, Leckhampton, about a couple of miles from hence. I went in to get the solemn thoughts that are sure to come. There is a tomb erected to Major Macready, brother of the actor. He died in Cheltenham in 1848. It was surrounded with beautiful iron rails, and a trellis-work of iron extending above them. Around it and in it is a garden border, full of most rare and carefully tended plants: roses, which bloom nowhere else, were blooming there. . . . .

Yesterday I rode out with Struan, Mr. Munro, and his niece, over some lovely country. We passed the scenes of many desperate leaps over walls and gates, taken by my brother and myself years ago. Munro said, "Why, Robertson, the farmers would not know you again, you ride so quietly." "I have been thinking," I replied, "several times during the ride, as I looked at a tempting wall or gate, of that line of Byron's applied to one who has spent his force, and was unmoved by beauty:—

'But now it moved him as it moves the wise.'"

I took a single leap to show him that it was in me, if I chose; but all day I was, as I have been all this visit, depressed and low. To-day—this afternoon, at least—I spent in rifle-shooting with Struan, against the side of the rocks of Leckhampton Hill, making very good practice, and putting six balls in the mark out of eight. Such has been my employment,—*distraction*, in the French sense, and so far only good or useful.

A merchant vessel has brought the news from the Cape that Major Wilmot, my brother's best friend, is killed.— Farewell.

Here he met Tennyson, but could not pursue the acquaintance, being forced to return to Brighton. "I feel," he says, "as low as a schoolboy going back to a school which he dislikes. I had not time to call on Tennyson."

On his arrival at Brighton, he proceeded to Lewes, to attend the assizes, at which he had been appointed chaplain to the sheriff. There is a graphic account, in his letters, of the trials held in the months of March and July. The sermons which he preached were first on St. John viii. 32, — "The kingdom of the truth"; secondly, on St. John vii. 17, — " Obedience the organ of spiritual knowledge." Both have been published. It was curious, I have been told, to watch the pew set apart for the judges, — Mr. Justice Coleridge and Mr. Baron Parke. Its occupants, on the conclusion of the "morning" service, expecting nothing to disturb their intellect, settled themselves into decent postures, full of ease, for their customary reverie. But before three minutes of the sermon had passed by, their attention was riveted, their position changed, and they listened with evident interest to a discourse of forty minutes in length. The conclusion of the first sermon was remembered well: —

In the name of Christ, I respectfully commend these thoughts, for the special consideration of the present week, to those who will be pledged by oath to witness to the whole truth they know, and nothing but the truth; to those who, permitted by the merciful spirit of English jurisprudence to watch that their clients, if condemned, shall be condemned only according to the law, are yet not justified by the spirit of the life of Christ in falsifying or obscuring facts, and who, owing a high duty to a client, owe one yet higher to the truth; and lastly, to those whom the severe intellectual and, much more, moral training of the English bar has qualified for the high office of disentangling truth from the mazes of conflicting testimony.

From the trial hour of Christ, — from the Cross of the Son of God, — there arises the principle, to which His life bore witness, that the first lesson of Christian life is this, — be true; and the second this, — be true; and the third this, — be true.

In April he took the chair at a meeting in which Professor Zaba, a Pole, expounded a new system of mnemonics. He introduced this gentleman with a speech which he afterwards reduced in a condensed form to writing. It will be found Letter XLV.

Shortly afterwards, perhaps the most interesting occurrence in his ministerial career took place. He narrates the occasion of it, and exposes the subjects on which he intended to speak. He sums up in a few words the principles of his teaching, and it is deeply to be regretted that an over-sensitiveness prevented him from carrying out his intention.

Tuesday, April 14.

The young men of my congregation have invited me to meet them on Tuesday evening next, on which occasion I understand they mean to present an address expressive of gratitude for the instruction they have received from the pulpit and the platform. It is kindly meant; and I hope it may not be marred by any misunderstanding amongst themselves, or by any compromise of myself in the wording of the address, into which zeal may easily hurry them. As I am not to know the contents beforehand, I cannot prepare a reply; but I am thinking of briefly reviewing some of the leading principles which I have aimed at inculcating, such as the soul of goodness in things evil, — positive truth instead of negative error, — belief in the Divine *character* of Christ's humanity, antecedent to belief in its Divine origin, — spiritual truth discerned by the soul instead of the intellect, in opposition to rationalism, — truth made up of two opposite propositions, instead of a *via media* between the two. Perhaps I may take the opportunity of crushing the attacks of the "Record" on me, and its allegations of my belonging to the Kingsley school; but of this I am not quite sure. I am not likely to have such another opportunity.

The address, a portion of which is quoted below,* was presented to him at the Town Hall, on April 21st.

---

* "We desire to express to you the high and affectionate esteem in which your name is and has long been held among us, and also to render you sensible of our gratitude for the advantages we have derived from your labors both in and out of the pulpit.

"There is entertained among us a strong feeling of obligation for the exalted views of all that is highest and holiest in religion with which you have familiarized our minds, for the elevated standard of morality to which you have taught us to conform our lives, and no less for those les-

More than eighty signatures were appended to it, and every signature was written from the heart. The meeting was unique in Brighton. Ever since his arrival in that town, Mr. Robertson had given much time and thought to the elevation of the young men of his congregation, especially those belonging to the class of clerks, assistants in shops, servants, and others. Gradually his influence over them became permanent. We have seen by his conduct at the meeting of the Early Closing Association, that he did not purchase that influence by flattering their views, or joining in their popular clamor. His sincerity of purpose at that meeting, which at first had partially repelled them, afterwards attracted them. They felt sure of him. They knew that they were loved not too well, but wisely. And Christianity became dear to them through him. They saw before their eyes continually how manly and noble a Christian life might be. Nor did he cease to urge this life upon them. "With all the earnestness he possessed," said one of them, "and how great that was! he exhorted us to begin in our youth to say with David, O God! thou art *my* God! early will I seek Thee." Many of his sermons were especially addressed

sons of philosophy and secular wisdom which it has been so often our privilege to learn from your lips.

"We would also assure you, honored sir, of our due appreciation of your ready sympathy with the cause of the young men in this town, your undeviating courtesy and kindness in conforming to their wishes and requirements, and your cordial exertions to promote their welfare.

"Permit us, in conclusion, respectfully, but most sincerely, to express a hope that we may long continue to enjoy the advantages of your residence amongst us, and that unfailing health and domestic happiness, o'ershadowed by no cloud of care or sorrow, may enable you with entire satisfaction to pursue the studies and fulfil the duties incident to that exalted calling to which you are devoted."

to them. It was easy to excite and interest them, but he was not content with that. He urged them to discredit feeling unless it passed into and was aroused by action for Christ. The novelty of his views, and the youthfulness of his character, were calculated to make young men adopt him as a leader. But he would not have them rest on him; he warned them that if they would be spiritually strong, they must learn how to stand alone with God and their own soul. He refused to claim dominion over their faith. "One was their Master," he said, "even Christ." Thus he endeavored to guide them into Christian manhood; and he succeeded. He had the rare pleasure of seeing the trees he had planted bearing matured and goodly fruit.

He answered the address in a few words. As he spoke, all rose, full of sincere emotion, and bound by the unity of that emotion into one body, in which the different ranks, the different opinions, and the various interests which in common life made them jar with one another, — were forgotten. They were all fused together by the fire of a common love. He himself was deeply moved. He said in words which were never forgotten, and which drew forth enthusiastic and heartfelt cheers: —

We are not here to bandy compliments with one another; you have not come to flatter me, and I have not come with any affected coyness, to pretend to disclaim your flattery, in order that it may be repeated. You have told me in the frank spirit of an Englishman that my ministry has done you good. Frankly, as an Englishman, I tell you with all my heart I do believe it. I know that there are men who once wandered in darkness and doubt, and could find no light, who have now found an anchor and a rock and a resting-place. I know that there are men who were feeling bitterly and angrily what seemed to them the unfair differences of society, who now regard them in a gentle, more humble, and more tender spirit. I know that there are rich who have been led to feel more generously towards the poor. I know that there are poor who have been taught to feel more truly and more fairly towards the rich. I *believe* — for on such a point God can only *know* — that there are men who have been induced to place before themselves a higher standard and perhaps, I may venture to add, have conformed their lives more truly to that standard. I dare not hide my belief in this. I am deeply grateful in being able to say that, if my ministry were to close to-morrow, it would not have been, in this town at least, altogether a failure.

He concluded with a sentence, which was the only answer he deigned to give to the taunts which had been levelled against him for his interest in young men, and in the subjects, both theological and social, which then engrossed them: —

"Let the words of that young man" (Mr. C. Evans, who had presented the address) "answer for it, whether there is Rationalism or Socialism in my teaching."

Yet in this, the most triumphant moment apparently of his ministry, he was at heart profoundly sad and wearied, partly from the loneliness of his life, and partly, as he hints himself in the following letter, from physical exhaustion and disease. It is sorrowful and strange to think how little men knew what lay beneath that quiet and resolute exterior: —

Wednesday, April 21.

The meeting of last night passed off as heavily as it was possible to conceive. One of the young men rose and presented the address with a warm and cordial speech, to which

I replied. The best thing of the evening was a very short speech in three sentences from one of the young men, who said he had been to the Great Exhibition, and had received from it a comment upon the doctrine which lay at the bottom of Mr. Robertson's teaching,—not to call anything common or unclean. It showed a finer and more masterly appreciation of what I aim at than I had expected. I returned thanks; but certain things which had been said had so damped all power of enjoying, that I left unsaid all I had meant to say, and confined myself to mere thanks. I had intended to state the principles of my teaching, such as the establishment of truth, instead of the negative destruction of error,—suggestive teaching, instead of dogmatic,—working from within outwards instead of the converse, &c.

I send you a "Guardian" with the account. It has somewhat mangled what I said, by putting in pithless and unmeaning words and epithets, as well as by altering and inserting sentences; but, on the whole, except the last sentence, it is tolerably correct. I wish I could describe the dreary feelings of yesterday evening. Eighty persons were present to do me honor, and express kindly feelings to me; the applause was enthusiastic, yet all seemed weary, stale, flat, unprofitable. In the midst of the homage of a crowd, I felt alone, and as if friendless.

The first sheet of this letter was written in a very gloomy mood,—the result partly of the excitement of the preceding evening, and the preaching and speaking of the last two days. It still remains. I think it only just to myself to ask you to read this sheet first, as I cannot judge at all whether I am seeing fairly or through a distorted medium, — whether I am myself, or in an unnatural mood. Do not, therefore, read what I have written without this allowance.

Mr. J—— Y—— and Mr. B——, whom I knew in Heidelberg, are coming to take tea with me this evening, so I shall forget my low spirits and myself, and perhaps see things more justly; at least whenever I feel strongly, I make it a rule now to assume the probability that physical causes have something to do with the matter.

During the months of May and June he prepared his class of young persons for confirmation. The labor which every year he bestowed upon this work was great. He personally interested himself in all the candidates, whether they were bright or dull in intellect. Indeed, the heavier the clay, the more pains did he take in his tillage. He endeavored to make himself master of the peculiarities of character belonging to each of his class, and of the drift of their lives, that he might adapt to these his teaching. While brimming over with images and apt illustrations calculated to attract youth and to fix the truths he spoke of in the memory, that teaching was laid on so solid a basis of learning, and supported by such original thinking, that the most advanced scholar could listen to it with satisfied pleasure.

Nor was this teaching formal: lectures repeated each year without variation. It is true it did not alter from year to year in the main subjects, or their order, but in its form and in its illustrations it changed continually. It laid all the events of the day under contribution. The form it had was worn as loosely as possible, and never hindered him from expansion. Often, inspired by a question from his class, he would leave his regular course, and speak on the difficulty proposed, or the shade of feeling suggested, for more than half an hour, without pausing a moment, and that with a logical sequence, — a grasp, an eloquence, and a fire of imagination which were the same, whether he discussed a point of theology, a shade of criticism, or a subtle winding in the labyrinth of the heart. No one could listen without being stirred, excited, and feeling a higher life possible. He knew that he produced this effect, and hence arose his constant warnings against a religion of mere transient enthusiasm, always embodied the Sunday before the Confirmation in such sermons as "The Parable of the Sower,"* "Jacob's Wrestling."†

This year the preparation of the candidates exhausted him greatly.

I am undergoing the reaction (he writes) consequent upon strained anxieties and attention. When all was over yesterday at the Confirmation, I felt as if I had no work to turn to, and it was with extreme repugnance and aversion that I contemplated preparation for Sunday. It reminds me of the "Song of the Shirt,"—"work, work, work"; and the perpetual treadmill necessity of being forever ready twice a week with earnest thoughts on solemn subjects is a task which is quite enough to break down all originality, and convert a racehorse into a dray.

Fortunately for his health, an outward interest now broke in upon his life. The elections for Brighton came on in July, and they interested him as much as if he had been a violent political partisan. But it was in reality the quicker life of the town and the public excitement which delighted him, and took him for the time out of his restricted sphere of action. The struggle, the play of human passions, the battle, in which he wished to see only the contest and not the rascality, roused in him all the combative enthusiasm of his warrior nature. He was seen everywhere,—his blue eyes flashing, his brown hair thrown back from his forehead,

---

* First Series, p. 39.   † Ibid., p. 60.

his walk rapid, his words quick and stirring. "I have read and done nothing all this week," he writes, "the excitement about the election has been so great." With his usual practice of bringing the events of daily life under the influence of the pulpit, he preached a sermon on the duties of electors.* He took as his subject the election of Matthias in the room of Judas. A short quotation will best show the spirit in which he fulfilled his task: —

> Delicate and difficult as the introduction of such a subject from the pulpit must be, yet it seems to me the imperative duty of a minister of Christ, — from which he cannot, except in cowardice, shrink, — to endeavor to make clear the great Christian landmarks which belong to such an occurrence. But let me be understood. His duty is not to introduce politics in the common sense of the word, meaning thereby the views of some particular party. The pulpit is not to be degraded into the engine of a faction. Far, far above such questions, it ought to preserve the dignity of a voice which speaks for eternity, and not for time. If possible, not one word should drop by which a minister's own political leanings can be discovered.
>
> Yet there must be broad principles of right and wrong in such a transaction as in any other. And in discharge of my duty I desire to place those before you.

In this sermon he steadily kept out of sight his own political views. He only declared the great principles according to which a vote should be given. Beyond the pulpit his influence was not unimportant, and he did not hesitate to exert it fairly in behalf of the liberal candidates, Sir George Pechell and Mr. Trelawney. He was the only Church of England clergyman who

* Fifth Series, p. 97.

voted for these gentlemen; and, owing to all the rest of his brethren supporting the other side, and to some reports industriously circulated concerning Mr. Trelawney's opinions, it was a courageous vote. It enlisted against him the conservative and the "religious" militia of Brighton. The letter which follows refers to these events, and his share in them: —

July 10.

The election is over. Lord Alfred Hervey was elected with a majority of about 250 over Trelawney, who, however, polled nearly 1,200 votes (I write from vague memory). I suppose people will be shocked at my vote, even those who voted for Pechell, though there is no difference between his politics and Trelawney's. A stranger, quite a gentleman in appearance, held up his hands on being told it, and said, "Why, Trelawney is an atheist." — "Do you know that for a fact?" said I. "No, but I was told so." — "Then I must say that as it is a very solemn charge, you ought to inquire before you assert it." Five minutes after, a lady met me, and said, "Why, Mr. Trelawney is a Catholic." So, after thorough investigation, I wrote a note to this gentleman, and told him Trelawney was neither an atheist nor a Catholic, but a member of the Church of England, — a man, as I was credibly informed by Mr. Seymour, of high character. I concluded with the suggestion that it was due to his honor to contradict his own statement wherever it had been made.

I omitted to tell you the surprise at the polling-booth at my vote was quite amusing. I saw by the countenances of the by-standers that it excited much interest to know which way it would be given. There was quite a breathless attention while the name, address, &c., were being taken down; and when I said, "Pechell and Trelawney," voices cried out on all sides, "Thank you, sir," "Bravo," "Well done, indeed; that's a man!" and the respect was extreme. I could not help fancying, from the tone of the remarks, that they appreciated the difficulty of a clergyman in voting on that side. What struck me most was, there was no uproarious cheers, but an evidently respectful and grateful acceptance of the act and its motives. . . . .

On his return from his usual absence during October, he found Brighton boiling over with excitement on the Sabbath question. It had been proposed to open the Crystal Palace on Sundays. It was at once inferred that Christianity was in mortal danger, and to protect it from its death-wound, the whole religious phalanx of Brighton rallied round its standard. Large talking assemblies met together, and the wildest and most unfounded assertions were made. The "Times" was accused of the grossest venality, because it defended the throwing open of the Palace; but the accuser, a clergyman, was obliged to eat his words. Mr. Robertson alone stood against the torrent in behalf of Christian liberty. He did not, for several reasons, approve of the opening of the Palace on Sunday; but he did refuse to adopt arguments against it, based on the supposition of the non-abrogation of the Jewish Sabbath. He preached a sermon, "The Sydenham Palace, and the Religious Non-observance of the Sabbath," * on the whole subject, in which he declared that he had satisfied himself.

November 16, 1852.

MY DEAR TOWER: — As you will be here next week, I will not write you a volume, for nothing else would do. I preached on the subject on Sunday, satisfactorily to myself at least, — a thing which has occurred to me but once or

---

* Second Series, p. 198.

twice in all my ministry; so I am thoroughly prepared with an opinion on a matter I have well considered. I will say at present I am quite resolved to sign no petition. Dr. V.'s pamphlet does not go to the root of the matter. I agree with him in viewing the move, so far as it is an *avowed* innovation, with great jealousy; but I cannot ask for a state enactment to reimpose a law which Christianity has repealed, without yielding the very principle of Christianity. Historically, the Lord's Day was not a transference of the Jewish Sabbath at all from one day to another. St. Paul, in Rom. xiv. 5, 6, speaks of a *religious non-observance* of the Sabbath; I cannot say or think that the Crystal Palace affair is a *religious* non-observance, believing it to be merely a lucrative speculation: nevertheless, I have nothing to do with that. The Sabbath is abrogated, and the observance of a day of rest is only a most wise human law now, not to be enforced by *penalties*. Besides, how dare we refuse a public concession to the poor man of a right of recreation which has been long assumed by the rich man with no protest or outcry from the clergy, who seem touched to the quick only when desecration, as they call it, is noisy and vulgar.

Mr. Tower suggested, in answer, Bishop Horsley's critical treatment of the question, and to this letter he replied: —

" Horsley's Sermons " I only vaguely remember. I am quite at ease on the subject. The critical disposal of this or that text would not alter my views. I am certain of the genius and spirit of Christianity; certain of St. Paul's *root thoughts*, — far more certain than I can be of the correctness or incorrectness of any isolated interpretation: and I must reverse all my conceptions of Christianity — which is the mind of Christ — before I can believe the Evangelico-Judaic theory; which is that Mr. —— may, without infringement of the 4th Commandment, drive his carriage to church twice every Sunday, but a poor man may not drive his cart;—that the two or three hours spent in the evening by a noble lord over venison, champagne, dessert, and coffee, are no desecration of the command; but the same number spent by an artisan over cheese and beer in a tea-garden will bring down God's judgment on the land. It is worse than absurd. It is the very spirit of that Pharisaism which our Lord rebuked so sternly. And then men get up on platforms as —— did; and quietly assume that they are the religious, and that all who disagree, whether writers in the "Times," Sir R. Peel, or the "sad exceptions," of whom I was one, to which he alluded, are either neologians or hired writers! Better break a thousand sabbaths than lie and slander thus! But the Sabbath of the Christian is the consecration of all time to God: of which the Jewish Sabbath was but the type and shadow. See Col. ii. 16, 17. Bishop Horsley's attempt to get over that verse is miserable, I remember.

"Six hundred churches wanted." Yes! but when shall we have different hours for service and different congregations in one church, say one for three congregations; and so save two thirds of the money spent on stone and brick, that it may be spent on the truer temple, human beings, in whom God's Spirit dwells? They do this on the Continent, and with no inconvenience. Besides, the inconvenience and mutual giving way would be all so much gain for Christian life, instead of an objection to the plan.

A member of his congregation wrote to him on this subject. He replied:—

60 Montpelier Road : November 17.

My dear Mr. Wright:—I am very sorry indeed that I should have left my meaning ambiguous on Sunday. I will briefly recapitulate what I said, or meant to say.

I tried to show that in St. Paul's judgment the Sabbath is

abrogated, being, as he calls it (Col. ii. 16, 17), a shadow of which Christ is the substance. This Sabbath has given way to a larger, grander, more spiritual Sabbath, — the Rest of the people of God, — a life claimed, not in parts, but as a whole, for him, — a perpetual sacrifice.

To urge this abrogated Sabbath again on men's consciences as indispensable to salvation, St. Paul reckons as a giving up of the spirit of Christianity (Gal. iv. 10, 11). Nevertheless, it is perfectly competent for the Christian Church to appoint days and times, as she shall find them needful, to aid her infirmities or express her love, provided only that she does not bind them on human consciences as indispensable.

Such a day, among others, she did appoint in very early times, — the Lord's day. But it was not a transference of the Jewish Sabbath from Saturday to Sunday, but arose out of the great Christian principle, which views all life in reference to the Church's crucified and risen Lord. And thus time was divided into cycles, larger and smaller, the cycle of the week or the cycle of the year, each representing the death in which all daily die, — the resurrection in which all daily rise. Friday and Saturday, Good Friday and Easter day, were the epochs respectively of these cycles.

I hold this institution of the Lord's day to be a most precious and blessed one, not to be dispensed with except with danger; and I believe that no one who loves his country can look on any measure which is likely to desecrate its observance, or break through our English feelings towards it, without great misgiving and apprehension.

And St. Paul modifies his broad view of a repealed Sabbath, by acknowledging that there may be a religious and conscientious observance of that day. "One man esteemeth one day above another. Let every man be fully persuaded in his own mind. . . . . He that observeth the day observeth it to the Lord." On the other hand, he modifies it again, by emphatically requiring that the *non-observance* of the Sabbath must be a religious non-observance, — a conscientious, and not merely a licentious or latitudinarian one. He that observeth not the day, *to the Lord* he observeth it not.

Now here is my first objection to the spirit in which the Crystal Palace is proposed. It contemplates a non-observance of the Sabbath, but not a religious one. It is not non-observance to the Lord. It does not proceed from a sublime view of Christian life as one great Sabbath, but from laxity, indifference, and love of lucre. At least, I fear so, for it is put forward in the light of a speculation.

My second objection — not so much to the thing itself as to the grounds on which it is advocated — is the assumption, that to humanize the people is identical with Christianizing them. I am very anxious to humanize and polish the people; but I cannot shut my eyes to the lesson of history, — that the arts, such as painting, sculpture, music, poetry, have not in themselves ennobled, but often deteriorated nations. The worship of the Beautiful is not the worship of Holiness; and therefore to talk of statue-galleries and museums, as if they were to do the work which can only be done by the Cross of Christ, and to represent such æsthetic amusements as the true and right *religious* use of rest, I hold to be mere false sentimentality.

But with all this I am strongly opposed to every endeavor to put down the Crystal Palace by petition or legislative enactments, on the three following grounds, which I meant to distinctly name in my sermon: —

1. Because it is a return to Judaism to enforce, by human enactment, that which St. Paul declares repealed. I may much regret the probable tendencies of this measure; but still I cannot try to forbid by law a sort of recreation for the poor man in public gardens and public picture-galleries, which the rich man has freely allowed himself in private gardens and galleries, with no protest whatever from the clergy.

2. Because a severe and stringent law injures the con-

science. Whoever multiplies enactments beyond what is essential, tempts human consciences to transgression. For it *is* transgression when a man does a thing which he thinks wrong, even though it be not abstractedly wrong. Hence St. Peter speaks against "putting a yoke upon the neck of the disciples, which neither he nor his fathers had been able to bear." And hence St. Paul speaks of the "motions of sin which were by the law"; that is, caused and stirred into motion by the law. I am persuaded that much abandonment is caused by the strict severity of Sabbath observance, when others, who are not fit for it, are compelled to obey, at the risk of being treated as infidels. Many a criminal on the scaffold can trace his first declension in crime to such a restriction, and the feeling of hopelessness and defiance which seized him when he had once broken it.

And I refuse to sign such a petition, lastly, because to exalt a "law positive," that is, a law contrived for temporary and special ends, — into the rank of a moral law eternally binding, has always been the first step towards relaxing the reverence for that which is moral. Thus the Pharisees were very scrupulous about tithing mint, anise, and cummin: justice, judgment, and truth they cared little for. They were furious at a transgression of the Fourth Commandment, but they would allow a man to be as proud, and selfish, and tyrannical as he pleased. And so, in the same way, there is a tendency now to be very indignant about a poor man's spending Sunday afternoon in a tea-garden, whilst there is little zeal against the real damning sins of social life. Why do they not preach a crusade against noblemen driving in the park? Or why do they speak of God sending a judgment on this nation for a Crystal Palace, while they quietly ignore the fact, or are too polite to take notice of it, that four-fifths of our male population are living in a state of concubinage till they are married? Why do they hold up hands of pious indignation when a train runs by, while more than one religious person in this town drives regularly to church on fine days as well as wet? Why do they say that it is a crime to sacrifice a single policeman to the comfort of the community, by making him work on the Sabbath, when their own servants are "sacrificed" — if it be sacrifice — in making their beds, cleaning their rooms, boiling their luxurious hot potatoes, &c., &c., &c., none of which are either works of necessity or works of mercy, — the only works they say, which are excepted from the rule? Why do they not grapple with the slander, and the gossip, and the pride of society, and the crimes of the upper classes? Why are they touched to the quick only when desecration of the Sabbath puts on a *vulgar* form? Because, as I said before, scrupulosity about laws "positive" generally slides into laxity about the eternal laws of right and wrong.

For all these reasons, I am against the petition movement, and strongly against it. Besides, though I look jealously and suspiciously at the Crystal Palace plan, I am not yet certain that it may not be an improvement on the way in which the poorer classes at present spend their Sundays. I hope this is clear, my dear Mr. Wright. I have written it rapidly, having much to do, and concisely; but I trust it will be clear. You are quite welcome to show it to any one who thought my sermon ambiguous.

Of course, refusing to sign the petition for an enactment against the opening of the Palace on Sunday, he was openly and covertly attacked. One of his brother ministers alluded to him as the "sad exception" to the Christian unanimity of the clergymen of Brighton. And yet he was more particular in his observance of that day than many of his censurers. He has often walked ten miles and more to preach on a Sunday, rather than accept a carriage or take a fly, and this lest he should cause his brother to offend. But alas! what matters that, as long as men act and speak as if they held that true religion consists in holding orthodox views, and not in doing right actions? "This man could not be of God, because he did not keep the Sabbath day!"

In the midst of all this outward rebuke, and in spite of the increased loneliness of his position, his spirit seems to have been growing humbler, calmer, and more gentle. The following words may well close the history of his life in this year:—

The life of Christ and His death, after all, are the only true solution of the mystery of human life; to that, after all, all the discords of this world's wild music must be attuned at at last. There is sharp pain — past pain — in that letter which you sent me, but yet how instinctively one feels at once that the tone of Christianity is wanting. I do not mean the cant expressions, but the genuine tone which numbers of real men and women have learned by heart.

It may be hereafter mellowed into this, as I hope my tone will; but neither are as yet, though I have got what your correspondent has not, the words of the Song; only I have not the music. And what are the words without? Yet it is something to feel the deep, deep conviction, which has never failed me in the darkest moods, that Christ had the key to the mysteries of Life, and that they are not insoluble; also, that the spirit of the Cross is the condition which will put any one in possession of the same key: "Take my yoke upon you, and ye shall find rest for your souls." It is something, much, to know this, for, knowing it, I feel it to be unphilosophical and foolish to quarrel with my lot, for my wisdom is to transmute my lot by meekness into gold. With God I cannot quarrel, for I recognize the beauty and justice of His conditions. It is a grand comfort to feel that God is right, whatever and whoever else may be wrong. I *feel* St. Paul's words, "Let God be true and every man a liar."

LETTERS FROM JANUARY, 1852, TO DECEMBER, 1852.

XXXVII.

My Dear —— : — If I do not reply at once, I may possibly never reply at all, so much has the habit of procrastination or the *à quoi bon* question taken possession of me. Secondly, if I do not reply at once, I may in honesty, after reading your heterodoxy, be compelled to administer castigation. And, thirdly, a slight *épanchement de cœur* says, " I shall not last long in your bosom, cold sir, so write to your friend while the fit is on you."

Well, I am no heretic in my affections either, and my friendship is as truly yours as ever, my dear ——. As warmly? Hum, — why *all* was warm and effervescing once, now all is cold and flat. If a mouse could change into a frog, or a falcon into a penguin, would the affections be as *warm* as before, albeit they might remain unalterable? I trow not, so I only say you have as much as a cold-blooded animal can give, whose pulsations are something like one per minute.

I cannot agree with you in wishing for a war. It is very horrible, and though I think there is nothing of personal danger in it that appals, the thought of what would befall our *women* gives me many a sleepless night. I expect an invasion; nevertheless, I detest war. But Mr Cobden and Co.'s doctrines prostitute national honor to the " wealth of nations," and have left us unable to defend ourselves or even to arm our soldiers as well as savages can afford to arm themselves.

XXXVIII.

I do not remember exactly what I said on E—— V——'s birthday about God's designs. A conversation grows out of warm striking of mind on mind, and it is almost impossible to reproduce it. At this moment it has as entirely gone from me as if it had never been. I can only conjecture that I said something to the effect that God's plan was not thwarted by transgression and a new plan begun; as in a siege, the plan of the invader is frustrated by a sap meeting him, and then a counter-sap and fresh mines carried on below to foil that; but that God's *idea* of Humanity is, and ever was, Humanity as it is in Jesus Christ; that so far as it fails of that, His idea may be *said* to have not been realized; but we must be cautious of first using this language to express rudely our mode of conceiving a truth, and then arguing from it, as if it were real, and not merely a human mode of thought. The idea of a tree or plant, — say the vine, — is of the tree in its perfection. In the English climate you may say it has failed, that is, it has not attained the stature which of right belongs to the plant; it is a fallen, abortive thing; but you do not mean by that, that its Creator intended that particular plant to succeed, and was disappointed in the attempt. Fallen, man is, in comparison of the Divine idea of Humanity, but it was no failure. However, it is impossible to write out in cold blood, unstimulated by something naturally going before, on such a subject. It becomes a mere dry essay.

XXXIX.

Lewes: Friday, 7.45 p. m.

From Tuesday until this moment I have scarcely had an instant. We are in court by nine, and directly it is over I dine either with the judges or the high sheriff. We are this moment out, after eleven hours' sitting. A horrible murder has occupied them all day, which is not over yet. We begin to-morrow at eight, a. m. I shall write to you shortly, with an account of the last few days. I am thoroughly and completely tired.

* * * * *

I write during an interval of a most painful character, —

during the trial of an unhappy woman for the murder of her husband. She is at this moment in a swoon. The judge has stopped the case until her recovery. I am sitting close to him, and his observations to me from time to time seem to show that there is not the slightest chance of her escape. It is a horrible case. She poisoned him in order to marry a young man, or boy, who has just given evidence against her in a disgraceful way. His only excuse is, that she had already tried to throw the murder upon him, and indeed I believe he had a hand in it; so, too, Baron Parke has just told me he thinks. The last witness is now giving his evidence; and when the counsel for the defence has spoken, and the judge has given his charge, I imagine the jury cannot doubt ten minutes about their verdict,—that being "*guilty*," her fate is sealed. No, I am wrong, her own child is just called to witness against her,—a poor little boy seven years old. The poor miserable creature herself, during the trial, which lasted all yesterday, and for the hour which it has continued this morning, has been almost in a swooning state. A quarter of an hour ago Dr. Taylor, the celebrated analyst, descended into the dock, and prescribed for her, the court meanwhile waiting several minutes in dead silence for her recovery. Dr. Taylor gave most interesting medical evidence yesterday, respecting the chemical analysis by which he discovered the presence of arsenic in large quantities in the deceased. The judge said to me as he took the book, "Now you will hear some evidence worth listening to."

I am thankful to say the little boy has not been permitted to give evidence: he knew nothing about an oath. Nothing could have been more horrible than an only child taking his own mother's life away.

*   *   *   *   *

I could write no more yesterday: the trial became too intensely interesting and painful to do anything. The judge's charge lasted, I should think, an hour and a half. The jury retired. An hour and a half passed in terrible suspense. At last they came: the foreman said at once, "GUILTY." Baron Parke put on the black cap. The poor woman, with burning cheeks, and eyes as brilliant as fire with excitement, was held up between two turnkeys to receive her sentence. "My lord," said the clerk of arraigns, "you have omitted two essential words; you did not say what death she is to die." So the fainting thing was held up again, and the last sentence of the award repeated, with the words "hanged by the neck." I felt as if I were a guilty man in sitting by to see a woman murdered. But my eye caught the figure of the scoundrel Hickman, standing by to hear her who was suffering all for him condemned to die, without the slightest appearance of emotion. It was a most sickening spectacle from first to last; and there is not the smallest chance of her life being spared.

My sermon was delivered badly and hurriedly. On Friday and Saturday the sheriff was away, and I did his duty for him of escorting the judges. Every time I returned to my lodgings alone in the carriage-and-four I was not a little amused by the blast of trumpets which saluted me the moment I put my foot upon the carriage steps, and the mute awe of the crowd, who were imposed upon by my robes with the idea of something very grand. I felt half inclined to bid the row of javelin-men, who uncovered in a line as I passed, and the trumpeters, have done with the solemn absurdity, at least in my case: but I reflected that forms and pageants are of far deeper importance for the masses than at first sight appears. A judge in black robes, instead of scarlet, would not be half a judge. Many reflections of this kind occurred to my mind, some of which I put into my afternoon sermon; in the morning I was too hoarse and unwell to preach.

XL.

March 26.

That miserable murderess, it is said, has confessed her crime, and exonerated Hickman entirely; but the truth of this latter portion of her story I rather doubt. Hanging a woman is a hideous thought. The impressions of last week will, I think, reverse forever all my intellectual convictions of the need and obligation of capital punishment; yet I think I could have strung up Hickman with my own hands with considerable satisfaction; so strongly do natural instincts, partly dependent upon the mere difference between man and woman, bias, and even determine, judgments that seem purely intellectual, and framed in what Lord Bacon called "a dry light."

It shows, besides, how utterly unfit woman would be for innumerable functions which American speculation would open to her; for her feelings warp even more than ours, and that which is her glory in its place, would unfit her for all those duties which require the abeyance of the feelings. This is the very reason, viz., her deceivability through feeling, which St. Paul wisely assigns against her usurpation of the offices of public teaching, &c., that Adam was not deceived, but Eve, &c. How deep inspiration is! so deep that, like the clear sea around the West Indies, it seems shallow until you try to dive into it.

A thought occurred to me while writing about invasion, which escaped by the time I got to the end of the above paragraph. It was this, — the distinction between the French spirit in war and ours. Theirs is "La Gloire!" Ours is "Duty!" And this was the real source of England's sublime battle-cry at Trafalgar, and the reason, too, why English troops can *stand* to be mowed down, as well as rush to the charge. It is the latter only for which the French are remarkable. "Hard pounding, gentlemen," said the Duke, at Waterloo, coming to a regiment which had lost, as some did, 600 men before they drew a trigger; "we shall see who will pound the longest." "La Gloire" against "Duty." We shall see which will stand the longest, provided it is not all over at the first onset, which it is likely enough to be from the small practice of our best officers.

Poor —— has lost his wife in confinement. I spent three hours with him to-day; some of the most profitable, in every sense of the word, that I have spent for a long time. He was severely shocked about it; he had not the slightest anticipation of such a termination. She had been going on well, and it was only on the day she died that unfavorable symptoms presented themselves. What a mournful case such an one always is! and how mysterious, remembering that Woman is in her vocation of involuntary sacrifice, giving mute obedience to the law,—life only through suffering or death; the law to which her whole life, consciously or unconsciously, voluntarily or involuntarily, is a testimony. To me the event will be a great loss. I had promised myself a congenial acquaintance or friend,—a man,—for we have had several walks together and "cottoned" to each other. He is going to leave Brighton, and stay with his brother, a clergyman, to get away from sad associations and reminiscences.

I gave a lecture on Thursday to the catechumens, on Jacob's journey from home,—different from former times in treatment, and quite extempore; that is, the whole train of thought presented itself when I began, and I spoke for three-quarters of an hour, quite different from what I had intended: I have no notes.

XLI.

You are quite right in your estimate of the comparative value of Lord Carlisle's and Mr. Drummond's letter. I told you in a former letter how I valued the latter as the *only* indication I have received of a sympathy which had penetrated into the motive of my *Lectures*. If I did not believe that religion is poetry, and that all or most poetry is the half-way house to religion, inasmuch as the laws of both are the same, the opposites of both being Science, and the organ of both Intuition, I should not have spent my time on those *Lectures;* — indeed, this I had said beforehand.

* * * * *

My tastes are with the aristocrat, my principles with the mob. I know how the recoil from vulgarity and mobocracy, with thin-skinned and over-fastidious sensitiveness, has stood in the way of my doing the good I might do. My own sympathies and principles in this matter are in constant antagonism, and until these can be harmonized, true Christianity is impracticable. A greater felt the same, — Milton; but he worked far more ardently for his principles, though, as life went on, he shrank more and more from the persons with whom his principles associated him; and so at last never went even to church, detesting the dissenter's vulgarity and the republican's selfishness. It is now some time since I became *conscious* of this discord in me, which mars usefulness; but it is curious that two letters, one from my mother, and one from a Miss Perry, a sister of Sir Erskine Perry, who was President of the Board of Education in India, — a letter not written to me, — have both within ten days remarked the same thing, the latter very acutely, in a review of the poetry affair, and preaching, and pamphlets generally. Lord Falkland, — you see I select grand precedents to excuse myself, — lived and died in the same way; and I suspect that if the Crown were ever to tyrannize, and the people were to rise, I should be found fighting against the mob, — at least if, unfortunately, a queen were sovereign. To give a less august precedent: poor Balaam was in a similar antagonism, with tastes, love of poetry, &c., on the side of Balak; principles on the side of Israel: only gold inclined the scales to the wrong side, which happily is not my temptation.

* * * * *

XLII.

Your note did not reach me until the afternoon post to-day. I am thoroughly worn and sore with work: prayers last week, — preaching Thursday, Friday, and Sunday, — prayers again to-day. The usual result has followed, — low spirits and deep depression. In such moods, I can see nothing truly, — all is black and hopeless; but as I know the cause to be chiefly physical, I resolve to give no utterance to transient feeling, but wait until the cloud passes. Therefore if in this anything sounds harsh or misanthropic, think it is not I, but one of the azure demons whose property I myself am for the nonce.

I will extract now, as nearly as I can remember, what I said about the *Birkenhead*.

After showing that the glory of the Cross — the text being, "God forbid that I should glory," &c. — consisted in "Obedience unto death," and hence inferring that man's real greatness lies in Duty, I said: —

"And this surely is impressed upon us to-day with double power by the news which reached the shores of this country two days ago, of the sinking of 450 Britons within sight of the shore of Africa. And yet no Englishman could have read those letters who did not feel his heart swell with proud and grateful exultation in the country which gave him birth; for the two things which were conspicuous in the whole of that dire scene, and which redeemed the disaster from the character of common, vulgar death, — were the spirit of Duty and the spirit of high Sacrifice; when men, summoned suddenly from their hammocks, mustered in silence, and obeyed the word of command as calmly, and as silently, and as simply on the deck of a sinking vessel, as they would have done on the parade-ground on a gala day; and when men who had waited for permission to throw themselves overboard to save their lives, were arrested almost to a man by the first voice that warned them that they could only save themselves by the sacrifice of the women and children. God forbid that we should glory in our country's wealth, her renown, or her military successes, merely as such; God forbid that we should glory in aught of hers, save in that English spirit of Duty and of Sacrifice, on which are stamped so unmistakably the lineaments of the Redeemer's cross. It was this which constituted the real force of that sublime battle-cry which preceded one of the most terrific lessons ever given to the world by the lips of her artillery, and told men wherein lay the might and the majesty of a country which expects of her chosen sons, in the hour of death and danger, not that every man shall save his own life, — nor that every man shall seek his own glory, — but that 'every man shall do his own duty.'"

That is nearly what I said, and I never said anything more from my heart. I do love and honor my dear old country with all my heart and soul; her sons cannot sing, paint, nor carve, but they can die at their posts silently, without thinking that "forty centuries are looking down upon them" from the Pyramids.

The women of the *Birkenhead* had not the option of sacrifice for the men. They did not know beforehand the cost at which they must be saved. Besides, if the men could have so calculated, they would not have been worth the saving. It is their self-devotion which makes us feel how much worth they were; and therefore it is like the old ordeal: if they sank they deserved saving, and if they escaped they ought to have been drowned.

XLIII.

I am also reading Guizot's "Méditations et Études Morales," in which there are some valuable thoughts, at least in that on *Immortalité*, — which is the one I have read. It singularly coincides with the views I gave last Sunday, but was read since. He shows that the belief in a future life is not the result of inductive and inferential reasonings, — such as the incomplete justice here, or the dissatisfaction with all earthly good, — but that rather, these result from the instinctive belief in immortality. Savages and children never doubt it; and the nearer you approach the instinctive state, the more indubitable it is. It is only when refinement, civilization, and science come that it grows dim. The attempt to rest our intuitions on a scientific basis, inevitable as the attempt is, brings with it doubt, — and you get back faith again when you quit logic and science, and suffer the soul to take counsel with itself, or, in Scripture language, "when you become again a little child." Do read Wordsworth's glorious ode in connection with this thought, which, indeed, is *the* thought of the whole ode.

XLIV.

They tell me that it is impossible for one in the vortex of London gayety to stop; that at last a single evening at home is intolerably *ennuyeux*. I partly believe it, and can only say that if it be so, it kills body and soul, and the severe restrictions which seemed to me to be excessive, of persons whom I reckoned righteous over-much, have more sense and reason in them than I supposed. And it appears to have been the same case with the fine ladies, and, to use the cant phrase, the smart people of Antioch, Corinth, &c., &c. I suppose the Apostle had been contemplating the exhausted countenances and languid listlessness of the fashionables of the metropolis, when he said so vehemently, "She which liveth in pleasure is dead while she liveth." I do not wonder at the success of Tractarianism among the Belgravians. Chanted services and innocent gentlemen with lilies of the valley in their dresses, must afford something of the same cooling and sedative effect which I have felt in the burning south of France, in going from a garden, on the walls of which innumerable lizards basked, and the sun's rays beat down intolerably, at once into the coolness of an artificial cave.

I am not calm, yet I do try earnestly, and against many hindrances, within and without, to rule my life by Law, and to win that composure without which nothing can be done; but much is against me, and my very duties hinder me. Here am I, on Monday morning, as languid and wretched as a London lady who has come down from her room at 11 A. M., pale and wan after an evening of dissipation; but my languor and the over-strung state of brain which will make the next two days mere endurance of life, come not from pleasure, but from public speaking. I can only get rid of my exhaustion by getting rid of my duty. To-day it is rather worse than usual, because I was obliged to give an hour last night, and on every Sunday until confirmation, to prepare some young men who cannot come on any other evening. After that I drank tea with the V——s, and found them all suffering more or less from the effects of this sand-impregnated wind. I was too tired to talk. I am going to take a solitary walk on the Downs, untempting as the day and atmosphere are, to try to invigorate after yesterday, and to get up resolution for a speech at a meeting this evening, in which I take the chair.

XLV.

Prefatory Observations to Mons. Zaba's Lecture on Polish Mnemonics.

Memory depends on two circumstances,—attention and the laws of association.

I. Attention.

Doubtless we are born with different natural capacities of memory. I leave this to the physiologist to explain, to show why, with an equal volume of brain, one man may have judgment, and another memory; why, in certain states of health, we can remember better than in others.

It is unquestionable, however, that memory can be improved; and it will generally, I believe, be found that this improvement arises from increased power of fixing the attention. No one can hope to remember who has not acquired the power of concentrating his attention.

A proof that this is one of the conditions of recollecting, we have in the fact that we recollect circumstances witnessed and things learnt in childhood, whereas we forget the events of yesterday; and this because when we come into the world all is new, startling, and arrests the attention. In later life we see as if we saw not, and hear as if we heard not. All is dulled; we are familiar with all, and our attention is languid and flags.

Another proof lies in the fact that people remember chiefly those points in which their profession or circumstances most interest them. For instance, one of the witnesses in the case of Rush, the murderer, deposed that the murderer wore a mask, or vizor, made of linen or some soft material. On being cross-examined and asked how she could swear that it was not of paper, as the event occurred in a darkened house, she replied that she had observed of the mask that it did not rustle. There spoke the *woman's* memory dependent on feminine observation. No man would have remarked the material of the mask. It was the woman's province.

Another illustration occurs in the history of Jedediah Buxton, the ploughman, of wonderful arithmetical capacities. You might have given him the size of the circumference of a wheel, and he would have told you on the spot how many circumvolutions it would make in going round the globe. This was his only forte. In almost all other points he was deficient. As usual in England, they lionized the wonderful ploughman. Among other places, they took him to the Opera. Upon inquiring what he thought of the celebrated dancer, he replied, " Wonderful! she danced ... steps in so many minutes!" That was all that he had attended to; that was all that he remembered. The gracefulness, the attitudes, the science, were all thrown away on him, and would be soon forgotten. Only in his own particular department of numbers, where his attention was stimulated by habit, did he see or remember anything.

II. Memory, again, depends upon the laws of association. What we mean by association is easily explained. When two things have been remarked together, in connection, it is a law of the mind that the presentation of the one at any future time will suggest the other. Thus, if an accident has occured at a certain turning of a road to me, I shall never be able to pass that spot without the spontaneous reappearance in my memory of the accident; or, if my friend has been in the habit of using a particular cane, the sight of the cane will conjure up a vivid recollection of my friend.

A great anatomist of the mind * has told us that the conditions of mental association are principally three:—

1. That of analogy.
2. That of contrast.
3. That of juxtaposition.

Juxtaposition, or contiguity. As, for instance, if you were in the habit, for six weeks consecutively, of seeing two men walk arm in arm, the sight of the one would force you to think instantaneously of the other.

And this is the kind of association on which verbal memory depends. Words that have been in connection suggest each other. One sentence brings up the sentence that has been read before in contiguity with it. It is not the highest memory, but a very useful one.

Contrast,— as when smallness suggests the thought of greatness, or a mean action compels you to the thought of nobleness.

The highest of all is that memory which suggests by *analogy*. It is this habit which furnishes the orator with

* Aristotle.

illustrations and parallels. It is this which essentially characterizes the inventor and creator; as when the bole of a spreading oak suggested itself to Smeaton, the architect of the Eddystone Lighthouse, when he desired to build an edifice which should brave the storm. And it is this which makes the great historian. Let me illustrate it from the life of Dr. Arnold. When Dr. Hampden was, as it seemed to him, persecuted for his opinions, the zeal with which he espoused his cause was not merely the result of affection for his friend, or love of his views. To Arnold it recalled the innumerable parallels of the past. He saw in Hampden's judges a resurrection of the spirit which had presided in many a council like that of Constance. All the past persecution of opinion rose like a phantom before his mind's eye. Thus does the historian write the present and the past, by the analogy of principles; yet between the name of Huss and Hampden how little resemblance! Between the opinions of the two men how wide a difference!

These are the internal laws of memory, — universal laws; the laws of suggestion.

Now, M. Zaba has invented a plan by which he proposes to assist memory by its own laws: a species of *memoria technica*, or artificial memory.

Its principles, as far as I collected from a hasty sketch he gave me, are twofold : —

1. It relies upon the additional aid furnished to mental memory by the eye. The importance of this aid all know who have studied history with or without a map. In the latter case memory will simply depend on the association of juxtaposition. Events and words follow one another in a certain order. If your verbal or your contiguous memory be tenacious, you may retain the circumstances; but if not, all you recollect will be confused. But if you call in the aid of eyesight, localizing this battle there, and tracing that invasion from town to town, you have got a local habitation as well as

a name for your facts,— the map is transferred to the inward eye.

Or you might skim over unobservantly the account of the locality of the birth of the first Prince of Wales; but if you had stood in the chamber in Carnarvon Castle, where the event took place, it would be engraven there for life; or, if you had seen the axe or block in the Tower on which some historical personage suffered, how much more vivid would your recollection of his fate become!

It is a passage often quoted from an ancient poet, that objects presented to the eye stimulate the attention and the mind far more keenly than those which are merely offered to the ear or the intellect.

M. Zaba's system maps out, as you see, all the past, localizing every event; and so you have in its proper shelf, or pigeon-hole, all that you would remember.

The next principle which he has summoned to his aid is that of method.

Now, without method memory is useless. Detached facts are practically valueless. All public speakers know the value of method. Persons not accustomed to it imagine that a speech is learnt by heart. Knowing a little about the matter, I will venture to say that if any one attempted that plan, either he must have a marvellous memory, or else he would break down three times out of five. It simply depends upon correct arrangement. The words and sentences are left to the moment; the thoughts methodized beforehand; and the words, if rightly arranged, will place themselves.

But upon the truthfulness of the arrangement all depends. Sometimes a man will find that his divisions have been artificial, and not natural. A thought is put down under a certain head, but there is no reason why it had not been in an earlier division. It belongs to both,— a sure proof that the division has been false and confused. Then, in speaking, perhaps it suggests itself under the first head; and when he comes to the one where it was to have been, there is a gap, and he stumbles and blunders.

Artificial arrangement must rest on a real and natural basis, or else it will be only partially useful. Dr. Whewell, in his pamphlet, — which forms one of a series delivered at the suggestion of Prince Albert, on the different departments of the Great Exhibition, — shows in a very interesting way how real and *natural* the arrangement of the Exhibition was; how perfectly successful in consequence; and how they gradually fell into the natural arrangement, after former Exhibitions had gradually corrected the mistakes of a more arbitrary and artificial division.

Now, the practicability and value of M. Zaba's scheme will mainly depend upon the question whether his method is simply artificial, or whether the arbitrary division rests upon a natural reason. For instance, each year is divided into nine compartments, — one representing a sovereign; a second, resolution; a third, invention; and so on. I invite him to explain this. Nine is an artificial number. Do nine particulars exhaust the chief subjects that are memorable? Do they interfere with each other? &c., &c.

One thing more. I trust he will recollect the difference between the English and the Polish intellect. Our national character excels in perseverance; theirs in talent. They can learn many languages with facility. A friend — I may call him such — of my own, a Pole, had extraordinary faculties of this kind. He told me all his countrymen shared it. The name of Count Streleczki is known to some of you. His talent is multifarious, universal. From the colonial capacities of Australia to the diameter of an extinct crater in one of the Polynesian islands, from the details of an Irish poor-law to the chemical composition of malachite, he is at home; in all departments of literature and science. M. Zaba's son — a most intelligent young gentleman — has exhibited wonderful knowledge. But I ask — he has had experience — how far is the system applicable to our obtuse and low English intellects? How long will an Anglo-Saxon boy be occupied in mastering the system?

XLVI.

Last night I began Margaret Fuller Ossoli. The reviews had prejudiced me against her by most unfair extracts, which give no idea whatever of her character as a whole; and it is only one more out of many lessons to judge for one's self; and not to accept the offices of a taster. I got through the first volume almost before I went to bed. I was much pleased; an exceedingly rich nature, — growing weeds luxuriantly, but fewer than might have been expected. At the commencement are some remarkably well-put observations respecting the hackneyed subject of the Greeks and Romans; but I agree with one of the editors in what he says about being "*almost*" Christian. For self-development is not the aim of Christianity, much higher though it be than ordinary paganism, and better too than evangelicalism, which does not mean quite so much by its watchword, "Save your own soul."

Old friends are quite as easy to put off as old gloves, but not quite so easy to draw on again, — they have been damped, dried, and cannot open themselves as largely as before. How few can, like Margaret Ossoli, keep the threads of many acquaintances and friendships in the hand, without breaking any, or entangling any? I have begun the third volume, — her "Residence in Europe": in the first pages are some beautiful passages; but her "Residence in Paris" rather startles and revolts me. The words "noble," "good," &c., &c., which she bestows upon that profligate and licentious George Sand, are profanation. What are they worth if they are given indiscriminately? Paris seems to warp and injure every spirit that comes within its unnatural atmosphere. It is the natural birthplace of Phædras and Pasiphaës, and all that is refinedly brutal. My beau-ideal of a Devil, or rather imp nature, is a Parisian woman, thoroughly refined and thoroughly corrupted. And I knew one or two who were admirable approximations.

XLVII.

I have nearly read through Latham on the "English Language," a tough book; and also his "English Grammar." I have begun them again, in the way of slow and patient study. Once master of the subject, I shall be able to teach it. The great mistake in teaching is to suppose that, in order to teach elements, only rudimentary knowledge is required. I believe the foundations must have been *approfondis*; not that such teaching need be deep, but it must rest on depths. Results are for production, and the public; but it may cost years to get the freedom of stroke which passes for an off-hand inspiration of the moment; and long familiarity with a subject is the only condition on which facility of expression, abundance of illustration, and power of connecting the smallest parts with principles and with the whole, can be obtained.

I have resolved to master Latham, Physical Geography, and Wallenstein, before I leave for Ireland; also to get through the visiting of my congregation. It is always a good plan to fix definite periods for completing work, else it drags on uncompleted for months, perhaps forever. This, with my other work, will be all that I can manage, for I am no longer able to read hard. I sat up late two nights ago, and am suffering from it still.

How admirable those extracts are which you quote from Margaret F. Ossoli's "Life"! I agree with what she says about diffuseness in giving out an idea. I am sure the opposite has been my fault, and caused much to fall to the ground inoperatively. I am trying to get over it, and will yet more.

XLVIII.

It is now nearly midnight,—the only enjoyable time for writing, thought, or contemplation during this intense heat. By the side of a wall with a southern aspect the heat is of tropical sultriness, the sunbeams striking off almost as in the focus of a convex glass, and you look along the stones expecting to see the lizards basking in numbers as in the South of Europe. Several persons, I am told, have fallen dead in the open field: yet, severe as it is here, they say it is much worse inland, for during some hours of the day we have a refreshing sea-breeze. Indeed, I am speaking more of others' feelings than my own, for to me the intensest heat is always delightful. At this moment sheet-lightnings are, from time to time, transforming a very dark sky into a brilliant sheet of fire.

What you remark about Margaret Ossoli's "Life" is quite true. I think there is an apparent decline in power and intellect during her stay in Italy; but then it is, to be remembered, in the first place, that the painful and stirring scenes of war and revolution in which she was called to act, called out the woman's heart more than the brain, and the sad realities of the hospital dulled all inclination to soar into realms of speculation, philosophy, and past history. What was the question of "woman's future position" side by side with splints and bandages, and all things apparently going backwards? Then, in the second place, we must not forget that the whole of her papers concerning Italy were lost in the shipwreck, and in them alone could we expect her intellectual powers to have found a field. It is a life suggestive of much, and that not all pleasing. There is much out of joint in the body social and politic; say rather in our own hearts.

I have received a letter from an intelligent lady, which, I confess, pained me. In reply, I told her there was one thing of which she could not deprive me, — the certainty of having done her much good; that, having listened for years with reliance and trust, the truths of feeling and life which I have taught must have mixed with her life, — cannot be separated from her being, — must grow and produce a harvest which I shall claim hereafter as my harvest, and of which no power in the universe can rob me. I briefly explained her misconception of my views, telling her that the difference between them and those of the party whose views she expounds does not lie in the question of the Atonement, — we agree in this, — but in the question *what* in that atonement was the element that satisfied God? They say pain. I say, because I think the Scriptures say so, the surrender of self-will, as is clearly and distinctly asserted in John x. 17: and also in Hebrews x. 5, 6, 7, 10, where the distinction is drawn between the sacrifices of blood and suffering, which were mere butchery, and the Sacrifice which atones, in this special point, that one is moral, an act of "WILL," — the other un-moral, merely physical, and therefore worthless. Indeed, this is the whole argument of the Epistle to the Hebrews, and a glorious one it is. But I strongly recommended her to persevere in her resolve to quit Trinity, since it is not views which mould character, but a spirit; since our mysterious being is only capable of being stirred by the higher springs of action, trust, reliance, reverence, love; and when trust is gone, neither wisdom nor truth from the lips of a teacher can avail anything.

However, as a specimen of a Class, the circumstance pained me. How long will the rest remain? Only until they clearly comprehend what I surely try to make plain as my meaning; then I shall be alone, as I expected years ago. Still, this desertion one by one is painful.

> Truths would you teach, or save a sinking land?
> All fear, none aid you, and few understand.

Well, all the dearer will be the true and few who remain. So it was with Him.

The friends thou hast, and their adoption tried,
Grapple them to thy heart with hooks of steel.

Wise, profound Shakespeare!

XLIX.

My Dear ——:— Receive all grateful thanks for your nice list, nearly all of which I have already selected for my brother, and sent by this day's post. I feel bound in honor to make the *amende honorable* for my hasty acceptance of the verdict of reviews on Margaret Fuller Ossoli, and acknowledge that she was a noble creature, and that I have read her life with increasing depth of interest, with respect, admiration, and,—no! not with tears, but—a certain moisture on the eyelids, the result of reading by a bad light, or too long, or too late,—nothing else! I honor her because she was not a man, and could not have been if she had tried; nor a blue, but a woman, whose brain was all heart, and who fulfilled her mission of the friend, and her more sacred mission of the comforter, right nobly. There,—I was wrong, and you can make as ungenerous a use of the acknowledgment as you can,—that is, as you have it in you to make; which is a moral inability. But it only corroborates my convictions on the general subject. Margaret never looked at one single subject from the point of view from which a man would have contemplated it, and her high-sounding abstractions only veiled her intense belief in and love of living personalities. She was a splendid proof of "how divine a thing a woman may be made."

L.

The poor ignorant Roman Catholics, are they to be taught their duty by leaving them to the priests, or by living among them and showing them who are their true friends? There is a fearful debt due to Ireland, which has been accumulating for centuries, through absenteeism and landlords, whose interests have been in England, and not in Ireland. By the unalterable law of retribution it has all come on this generation; and the way to perpetuate it with ever-accumulating interest on the next generation is to pursue the same old false vicious system which has made Ireland what she is.

As to the Roman Catholic Emancipation Bill, nothing has altered my opinion. The old system was monstrous, and the Act was only one of justice. Roman Catholics in France are more attached to their country than to the Papacy, and so they are in Germany. But the mad Orange system, which would wean the affections of a persecuted and unprivileged Roman Catholic from his country and fix them on Rome, — banish them from Maynooth to be educated at St. Omer or other foreign seminaries, — forces him to be an Ultramontane. I earnestly trust England will never pause, much less retrograde, in the path of fairness and justice on which she has entered. No doubt many immediate consequences will seem bad, but trust to principle and time. Stockport riots, ferocious altar-pieces, — what do they come from but Ecclesiastical Titles Bills and proclamations against Roman Catholic worship? No; the old "root-and-branch" system of extermination must either be done thoroughly, or else you must not exasperate a foe whom you have not crippled. Extermination is possible. It succeeded in the revocation of the Edict of Nantes. But, then, it must be thorough, with fire and sword, and banishment. If not, there is nothing left but the concession of full political privileges. Make them Britons before you attempt to make them Protestants: once Britons, half the venom of their Romanism will be extracted. And then secular education is your sure ally to do the rest, — sure and safe, because it does not attack their religion directly, and you will have the people on your side against the priests as in the Thurley affair.

What appals me is to see the way in which people, once liberal, are now recoiling from their own principles, terrified by the state of the Continent, and saying we must stem the tide of democracy, and therefore support the Conservatives. Why, what has ever made democracy dangerous but Conservatism? French revolutions,—socialism,—why, people really seem to forget that these things came out of Toryism, which forced the people into madness. What makes rivers and canals overflow?—Deep channels cut ever deeper, or dams put across by wise people to stop them?

LI.

It is only one hour or two since I left Lewes, the work of the Assize being over, and to me it was rather a wearisome work. Yet I do not regret having had this office this year, for it has given me an insight into criminal court practice, which I never should have had but for this occasion, for nothing else would have compelled me to sit twice for four or five days together through every case. The general result of my experience is, that although Burke says, "the whole end and aim of legislation is to get twelve men into a jury-box," yet the jury system, beautiful as it is in theory, is in itself neither good nor bad, but depends upon two things,—first, the national character; secondly, the judge; and on this last almost entirely. The chief justice, Sir John Jervis, was the criminal judge this time, and his charges to the jury surpassed in brilliance, clearness, interest, and conciseness anything I ever could have conceived. The dullest cases became interesting directly he began to speak, —the most intricate and bewildered clear. I do not think above one verdict was questionable in the whole thirty-six cases which he tried. One was a very curious one, in which a young man of large property had been fleeced by a gang of blacklegs on the turf, and at cards. Nothing could exceed the masterly way in which Sir John Jervis untwined the web of sophistries with which a very clever counsel had bewildered the jury. A private note-book, with initials for names, and complicated gambling accounts, was found on one of the prisoners. No one seemed to be able to make head or tail of it. The chief justice looked it over and most ingeniously explained it all to the jury. Then there was a pack of cards which had been pronounced by the London detectives to be a perfectly fair pack. They were examined in court; every one thought them to be so, and no stress was laid upon the circumstance. However, they were handed to the chief justice. I saw his keen eye glance very inquiringly over them while the evidence was going on. However he said nothing, and quietly put them aside. When the trial was over and the charge began, he went over all the circumstances, till he got to the objects found upon the prisoners. "Gentlemen," said he, "I will engage to tell you, without looking at the faces, the name of every card upon this pack." A strong exclamation of surprise went through the court. The prisoners looked aghast. He then pointed out that on the backs, which were figured with wreaths and flowers in dotted lines all over, there was a small flower in the right-hand corner of each like this :— ..⁚

The number of dots in this flower was the same on all the kings, and so on, in every card through the pack. A knave would be perhaps marked thus :— ... ... An ace thus: —·.· And so on; the difference being so slight, and the flowers on the back so many, that even if you had been told the general principle, it would have taken a considerable time to find out which was the particular flower which differed. He told me afterwards that he recollected a similar expedient in Lord De Ros's case, and therefore set to work to discover the trick. But he did it while the evidence was going on, which he himself had to take down in writing.

Another thing he did very well. A man was robbed. Among the coins he had was a sou, a Portsea token, and another the name of which I forget,—a sort of halfpenny. A man was taken up on suspicion, and in his pocket, with some other money, were three such coins. The prosecutor could only swear that he had had three such. He could not identify, nor could he swear to any of the other pieces. The counsel for the defence proved in evidence that all these coins are extremely common in Brighton, where the robbery took place, and the case seemed to have broken down, by the countenances of the jury. "Gentlemen," said the Chief Justice, "the question has to be tried by the doctrine of chances. The sou is common, the token is common, and the third coin too. The chances are, that perhaps a thousand sous are in the pockets of different people in Brighton; that five hundred tokens are so too, and perhaps fifteen hundred of the other; but the chances are very great against two men in Brighton having each a sou and a token, and almost infinite against two men having each in his pocket at the same time a sou, a token, and the third coin. You must, therefore, add this to the rest of the evidence, not as a weak link, but as a very strong one."

My sermon was from John vii. 17, not the one I had intended to take, as I meant to preach from John xviii. 38,—"What is truth?" but I did not feel up to it. I therefore took the old one, and considerably improved as a composition, leaving the main features unaltered, and it forms a very good sequence to the sermon at the first assizes.

LII.

July 30.

This week has been spent in visiting my people, all of whom I hope to see before I leave Brighton.

Mr. V—— dined with me yesterday, and the day before. I was in very good spirits: I walked home with him by the soft light of a most lovely moon, and thought I had never seen the silver flood on the sea more tender in its lustre,— the sound of the waves was more plangent than usual.

Martineau's views about Inspiration I think, on the whole, correct. He would not, I presume, deny that artistic power, &c., can be called in a sense inspiration; but he rightly draws a distinction between that kind of power and the power to which we, by common consent, chiefly consign the word. All power is from God. In the Epistle to the Corinthians, the gifts of the Spirit take in healing, &c., as in the Old Testament Bezaleel and Aholiab are said to be taught by God. In opposition to such as limit to spiritual truth the results of Divine agency, it appears to be important to assert the great truth, "Every good gift and every perfect gift is from above"; but, then, I do think that those who have most volubly reasserted this forgotten truth have been in danger of levelling these gifts of the intellect with the moral gifts of character. Both come from God, and therefore they assume that both are equally Divine, which is as fallacious as to say, God created men and worms, and therefore worms are equal to men. To assert that the sphere of the Divinest is in moral gifts, is almost identical with Christianity; to assert that the Divine is only in them, is an exaggeration dangerous and false. About a year ago I strongly urged this distinction on a man of some ability who published a little *brochure* on the Prophets,— a workingman,— and made him insert it in his preface to correct the tendency of his book in the other direction. Did I not give you one with a dedication to myself?

One of Carlyle's faults, as it seems to me, is this very tendency to see the Divine everywhere, and to make little distinction between the amount of Divinity which is contained in different forces, provided only that they be Force. Now the prophetic power, in which I suppose is chiefly exhibited that which we mean by inspiration, depends almost entirely on moral greatness. The prophet discerned large principles, true for all time, — principles social, political, ecclesiastical, and principles of life, — chiefly by largeness of heart and sympathy of spirit with God's spirit. That is my conception of inspiration. Much that Theodore Parker says is very valuable, though I am of opinion that Martineau has, with much sagacity and subtlety, corrected in that review certain expressions which are too unguarded, and which, unless modified, are untrue. "My judgment is just because I seek not my own will, but the Will of Him that sent me"; that is the very canon of inspiration. Sometimes I feel inclined to write a treatise on the subject; but then indolence, hopelessness, and self-distrust come in the way and nip the resolve in the bud, or, rather, nip it before it sets into resolve.

LIII.

The Apostles lived in anticipation of an immediate end of the world, no doubt; but I cannot see that this, on the whole, was anything but good. It was this which drew the Christians so closely together, — made their union so remarkable, and startled the world, to which, otherwise, the new religion would have appeared merely a Philosophy, and not a Life. Besides, are we sure that aught less strong than this hope could have detached men so instantly and entirely from the habits of long sin; or that, on natural principles and without a miracle, even the Apostles could have been induced to crowd so much superhuman energy into so small a compass?

I think the great main doctrine of Christ is that Truth is Light, and they who love the light come to it; that wisdom is justified by her children; that the Jews did not hear Him because they were not His sheep; and, therefore, that the Gospel was truth appealing to the heart much more than demonstrable to the senses. Hence, "If they heard not

Moses and the Prophets, neither would they be persuaded" by the most marvellous miracle.

But this did not include a secondary kind of proof for a lower kind of mind; see, especially, John xiv. 11, where the two kinds of proofs are given, and one subordinated to the other. It is quite consistent with God's wisdom to reveal Himself to the senses as well as the soul; and if the Gospel were utterly deficient in this latter kind of proof, one great evidence that it is from God would be wanting, — an evidence which we are justified in expecting from the analogies of nature. God has written His glory, for instance, in the heart; at the same time, He has so constructed the visible universe that "the heavens declare the glory of God." And when the Eternal Word is manifested into the world, we naturally expect that divine power shall be shown as well as divine beneficence. Miracles, therefore, are exactly what we should expect, and I acknowledge, a great corroboration and verification of His claims to Sonship. Besides, they startled and aroused many to His claims who otherwise would not have attended to them. Still the great truth remains untouched, that they, appealing only to the natural man, cannot convey the spiritual certainty of truth which the spiritual man alone apprehends. However, as the natural and spiritual in us are both from God, why should not God have spoken both to the natural and spiritual part of us; and why should not Christ appeal to the natural works, subordinate always to the spiritual self-evidence of Truth itself?

You say, "St. Paul appeals in the Romans to divine sovereignty and might, and does it not prove that Might makes Right, and that it is right to act thus, and thus only, because the Supreme Power has willed it?" Not at all. The spirit of the sentence seems to me only that of another expression of his, "Let God be true and every man a liar." It is a reply to some one finding fault captiously with the constitution of things, and asking the reason why higher privileges,

&c., are not given. And to this it is enough to say, "God has willed." But St. Paul takes for granted all through that the will is a holy will. Suppose two children disputing about a fact or a principle; one argues and disputes, the other cuts the whole matter short by saying, "I know it is so, — papa said so." Could we justly infer that that child considered its father's word to be the origin of truth, and enough to establish it, though it had not existed before? No; but it only takes for granted, from its father's known veracity, that the questionable matter must be so in spite of all appearances against it. Yet, as its expression is loosely worded, in reply only to a particular argument, an acute metaphysician, who was determined to extract metaphysics out of a child's argument, might easily make such a view appear to be unconsciously the child's view of truth. Now St. Paul, I believe, wrote in the same way. He is not dealing in any way with the metaphysical question of the foundation of Right, but only with the popular Jewish question, "What right have the Gentiles to the Messiah? — What claim have they to be chosen instead of the Jews?" He says, "Nay; but, O man, who art thou that repliest against God?" God has a right to do what He will with his creatures. But, observe, he never assumes or implies that God has a right to create moral evil; that simply does not enter into his conception, and would have been horrible and shocking to him.

The Inspiration of the Bible is a large subject. I hold it to be inspired, not dictated. It is the word of God, — the words of man: as the former, perfect; as the latter, imperfect. God the Spirit, as a Sanctifier, does not produce absolute perfection of human character; God the Spirit, as an Inspirer, does not produce absolute perfection of human knowledge; and for the same reason in both cases, — the human element which is mixed up, — else there could have been no progressive dispensations. Let us take a case, — the history of the creation. Now, I hold that a spiritual revelation from God *must* involve scientific incorrectness: it could not be from God unless it did. Suppose that the cosmogony had been given in terms which would satisfy our present scientific knowledge, or, say, rather the terms of absolute scientific truth : It is plain that, in this case, the men of that day would have rejected its authority: they would have said, " Here is a man who tells us the earth goes round the sun; and the sky, which we see to be a stereoma fixed and not far up, is infinite space, with no *firmament* at all, and so on. Can we trust one in matters unseen who is manifestly in error in things seen and level to the senses? Can we accept his revelation about God's nature and man's duty, when he is wrong in things like these?" Thus, the faith of this and subsequent ages must have been purchased at the expense of the unbelief of all previous ages. I hold it, therefore, as a proof of inspiration of the Bible, and divinely wise, to have given a spiritual revelation, i. e. a revelation concerning the truths of the soul and its relation to God, in popular and incorrect language. Do not mistake that word incorrect; incorrect is one thing, false another. It is scientifically incorrect to say that the sun rose this morning; but it is not false, because it conveys all that is required, for the nonce, to be known about the fact, time, &c. And if God were giving a revelation in this present day, He would give it in modern phraseology, and the men He inspired would talk of sunrise, sunset, &c. Men of science smile at the futile attempts to reconcile Moses and geology. I give up the attempt at once, and say, the inspiration of the Bible remains intact for all that, — nay, it would not have been inspired, except on this condition of incorrectness.

Neologianism is a large word, and embraces an almost endless variety of views; but to be candid, I look upon Bibliolatry with quite as much dislike as Arnold did, — as pernicious, dangerous to true views of God and His revelation to the human race, and the cause of much bitter Protestant

Popery, or claims to infallibility of interpretation, which nearly every party puts forth. I believe Bibliolatry to be as superstitious, as false, and almost as dangerous as Romanism.

Men try, you say, to find resting-places for Faith in Reason, rather than for Reason in Faith. If there has been a single principle which I have taught more emphatically than any other, it is that not by reason, — meaning, by reason, the understanding, — but by the spirit, that is, the heart, trained in meekness and love by God's Spirit, truth can be judged of at all. I hold that the attempt to rest Christianity upon miracles and fulfilments of prophecy is essentially the vilest rationalism; as if the trained intellect of a lawyer, which can investigate evidence, were that to which is trusted the soul's salvation; or, as if the evidence of the senses were more sure than the intuitions of the spirit, to which spiritual truths almost *alone* appeal. It is not in words (though they are constant), but in the deepest convictions and first principles of my soul, that I feel the failure of intellect in this matter. Indeed, the common complaint against me is, that I make too little of the proofs addressed to the understanding. I complain of Evangelicalism because it tries to explain the Atonement by Reason, — a debtor's and creditor's account. As to the desire after breadth and comprehension, that I confess. I am sick of hatred, suspicion, slander, and condemnation of one another, and long to believe in men's good rather than in their evil, in God rather than in the Devil. I believe I hold "the distinctive features of my religion" sharply enough, too sharply for a great many people; but I cannot and will not judge those who do not hold them as I do; nay, I go further, I will not cease trying to love them, and believing that, under other words, they often express the truths that I hold most dear. To the question, Who is my neighbor? I reply, as my Master did, by the example that He gave, "The alien and the heretic." And I do not think that He will say my charity is too large, or my inclusiveness too great. Alas! alas!

when I see Romanists cursing the Church of England, Evangelicals shaking their heads about the Christianity of Tractarians, Tractarians banning Dissenters, Dissenters anathematizing Unitarians, and Unitarians of the old school condemning the more spiritual ones of the new; I am forced to hope that there is more inclusiveness in the Love of God than in the bitter orthodoxy of sects and churches. I find only two classes who roused His divine indignation when on earth: those who excluded bitterly,—the Scribes, and those of a religious name,—*the* popular religious party of the day, who judged frailty and error bitterly,—the Pharisees. I am certain that I do not "dilute" truth, at least what I count truth, nor hold lax views about opinions; but I am certain that men are often better than their creed, and that Our Lord's mode of judging of the tree by its fruits is the only true one.

LIV.

Your welcome letter reached me safely yesterday afternoon, surrounded with business. The calmness of weather of which you speak did not extend to the Irish Channel, for it was blowing hard out of harbor, and, besides, the effects of the late gales remained upon the surface of the sea, which was like a boiling cauldron. I never felt so ill at sea in my life. I sent off a telegraphic despatch to B—— to say I should probably not be at home on Sunday, but I afterwards resolved to overcome the weakness, and reached London just in time.

I feel already the lack of severe exercise,—the only remedy for excitable nerves. On my way in the train I purchased and partly read Prescott's articles, collected from the "North American Review." They are good, but not so much out of the common as I expected. Indeed, except for the refreshing character of everything American, which is young and not *blasé*, like European literature, I should say they are not above par; but the above peculiarity makes all that comes from the New World interesting. How devoutly it is to be hoped that, in the coming conflict of the nations, America and England will stand side by side, instead of opposite; for, if not, it will be all over with the cause of liberty, for some centuries at least. The conqueror in the strife will be then a military power, and must perforce crush the peoples under a tyranny. And as to a universal war, that is inevitable, and in every direction men's minds are foreboding it,— a very strange symptom of the times to be so prevalent long before a single *casus belli* has made its appearance. It is one of those mysterious phenomena which plunge you into the deep question of Prophecy,— what it is in our human nature, and how and why it works. At present this anticipation resembles the inexplicable awe and sense of coming danger which makes the dumb unreasoning cattle restless at the approach of a thunder-storm. I am told that the Ministry are full of apprehensions, and that even the late Cabinet would have taken much more decisive measures but for their fear of that infatuated Manchester Peace school. Strange, that people with so much to lose in case of war should be so blindly unwilling to pay in the present for the means of peace!

I mean to work very hard soon at Wordsworth, his life, principles, and poetry, — a large subject.

Another most strange thing: a young man has been longing only to live until my return. " When will Mr. Robertson be back? I must hear his voice again." He is dying; and a lady has been waiting in the same way,— a Mrs. —— saw me at 9, A. M., yesterday, and died at six. I must not, and ought not, to regret that I did not stay.

LV.

There is an old friend of mine whose income does not exceed 2,000*l*., and whose charities are at least 1,200*l*. annually. Certainly, with examples such as hers, and comparing what most of us spend upon ourselves, it does seem the very acme of effrontery and impudence to call ourselves Christians. A young gentleman's cigars, or a young lady's ribbons, would save a human creature's life, and make ten happy. I am tempted sometimes to resolve I will never again suffer the word " self-sacrifice " to pass my lips, which now so often and so smoothly runs from them, and that I will not suffer it to fall unchallenged from the lips of others. In Christ's day people used similar unmeaning sentimentalisms, but He always took them up, as it were, and forced them to weigh the meaning of their words: as, for instance, to the woman who came out with a fine piece of sentiment, "Blessed is the womb that bare Thee," He replied, "Yea rather, blessed are they who know the word of God and keep it"; and to the man who said, "Blessed is he that shall eat meat in the kingdom of God," He spoke forthwith the parable of the Wedding-Guest Expelled, with the obvious application, — "Yes, true enough, but do you know *how* true what you say is 'Blessed,' for many shall *not eat* bread in that kingdom?"

LVI.

There are some persons whose language respecting Ireland is positively unchristian, and only to be paralleled by the tone used of the *canaille* by the French nobles just before the terrible retribution of the Revolution. Women are taught history in a way that is utterly useless and unpractical, else the past wrongs of Ireland would forever haunt them, and the present squalidness, beggary, and demoralization would conjure up a hideous picture of the past, and, reminding of the law of retribution, tie the tongue when it was inclined to abuse. What are the antecedents of the present state of things? At whose door must the guilt lie but at that of the ancestors of those who now inherit the soil? But French revolutions teach nobody! And the study of the history of bees and ants would do people, I verily believe, as much good as the study of human history. So with the Jews of old: they were very weather-wise, but could not read "the signs of the times." Jewish ladies were a good deal surprised when they found themselves sold as slaves to Romish voluptuaries; and Parisian ladies were equally astonished when, having spent such enormous sums on their *coiffures* and ribbons, they one fine day found their head-dresses arranged for them at the national expense, *à la guillotine*. Jewish prophets reminded people pretty clearly of what had been, and Isaiah went somewhat minutely into the expenditure of the Jewish ladies on their pretty persons, while the cause of the widow and fatherless was uncared for; but they laughed at him till he became importunate, and then they thought it *un peu trop fort*, and poor Isaiah was sawn in two, and he bothered them no longer about their "chains," and their "bracelets," and their "mufflers," their "changeable suits of apparel," the "glasses" and the "fine linens," the "hoods" and the "veils." I wonder what they thought when Nebuchadnezzar invaded the country and their own *canaille* betrayed them to the conqueror! Do not give way to impatience about poor Ireland; likely enough Mr. C—— may have failed partially. Why, God's own Son failed,—and if, after His failures with you and me, He were to give us up as incorrigible, I wonder where we should be to-morrow. And yet we think a few charitable efforts are to succeed at once, and undo the accumulated vice of years. I knew a young lady whose views on this subject were the most *naïves* I ever heard. She went down once to ——, and lectured the poor wretches upon their dirt and uncomfortable habits and houses, and — hear it, earth and heaven! — they did not repent them of their evil ways, and reform at the voice of that angelic visitation. It is just possible that, never having *seen* cleanliness or comfort, they did not know *what* she wanted them to aim at, or *how* to begin. Mrs. Fry would have bought them a bit of soap, and washed a child's fingers with her own hands as a specimen, and drawn out a little set of rules, and paraded the family once a week, half in fun and good-humoredly, to see that her orders were obeyed; and she would have gone on for a year, and if at the end of a year she saw a little dawn of improvement, she would have thanked God and taken courage. But fine young ladies think that an eloquent cut of a riding-whip through the air in the last Belgravian fashion is to electrify a Celtic village, and convert a whole population of savages to civilized tastes and English habits.

The patient drudgery of love which does God's work, however, is not learned in Belgravia. Well, the aristocracy of the next world will be the Frys, and the Chisholms, and the people who do not care for being smart, and are not afraid, like their Master, "to lay their hands" upon the wretches whom they would rescue. I do not know that anything in "Uncle Tom's Cabin" struck me so much as that remark! — it was one of those which are suggestive of worlds of thought, and send a whole flood of light into a subject.

Mr. C——, you say, has spent his life on his property, trying to ameliorate, &c., and he has failed. "Well," as Lord Carlisle said, " Heaven is for those who have failed on earth," — failed *so*. Is Mr. C——, disgusted with ingratitude, going to throw up all, and give himself up to a life of pleasure? Well, quote to him, " Look to yourselves that we lose not the things that we have wrought, but that we receive a full reward." Quote to him, " Servant of God, well done; well hast thou fought the better fight who singly hast maintained." Quote to him, " Into whatever house ye enter, salute that house; and if the son of peace be there, your blessing shall remain; if not, it shall return to you again."

In the moments when life presents itself to me in its true solemn aspect, I feel that I would rather be the author of such a failure than of all the success and glory of Wellington; and I suspect one or two more will think so in the Day of Judgment.

You wonder at my wish to go to the war at the Cape. I think it is because my feeling of life is antagonism rather than tenderness. I suppose to see, in visible flesh and blood, that which I might legitimately call my foe, would be a relief from that vague sense of invisible opposition with which my life is encompassed. No doubt the true end to which this feeling is meant to conduct is the hostility of Evil; but Evil in the abstract is so hard to hate that we are forever identifying it with the concrete, and longing to grapple with it in a form. Such, I suppose, is the true interpretation of the Psalms, where so much hatred is expended on God's enemies, — meaning men, — and which modern writers have rightly spiritualized, though on most loose and inconsistent principles. They take Moab and Ammon and Babylon to mean certain modern persons or principles, feeling that, taken literally, the spirit of denunciation is irreligious. But the Psalmists did not mean this. David and others meant Moab, &c.; but that which was true in their feeling was the human indignation against the Evil in Moab and Ammon, and which they could not separate in idea from them. It is this, stripped of the local, transitory, and Jewish form in which it appears, which is everlastingly true: in other words, the prophetic spirit. And as such, to say that, transferred to our times, our Babylon, our Ammon, are such-and-such evils, is perfectly true, and that to hate them is the real essence of the lesson of those Psalms, and is that which is true and eternal in them. All this out of my instinctive love of war!

I sat with the S———s for half an hour two days ago, just after the sublimest and most wonderful sunset I ever saw in my life. S. T. quite agreed that it was so. A mighty mass of blood-red crimson, mottled richly with gold, spread over the whole west, miles broad and many degrees high. In this were lakes of purest green, like that of the lakes of Switzerland. It was startling from its mass and majesty. Turning a corner, I came on it suddenly, and absolutely gasped for a moment.

LVII.

To-morrow is the funeral of the Great Duke. I do not think I shall go up, though I am tempted by the thought that it might be an impression for life for Charlie. Old England has departed for once from her habit of unostentatious funerals, and I am not one who think that in this case she has done unwisely: to bury the Duke as common greatness is buried would be out of place. Such men take a century to grow, and we cannot have another such in this generation. If you could find a man equal in genius, you could no thave the tried of eighty years until eighty years are gone. This old, dull country, which the filigree nations laugh at, with her inconsistencies and her prejudices, how sound at heart she is in the way she does her hero-worship, and what unique heroes hers are! — Duty, the watchword of Nelson and Wellington, — the last sublime battle-cry of the one and long life-law of the other, — and no splash nor dash nor French theatricals about either of them.

His long self-sacrifice of life is o'er.

Tennyson has put it all into one pregnant line. Nelson, Adelaide, Wellington, — these have been the *great* mournings of England in this century; and Peel, because men thought there was sacrifice in him too, in his degree. Yes, Goodness, Duty, Sacrifice, — these are the qualities that England honors. She gapes and wonders every now and then, like an awkward peasant, at some other things, — railway kings, electro-biology, and other trumperies, — but nothing stirs her grand old heart down to its central deeps universally and long except the Right. She puts on her shawl very badly, and she is awkward enough in a concert-room, scarcely knowing a Swedish nightingale from a jackdaw; but — blessings large and long upon her! — she knows how to teach her sons to sink like men amongst sharks and billows, without parade, without display, as if duty were the most natural thing in the world, and she never mistakes long an actor for a hero or a hero for an actor. Men like Arnold and Wordsworth she recognizes at last, — men like Wellington, more visibly right, at once, and with unalterable fidelity. I do love my dear old blundering Country, and I forgive her the few deaths caused at the lying-in state by her awkwardness and want of experience in spectacles, and with plenary indulgence prospective all the mistakes and even absurdities she will probably be guilty of to-morrow.

CHAPTER III.

1853.

Friendship of Mr. Robertson with Lady Byron. — State of his Health. — Advance of Disease. — Sermons of this Year. — The Principles which underlie his Teaching. — Adoration of the Virgin. — Sacrament of the Mass. — Purgatory. — Apostolical Succession. — The Seven Sacraments. — Suggestive, not dogmatic Teaching. — The Peacemaker. — Foundation of his Teaching. — His Position with regard to Unitarianism. — Lecture on Wordsworth. — Letter in answer to a Criticism, in which he discloses the Loneliness of his Heart. — Wordsworth and High Churchism. — Letter replying to one of the High-Church Party who urged him to unite himself to them. — Increasing Weakness. — Visit to Cheltenham. — His Congregation offers him a Curate. — The Vicar puts a Veto on his Choice. — Last Sermons preached in Trinity Chapel, May 29, 1853.

DURING the first few months of 1853, Mr. Robertson seems to have been frequently at Esher, where Lady Byron lived. He had known her almost from the time of his arrival at Brighton, and acquaintance soon passed into a deep and lasting friendship. He said of her that she was one of the noblest and purest women he had ever met. "Her calm subdued character," he writes, "warm sympathy, and manifold wisdom have been one of my greatest privileges here." He heard from her the whole history of her life, and she committed into his hands the charge of publishing, after her decease, her memoirs and letters. This was, to her great regret, frustrated by his death. While he lived he sought her sympathy, and always received it. Her friendship gave him new life, and supplied him with strength to conquer his trials.

And, indeed, he needed at this time both sympathy and assistance. He was almost worn out. His state of health was dangerous in the extreme. The annexed letter, written in January, 1853, is a true account of his condition:—

January 13, 1853.

To-day I have done little; Titus would have written, "I have lost a day." I prepared for Sunday with little zest and much lassitude of mind, walked with S——, read the newspaper, and scarcely anything else besides. It is strange how much more loss I feel in me of life's vital force than a year or two ago; it seems a tortoise existence; the truth of which *simile* you will appreciate, if you remember that the pulse of that creature beats about once to twenty pulsations of our blood, and every function of his nature, walking, &c., is performed in the slowest way, as if existence were dragged out.

Already the disease which slew him began to declare itself plainly. Loss of the old power and quickness of thought; the necessity for a laborious exercise of will in order to stimulate thought, and appalling exhaustion after such an effort, were some of the first symptoms. It is sad to see that a change in the day appointed for his lecture on Wordsworth was sufficient to throw him into mental confusion; that his memory, which once could retain for years together the order of his reasoning and thinking on any subject, was now so far enfeebled that the whole work of his lecture had to be done over again. Torturing pains in the back of his head and neck, as if an eagle were rending there with its talons, made life dreadful to him. During Monday, Tuesday, and the greater part of Wednesday in every week he suffered severely. Alone in his room he lay on the rug, his head resting on the bar of a chair, clenching his teeth to prevent the groans which, even through the sleepless length of solitary nights, the ravaging pain could never draw from his manliness. It is miserable to read, week by week, the records of his advancing illness, and to know that it might have been arrested by the repose which he did not and could not take.

Yet among his discourses of this year are some of the most striking that he ever preached. The sermon on "The Glory of the Virgin Mother" is as original as it is remarkable, for the new method in which he proposed to treat the subjects of controversy between our Church and that of Rome. He intended that it should be the first of a series in which the positive truths underlying the Roman Catholic errors should be brought into clear light. This plan he would have carried out with the help of the two first of the principles which he lays down himself as characteristic of his teaching. I quote the whole of the passage (numbering the principles, for the sake of clearness), as important for a just comprehension of his writings:—

The principles on which I have taught:—

First. The establishment of positive truth, instead of the negative destruction of error. Secondly. That truth is made up of two opposite propositions, and not found in a *viâ media* between the two. Thirdly. That spiritual truth is discerned by the spirit, instead of intellectually in propositions; and, therefore, Truth should be taught suggestively, not dogmatically. Fourthly. That belief in the Human character of Christ's Humanity must be antecedent to belief in His Divine origin. Fifthly. That Christianity, as its teachers should, works from the inward to the outward, and not *vice versâ*. Sixthly. The soul of goodness in things evil.

On the first of these, the whole of his controversial teaching was founded. By the formula of the second he eliminated the positive truth with which he confronted the errors he opposed. The best illustration which can be given of the working of this method is his examination of the Roman Catholic doctrine of the Adoration of the Virgin in the sermon mentioned above. A slight note supplies the information that it was his intention to have applied this method of analysis to all the Roman Catholic dogmas. The passage is as follows: —

Purgatory, Mariolatry, Absolution, Apostolical Succession, Seven sacraments instead of two, Transubstantiation, Baptismal Regeneration, Invocation of saints, — each are based upon a truth; but crystallized into form, petrified into dogmas, they are false. Endeavor to trace the meaning contained in Romish institutions: do not meet them with anathemas. Discover what the Roman Catholic means, translate to him his longing, interpret to him what he wants. I can conceive no more blessed work than this for the man of large heart and clear, vigorous intellect.

The sermons on Baptism and Absolution are also elaborate examples of the way in which he performed his work.

From notes, with which I have been supplied, of conversations with him, other instances of his application of this method are extracted. . .

On the sacrament of the Lord's Supper, he says: —

In opposition to the Dissenting view, it *is* Christ's body

and blood received; in opposition to the Romanists' view, *it is not* Christ's body and blood to those who receive it unworthily. We do not go between the two. Each of these opposite statements of the Dissenter or of the Roman Catholic are truths, and we retain them. It is not merely bread and wine; it is, spiritually, Christ's body and blood: God present spiritually, not materially, to those who receive it worthily, — i. e. to the faithful. It is not Christ's body and blood to those on whose feelings and conduct it does not tell.

It is well known that he went further than this. He held, with our Church, that the Sacrifice of Christ was once offered and no more. But he held also, that ultra-Protestantism missed the truth contained in transubstantiation; that that sacrifice is repeated daily, in a spiritual manner, in the hearts of all faithful people. The Romanist is right in the principle, — wrong in his application of the principle. The Sacrifice of Christ is forever going on, but not in the sacrifice of the Mass.

He met the doctrine of Purgatory as follows: —

The ultra-Protestant utterly denies it. But the law of the universe is progress. Is there no more pain for the redeemed? Is there nothing good in store for the bad? We ask ourselves such questions when we observe the large class of human beings who are neither heavenly nor damnable. We know here that affliction and pain soften some, while they harden others, as heat which softens iron, hardens clay. We are told that as men die so they rise. Some few die ripe for the presence of God; others, as in the case of the Pharisees, to whom good appeared only as Satanic evil, need only go on to find, as Milton has expressed it, "myself is hell." But, in the case of the first class mentioned, does not analogy make it more than conceivable that their pain should be remedial, not penal? Here, then, we have the principle of purgatory.

I have stated this hypothetically; the Roman Catholic states it as a dogma. Our fate is decided here. This is said rigorously by the ultra-Protestant. *So it is;* there is the Protestant truth. The Romanist states the opposite truth, and says, "Our destiny is determined beyond the grave." So long as either is a positive statement of a truth, it is right; but the moment either denies the truth of the other, it becomes falsehood.

Mr. Robertson, as may be seen from his instance of the Pharisees, was not a Universalist in doctrine, however he may have hoped that Universalism was true. "My only difficulty," he once said to a friend, "is how not to believe in everlasting punishment."

With regard to the doctrine of Apostolical Succession, he says, using the principle given above: —

There is an Apostolical Succession. It is not the power of God conveyed by physical contact, — it is not a line of priests; it is a succession of prophets, — a broken, scattered one, but a real one. John was the successor of Elias's spirit. In the spiritual birth Luther was the offspring of the mind of St. Paul. Mind acts on mind, whether by ideas or character: herein is the spiritual succession.

He made use of the same principle in speaking of the Romish doctrine of Seven Sacraments: —

The Roman Catholic has seven sacraments; we have but two. We can rise to a higher truth than either. The sacraments, Baptism and the Supper of the Lord, are representative symbols. One day was set apart to sanctify all time; one tribe to make all the nation holy; one nation to make the whole world the kingdom of God. In this way the race was educated. On the same principle God has divinely ordained two material acts, to represent the truth that all nature is holy when everything in it reveals His sacredness to men:

that acts are holy when done in the spirit of Christ. Water, the simplest element, represents the sacredness and awfulness of all things. By the consecration of the commonest act of life, — a meal, — every act is made holy. By the extension of these symbols from two to seven, we really limit their meaning, — we say that seven *alone* are holy; but when we retain only one *element*, and one *act* as set apart to be holy by Christ, we see in these symbols the statement of two universal truths, — that all the material Universe and all acts ought to be holy to the Lord.

This argument, which has been condensed out of many scattered hints, he closes thus: —

The Protestant truth is that two symbols only are ecclesiastically set apart; the Roman Catholic truth is that many more than these are channels of divine communication to our spirits. These two views make up the whole truth. The Protestant falsehood is limiting to these two the grace (here meaning a strong and vivid impression) of God; the Romanist falsehood is the negation of the Protestant truth: these two are not the only ecclesiastical sacraments, — there are five more; by which assertion he has got into superstition, and lost the general meaning of the sacraments.

The third principle of his teaching, that spiritual truth is discerned by the spirit, and not intellectually in propositions, pervades all his writings, and is especially laid down in a sermon preached in this year, 1853, on "The Good Shepherd," in a passage beginning, "The Son of Man claims to himself the name of Shepherd," &c.[*] He believed that the highest truths were poetry, — to be felt, not proved; resting *ultimately*, not on the authority of the Bible or the Church, but on that witness of God's Spirit in the heart of man which is to be

---

[*] Second Series, p. 295.

realized, not through the cultivation of the understanding, but by the loving obedience of the heart. Therefore his own personal teaching was suggestive, not dogmatic. He did not choose his text in order to wring a doctrine out of it, but he penetrated to its centre, and seized the principle it contained. It was the kernel, not the shell, for which he cared. He taught no schemes of doctrine. His thoughts could not flow in cut channels, but only like a river, livingly, and "at their own sweet will." Owing to this, he never became the leader of a sect or the follower of any religious school. He stood aside from all parties, and yet, standing aside, he was formed to be the reconciler and uniter of parties.

While he sternly denounced moral evil, he was tolerant of intellectual error; while he spoke severely against the bigotry of sects, he conciliated minor differences of opinion. His peculiarly receptive character, which reflected what was good as naturally as a calm lake reflects its shores; his intuitive grasp of truth; his large love, which felt all that was real in men, formed, unconsciously to himself, a common ground where divided parties might unite. Starting from different points, they found a centre in him. They found all that was good in them acknowledged and brought out by him into clearer prominence; and in their satisfaction grew tolerant of the errors and quick to recognize the truths which others taught. For he represented to men not sharp distinct outlines of doctrine, but the fulness and depth of the Spirit of Christianity, which, allowing in his view of outward difference of opinion, united men by a pervasive spirit of love to Christ and to one another. He thus became the peacemaker.

This was the great work of his life. But it was hindered and stifled at Brighton by the opposition and the factiousness of his professional brethren, who could neither see the meaning of his life nor the signs of the times. But since his death this aspect of his work has been advancing into prominence. He cannot be claimed especially by any one of our conflicting parties. But all thoughtful men, however divided in opinion, find in his writings a point of contact. He has been made one of God's instruments to preserve the unity of the Christian Church in this country, and to avert the vagrancy of mind and the loss of working power which are the natural results of schism. For, instead of by violent dogmatic teaching promoting mutual rancor, and therefore uselessness, he taught principles which established mutual love, and therefore practical usefulness for Christ. This will be the main result of his life upon this age.

But, though his teaching was more suggestive than dogmatic, he did not shrink from meeting in the pulpit the difficulties involved in many of the doctrines of the English Church. His explanations of the Atonement; of the way in which Christ suffered, being tempted; of the doctrine of sin; of the doctrine of the sacraments; of absolution; of imputed righteousness; of the freedom of the Gospel in contrast to the bondage of the Law, — have solved the difficulties of many. He believed himself that they were true solutions. But he also believed that the time might come when they would cease to be adequate solutions. He recognized that the solution which was fitting for one age might be unfitting for another; that his solutions were perhaps, only grounds for more comprehensive ones. There is another reason why he never founded a school. He would not say, "My explanations are final," for he looked forward to an advance of the Christian Church, not into new truths, but into wider or more tolerant views of those old truths which in themselves are incapable of change.

Yet, notwithstanding all this, — which men called, while he lived, and now when he is dead will call, want of a clear and defined system of theology, — he had a fixed basis for his teaching. It was the divine-human Life of Christ. This is the fourth principle mentioned in his letter, "that belief in the human character of Christ must be antecedent to belief in His divine origin." He felt that an historical Christianity was absolutely essential; that only through a visible life of the Divinest in the flesh could God become intelligible to men; that Christ was God's idea of our nature realized; that only when we fall back upon the glorious portrait that has been, can we be delivered from despair of Humanity; that in Christ "all the blood of all the nations ran," and all the powers of man were redeemed. Therefore he grasped, as the highest truth on which to rest life and thought, the reality expressed in the words, "The Word was made flesh." The Incarnation was to him the centre of all history, the blossoming of Humanity. The Life which followed the Incarnation was the explanation of the life of God, and the only solution of the problem of the life of man. He did not speak much of loving Christ; his love was fitly mingled with that veneration which makes love perfect; his voice was solemn, and he paused before he spoke His name in common talk; for what that Name meant had become the central thought of his intellect, and the deepest realization of his spirit. He had spent a world of study, of reverent meditation, of adoring contemplation on the Gospel history. Nothing comes forward more visibly in his letters than the way in which he had entered into the human life of Christ. To that everything is referred, — by that everything is explained. The gossip of a drawing-room, the tendencies of the time, the religious questions of the day, especially the Sabbath question, the loneliness and the difficulties of his work, were not so much argued upon or combated, as at once and instinctively brought to the test of a Life which was lived out eighteen centuries ago, but which went everywhere with him. Out of this intuitive reception of Christ, and from this ceaseless silence of meditation which makes the blessedness of great love, there grew up in him a deep comprehension of the whole, as well as a minute sympathy with all the delicate details of the character of Christ. Day by day, with passionate imitation, he followed his Master, musing on every action, revolving in thought the interdependence of all that Christ had said or done, weaving into the fibres of his heart the principles of the Life he worshipped, till he had received into his being the very impression and image of that unique Personality. His very doctrines were the Life of Christ expressed in words. The Incarnation, Atonement, and Resurrection of Christ were not dogmas to him. In himself he was daily realizing them. They were in him a life, a power, a light. This was his Christian consciousness.

Out of this study and reception of the Humanity arose his conviction of the Divinity of Christ.

The following striking passage, from an unpublished sermon, is very characteristic of his teaching on this subject. It establishes a *method* of arriving at a conviction of the Divinity of the Son of Man, which, were it oftener employed, were well. I know one, at least, whom this view has saved from Unitarianism.

Christ was the Son of God. But remember in what sense He ever used this name, — Son of God because Son of Man. He claims Sonship in virtue of His Humanity. Now, in the whole previous revelation through the Prophets, &c., one thing was implied, — only through man can God be known; only through a perfect man, perfectly revealed. Hence He came, "the brightness of His Father's Glory, the *express image* of His person." Christ then must be loved as Son of Man before He can be adored as Son of God. In personal love and adoration of Christ the Christian religion consists, not in correct morality, or in correct doctrines, but in a homage to the King.

Now, unquestionably, the belief in the Divinity of Christ is waning among us. They who hold it have petrified it into a theological dogma without life or warmth, and thoughtful men are more and more beginning to put it aside. How are we then to get back this belief in the Son of God? — by authority or by the old way of persecution? The time for these has passed. The other way is to begin at the beginning. Begin as the Bible begins, with Christ the Son of Man. Begin with Him as God's character revealed under the limitations of humanity. Lay the foundations of a higher faith deeply in a belief of His Humanity. See Him as He was. Breathe His Spirit. After that, try to comprehend His Life. Enter into His Childhood. Feel with Him when he looked round about Him in anger, when he vindicated the crushed woman from the powerless venom of her ferocious accusers; when He stood alone in the solitary Majesty of

Truth in Pilate's judgment-hall; when the light of the Roman soldier's torches flashed on Kedron in the dark night, and He knew that watching was too late; when His heartstrings gave way upon the Cross. Walk with Him through the Marriage Feast. See how the sick and weary came to Him instinctively; how men when they saw Him, felt their sin, they knew not why, and fell at His feet; how guilt unconsciously revealed itself, and all that was good in men was drawn out, and they became higher than themselves in His presence. Realize this. Live with Him till He becomes a living thought, — ever present, — and you will find a reverence growing up which compares with nothing else in human feeling. You will feel that a slighting word spoken of Him wounds with a dart more sharp than personal insult. You will feel that to bow at the name of Jesus is no form at will of others, but a relief and welcome. And if it should ever chance that, finding yourself thrown upon your own self, and cut off from sects, — suspected, in quest of a truth which no man gives, — then that wondrous sense of strength and friendship comes, — the being alone with Christ, with the strength of a manlier independence. Slowly then, this almost insensibly merges into adoration. For what is it to adore Christ? To call Him God; to say, Lord, Lord? No. Adoration is the mightiest love the soul can give, — call it by what name you will. Many a Unitarian, as Channing, has adored, calling it only admiration; and many an orthodox Christian, calling Christ God with most accurate theology, has given him only a cool intellectual homage.

It will be seen from this with what wisdom and toleration he spoke of the Unitarians without surrendering an iota of his own faith. With the violent, bigoted, and unspiritual portion of their school he had no sympathy; but with those who occupied a higher region he had much sympathy, and to them he owed much. He read

James Martineau's books with pleasure and profit. The influence of "The Endeavors after a Christian Life" can be traced through many of his sermons. Theodore Parker he admired for the eloquence, earnestness, learning, and indignation against evil, and against forms without a spirit, which mark his writings. But he deprecated the want of reverence and the rationalizing spirit of Parker.

He revered and spoke of Dr. Channing as one of the noblest and truest Christians of America. He was deeply indebted to his writings. He read them carefully, and borrowed from them largely. He spoke with indignation against those who would un-Christianize Channing, because in words he denied the coequal divinity of Christ with the Father. He said, if the deepest love is the deepest worship, no man adored Christ more sincerely than Channing. He would have been more amused than hurt at the accusation brought against him after his death, that in praising Channing he was praising a Socinian. He would have said, to call Channing a Socinian, is like calling Fichte a materialistic Pantheist. He would have replied to the insinuation that he had a tendency to Unitarianism because he admired Channing, that on the same grounds he might be said to have a tendency to Roman Catholicism because he admired Pascal, or a tendency to believe in particular redemption because he studied and reverenced Jonathan Edwards.

The truth is, that he recognized the value of Unitarianism up to a certain point. To the Unitarians had been committed the task of exhibiting more fully than others the truth of the Humanity of Christ. But while receiving with thankfulness their full declaration of this truth, he could not *remain* with them on their platform. Comprehending with great clearness and sympathy their stand-point, he was able to distinctly realize its want. He felt, that if Christianity were to become a universal power among men, — if Human Nature were ever to be entirely ennobled, there must be added to the Humanity of Christ the Divinity of Christ. Nor was he content with merely saying " Christ must be divine, because I *feel* he must be so." Contrary to his usual custom, he brings argument to bear upon the doctrine, and endeavors to prove it in his lectures on the Corinthians, and in several of his sermons.

With regard to the two other principles which he mentions, " that Christianity, as its teachers should, works from the inward to the outward," and " that there is a soul of goodness in things evil," no comment is required, for the first runs through everything he wrote and spoke, and the second ruled his life, his estimate of men, and his action upon them, as well as his view of the world, of history, and of nature.

The importance, not of explaining his doctrines, but of presenting a concentrated view of the principles of his teaching, may excuse the apparent irrelevancy of this digression.

On February 10, he delivered a lecture upon Wordsworth. It had been promised in the August of the previous year. He had then written a rough sketch of what he might possibly attempt.

The Athenæum people have again asked me to give them a lecture, — this time in place of James Anderson, who cannot come from some domestic affliction. I am rather tempted to comply. A subject is part of the difficulty, however. Two have occurred to me,— "The Influence of Fiction," and "Wordsworth, his Life and Poetry." This would be a large one, as it would require an investigation into the influences of the French Revolution on his mind in youth, both in its generous spirit and in its reaction. It would lead to the question how a life is to be led true to the idea of each man's own character, of which rare case Wordsworth is a remarkable example. It would bring in, too, the question of how far rhythm is essential to poetry, and what is its influence besides the main object of the whole, — Wordsworth's principles of poetry, faults and excellences.

In the first page of his lecture he lays down his plan of treatment: —

In order to treat fully the subject which I have to bring before you this evening, I believe there are three points to which I ought principally to direct your attention. The first is, the qualifications necessary for appreciating poetry in general, and for appreciating the poetry of Wordsworth in particular. The second is, the character and life of Wordsworth, so far as they bear upon his poetry, and so far as they may have been supposed to have formed or modified his peculiar poetical theories and principles. The third point is, the theories and poetical principles of Wordsworth, and how far they are true, how far they have been exaggerated, and how far Wordsworth has himself worked out the principles he has laid down.

The last, as he says, was the most important point of all, — *the* subject; but the second lecture, in which this was to be treated, was never delivered, owing to his increasing weakness.

The published lecture on Wordsworth is not so generally appreciated as the two lectures on poetry, partly because Wordsworth belongs to the few and not to the many, and partly because it wants Mr. Robertson's corrections. But it is a true and thoughtful review of Wordsworth's life, character, and work; and a fine defence of the Poet against the vulgar accusations of egotism and inconsistency. It has a further interest, as all that Mr. Robertson said has, in being more or less a revelation of his own character and heart. The qualifications he lays down as necessary for comprehending the poetry of Wordsworth were his own qualifications, — "unworldliness," — and the more he lived, the more he learnt to protest, and to act out his protest, that the spirit of the world was more destructive of a Christian life than even sin itself, — "feelings disciplined by nature," — and all his life long he endeavored to free himself from conventional views of art and beauty, and to keep his heart natural and pure enough to receive impressions direct from Nature, and to see her as she is, — "feelings disciplined through the minds of the great masters and poets," — and if there was one thing preeminent in his character, it was the beautiful and childlike reverence which he gave to those who were worthy, and his hatred of the unvenerating flippancy of modern criticism; — "a certain delicacy and depth of feeling,"— and the depth, subtlety, and gossamer strength of his feeling, is that which chiefly appears in his writings, as well in his keen analysis of the feelings of others, as in his morbid analysis of his own. He had another qualification, in that the passionate enthusiasm of his early days had given place to a calmer and sterner view of life; in that Feeling was no longer dominant in him, but Will; and Wordsworth is the poet of calm, and not of passion. He also felt deep sympathy with that want of the sense of the ridiculous in Wordsworth which made all the world, even to its meanest things, a consecrated world. "The ludicrous now rarely troubles me," he says: "all is awful."

He sympathized also with the variations of Wordsworth's heart between democracy and aristocracy. "Wordsworth's tastes," he says, "were all on the side of conservatism, his convictions all on that of democracy. Such a man, when it comes to the vulgarities of life, shrinks from democracy,— expects that all shall be as lofty as himself. Wordsworth was too fastidious. The only remedy was less contemplative and theoretical life, and more work among the workers."

The last portion of the lecture, in which he dilates on Wordsworth's love of England as the guardian of liberty, was written out of his own heart. Robertson was a man whose patriotism was based, not on the "blind hysterics" of feeling, but on the faith that England was the witness to the world of the glory of duty fulfilled even to death, — of freedom poised between Conservatism and Liberalism, — of truth in business, and purity in domestic life. His voice, when it most truly expressed his devotion in England, would have said of her, —

> I could not love thee, Dear, so much,
> Loved I not honor more.

The following are the only passages in his letters which relate to this lecture : —

January 25.

I have no journals of books read, or thoughts matured, to send you; for my whole journal has been thinking, — thinking,—thinking about Wordsworth. I wish I had written the lecture, but I had not time; it takes so long in the mere act of penmanship. It is all in my brain somehow or other; whether it will come out orderly or tremblingly, I do not know. Then there is the question whether health or strength will be such as to give a command of words, and these two questions make the whole experiment a hazardous one. However, I must shut my eyes and harden my heart, as they say to boys riding over their first leap. When you get this it will be all over. Is it not curious how involuntarily one uses language concerning such a task which would be applicable to some terrible surgical operation? I do hate, detest, and abhor, as the oath of royalty runs, all speechifying and all publicity.

I am not writing with zest, but it is only that wretchlessness,—an old expressive English word extant in the Thirty-nine Articles,—which comes from the tension of nerve in preparing for a lecture and delivering sermons.

I am becoming of opinion that no duty whatever has a right to interfere with a human existence. I am not myself on these days; I can see nothing in its true light, but all through a veil of black crape. This has now lasted ever since the Wednesday of that unfortunate postponement. It makes one selfish, and fastens attention upon the slow succession of ignoble sufferings within,—hour by hour, minute by minute, wearing, wearing, wearing.

Owing to some difficulty about the room, his lecture was postponed. He writes—

February 8.

The morning was occupied in a vain effort to work up my Wordsworth thoughts; for it is a mixed work,—parts of the old thoughts coming in scraps to the recollection, and badly joining themselves with the fresh thought of the present, so that no consistent living whole is formed,—the result of thought working itself out of thought,—or rather a building made up by the fragments of an old building, clumsily worked into the masonry of to-day. It is a patchwork of memory and excogitation,—neither wholly, and both incompletely. The laws of mind are very curious. How dissimilar those two operations of creating and remembering! and no joinership, however dexterous, can bring the edges together, so that the lines of junction shall not be seen.

February 11.

One line to tell you that my lecture went off last night successfully,—that is, I did not break down, and preserved self-possession throughout; the room a perfect cram, and hundreds went away; but I have been suffering from severe pain in the head ever since,—shooting thrills so sharp and sudden that I can scarcely forbear an exclamation. Whether people liked it or not, I do not know; and if I could only get rid of these stabs in the brain every ten minutes, I should not care. Two lights with reflectors were placed on the table, glaring in my face all the time, which prevented my seeing anybody. There was little or no applause, except now and then a low murmur; but, on the whole, I was glad of this, for the worst acknowledgment that can be made of an instructive lecture is to clap, and I think they showed their good taste. At the same time, it partly arose from my own rapidity, and, I trust, from the absence of any of those sentences constructed for clap-trap, which any public speaker at all practised can easily fabricate. One or two passages having reference to the invasion expected in 1802, connected with the reading of Wordsworth's sonnets on the subject, were the only points in the lecture that seemed to wake up any audible response from the audience.

The "South Church Union" criticised the lecture, alleging that it favored Pantheism, and misrepresented High Churchism. Mr. Robertson replied in the following letter. Along with the criticism there were some innuendoes, which induced him to write the latter portion of his letter. It was not like his usual practice to lay himself thus open to the public. He had borne misrepresentation and attack so long in silence, that such a sudden unveiling of his heart in the columns of a newspaper is startling. It reads as if it had been wrung from him against his will, — as if he knew that it was for the last time, — as if he had thought, "For once they shall know what their intolerance has done."

March 4, 1853.

Sir: — In the columns of the "Brighton Guardian," denominated the "South Church Union Chronicle," I see some strictures on certain expressions attributed to me in my lecture upon Wordsworth. With the tone of the strictures — excepting one sentence which I regret, not for my own sake, for it is untrue, but for the writer's sake, for it is rude and coarse — I can find no fault. The whole criticism, however, is based on a misconception. It proceeds on the assumption that I complained with blame that —

"High Churchism regarded with peculiar reverence a sanctity as connected with certain places, times, acts, and persons," &c.

I did not use those words. That was not my definition of High Churchism, and to have condemned it as so defined would have contradicted my argument, for I was actually at the moment justifying Wordsworth, who is well known to have entertained such feelings. Had I so spoken, I should have condemned a feeling of the *relative* sanctity of such things, — a feeling which I comprehend too entirely to have any inclination to interfere with.

What I did say was as follows: —

"The tendency of Pantheism is to see the godlike everywhere, the personal God nowhere. The tendency of High

Churchism is to localize the personal Deity in certain consecrated places, called churches; certain consecrated times called Sabbaths, fast-days, and so forth; certain consecrated acts, sacramental and quasi sacramental; certain consecrated persons, called priests."

I endeavored to show that the *tendency* is not necessarily the error; and that there are High Churchmen, like Wordsworth, who recognize in such places, persons, and acts, a sanctity only relative, and not intrinsic, — relative to the worshippers, without localizing or limiting Deity in or to the acts, times, or places; the Pantheistic and High-Church tendencies, each false alone, balancing each other in the particular case of such men.

I have no intention of entering into controversy on this point; and I should, according to my hitherto invariable practice, have left both the misrepresentation and the criticism unnoticed, were it not that the words, as they stand, if used by me, would have evidenced an unworthy desire of turning aside from my subject to pander to the passions of my audience, and seeking a miserable popularity by an attempt to feed that theological rancor which is the most detestable phase of the religion of the day.

I do not merely say that I was not guilty of this paltry work. I say it is simply impossible to me. To affirm, whatever may be taught by our savage polemics, whether Tractarian or Evangelical, that the new commandment is NOT this, — " that ye hate one another," and that discipleship to Christ is proved more by the intensity of love for good than by the vehemence of bitterness against error, is with me a desire too deep, too perpetual, and too unsatisfied, to have allowed the possibility of my joining even for one moment in the cowardly cry with which the terrors and the passions of the half-informed are lashed by platform rhetoric into hatred of High Churchmen.

I acknowledge the courtesy of the attack on myself; and

admit that in all attacks from the High-Church side I have ever met, and expect beforehand to meet, generous, fair, gentlemanlike, and Christian antagonism.

At the same time, I could not help smiling good-humoredly at the writer's utter misconception of my aims, views, and position. If he thinks that what he calls a philosophic height above contending parties is a position which any man can select for his own comfort and retirement, he miscalculates greatly. If he suppose that the desire to discern the "soul of goodness in things evil," to recognize the truth which lies at the root of error, and to assimilate the good in all sects and all men rather than magnify the evil, is a plan which will conciliate the regard of all, secure a man's own peace, " and of course bring with it great popularity with the multitude," I can earnestly assure the writer that, whenever he will try the experiment, he will find out his mistake. He will, perhaps, then see a new light reflected upon the expression, " when I speak of peace, they make them ready for the battle." He will find himself, to his painful surprise, charged on the one side for his earnestness with heresy, and on the other for his charity with latitudinarianism. His desire to exalt the spirit will be construed into irreverence for the letter, his setting light by maxims into a want of zeal for principles, his distinction between rules and spirit into lawlessness. He will find his attempt to love men, and his yearnings for their sympathy, met by suspicions of his motives and malignant slanders upon his life; his passionate desire to reach ideas instead of words, and get to the root of what men mean, he will find treated, even by those who think that they are candid, as the gratification of a literary taste and the affectation of philosophic height above the strife of human existence. I would not recommend him to try that "philosophic height" which he thinks so self-indulgent, unless he has the hardihood to face the keenest winds that blow over all lonely places, whether lonely heights, or lonely flats. If he can steel his heart against distrust and suspicion: if he can dare to be pronounced dangerous by the ignorant, hinted at by his brethren in public, and warned against in private; if he can resolve to be struck on every side and not strike again, giving all quarter and asking none; if he can struggle in the dark with the prayer for light of Ajax on his lips, in silence and alone, — then let him adopt the line which seems so easy, and be fair and generous and chivalrous to all. But if he expects from it "of course considerable self-applause and great popularity with the multitude," I can tell him they are not the rewards of *that* path. Rather let him be content to remain a partizan, and call himself by some name, Churchman, Evangelical, or Tractarian. Then he will be abused by many; but his party will defend him.

His definition of High Churchism called forth further remonstrance. One of his friends wrote to him upon the subject. He replied: —

My dear ——: — I gratefully accept your hint about the definition of High Churchmanship. I will modify what I said, to prevent misunderstanding. At the same time, as High Churchmanship, in the sense in which I was then speaking, is, in my view, an error, I must represent it in its most developed, not in its modified form, and as the exact opposite of Pantheism. All grand truth is the statement of two opposites, not a *via media* between them, nor either of them alone. I conceive Wordsworth to have held both, — the Personality of the Eternal Being, and also His diffusion through space. Now, I cannot conceal my conviction that it is the vice of High Churchism in its *tendency* to exaggerate the former of these, by localizing Deity in acts, places, &c. It is the vice of Pantheism to hold the latter alone.

When a High Churchman fully recognizes the latter, as Wordsworth did, I care little for any trifling exaggerations of the former, and I will always fight for him, and maintain that his High Churchism has no radical error in it, even though his *expressions* may to my mind seem to predicate locality of Gŏd much more than I should like to do it. But when he represents Personality as a limitation to time, space, acts, &c., instead of recognizing it in three essential points, all metaphysical and super-sensual, viz., consciousness, will, character,— then I must earnestly and firmly oppose High Churchism, and say that its tendency is to localize; and I must quote anxiously those texts which, taken alone, have a Pantheistic sound. "Howbeit, the Most High dwelleth not in temples made with hands. Heaven is my throne; Earth is my footstool: what house will ye build for me?"

And indeed I do think that this is a very common and very dangerous tendency. I will modify my definition by saying it is the *tendency* of High Churchism. That it is not inseparable from it, I showed by defending Wordsworth. High Churchism I hate. High Churchmen, many of them, I love, admire, and sympathize with.

The former of these two letters seems to have touched and excited some of the nobler spirits among the High-Church party. One of them wrote to him, urging him to unite himself to them, and drew from him the following reply, most valuable as the latest utterance of his convictions on many points of interest: —

60 Montpelier Road, Brighton: April 1, 1858.

DEAR SIR:— I thank you for your cordial and welcome letter. It is a joy to meet with any testimony to the veraciousness of a ministry beset with disappointments, and to read in such testimonies a prophecy of a coming day when we shall understand at least what each other means.

To the main question of your letter, respecting the duty of union,— that is, professed and active union with men whose earnestness is acknowledged,— and the apparent unreasonableness of standing aloof and alone, it would take many sheets to reply adequately.

It is my belief that in all the tenets and practices of the High-Church body there is an underlying truth; but then I confess that I should find as much difficulty in using their *forms* of statement in many points, as I should in using those of the Evangelicals in all points. With a thoughtful and large-minded High Churchman I believe I should sympathize more than with one of any section of the Church; but my recoil from the bare formalism of the half-educated and half-spiritualized of that school would, I fear, be stronger than from the extremes of any other party.

Spirit is Eternal, — Form is Transient; and when men stereotype the form and call it perpetual, or deny that under other and very different forms the self-same truth may lie (as the uncovering of Moses's feet is identically the same as our uncovering our heads, — ay, and I will even dare to say, often with the *covering* of the Quakers, when reverence for God is the cause for each), then I feel repelled at once, whether the form be a form of words or a form of observance.

To announce spiritual religion, as Christ announced it to the woman of Samaria, independent of place, on this mountain or that, — as Stephen announced it when they stoned him for blaspheming the temple, — this, I think, is the great work of a Christian minister in these days. He will joyfully recognize a reverence for the Invisible in the even exaggerated zeal with which good men, afraid of Rationalism, Pantheism, Germanism, and a hundred other things, strive to confine a sacredness to churches, rites, offices; but he cannot and will not join such efforts to preserve spiritual religion, because he knows by the experience of history in what they must inevitably end. He knows that the attempt to be independent of form is a vain effort for beings encased in flesh and blood, and in a world which is the Great Form by which God has manifested Himself. But, at the same time, he must feel that the special Church forms are only valuable as a protest for the Eternal Presence in and through all forms to the spirit that loves Him, and he will dread all attempts to limit and confine God's grace and presence to any authoritative forms, however time-honored.

Now, only giving these feelings as specimens, how could such a man join a party? He would soon be saying things which would make him a black sheep among them, every now and then protesting against their extremes with vehemence that would make him look like a renegade. What would he have gained by union? For himself and for others, — nothing.

Unless a man has a skin like a rhinoceros, and a heart like a stone-fruit, it is no easy thing to work alone; the bad feelings of pride or vanity get as little to feed them in such a struggle as the better ones of sympathy and charity; — and Elijah, stern and iron as he was, should be a warning to any common man to expect that many a day he will have to sit under his juniper-tree in despondency and bitter sense of isolation and uselessness.

Nevertheless it is my conviction that for some minds there is no other path open; they must speak such truth as is in them fearlessly and uncompromisingly, pleasing no mortal ear on purpose. They must try — not by eclecticism, but by a true application (not the Tractarian) of the canon, *quod semper, quod ubique, quod ab omnibus* — to discern the one truth which lies beneath various apparently antagonistic forms, as Cuvier discerned the fontal types of organization in things so diverse as leaves and lungs, tortoise-shells and human skeletons.

If God would raise up some man of rare largeness of heart and brain to do this work, and tell us what is the truth in each case which makes good men cleave to the error so tenaciously, a grand work of union might perhaps be accomplished, such as no "Protestant Defence Associations" nor

"South Church Unions" ever can accomplish; for all that they can do is to win a triumph for their party, and none of them will venture to say that their party contains all the liege men of the truth.

For a man or a body of men to do this I earnestly long and yearn; and in the absence of such large-hearted and largely-gifted man, I persist in trying, in my small blundering way, to do it for a few who will be candid enough to interpret what I mean. I believe the path in which I work is the true pass across the mountains, though the thought and the hand of the master-engineer are wanting to make it a road broad and safe for the people and the multitude to travel in; but that is not my fault or blame. God will provide His own workmen. I think I see how the work should be done, but I have neither the qualifications nor the strength to do it; but I can at least be faithful to my convictions and limited task, and I have cheerfully counted the cost, and have as cheerfully, for the most part, paid it.

This is a long letter; but I think the frankness of yours demands to be met with equal frankness.

It is really time now, after eighteen centuries, that we should get some better conception than we have of what Christianity is. If we could but comprehend the manifested Life of God, Christ in His earthly career, how He looked on things, and felt and thought, what He hated and what He pitied, we might have some chance of agreement. As it is, I suppose we shall go on biting and devouring one another, and thinking — alas for the mockery! — that we have realized a Kingdom of God upon earth.

To understand the Life and Spirit of Christ appears to me to be only the chance of remedy; but we have got doctrines about Christ, instead of Christ, and we call the bad metaphysics of Evangelicalism "the Gospel," and the temporary transient forms of Tractarianism "the Church."

To know Him, the power of His resurrection, and the fellowship of his sufferings,—that is all in all; and if the death and life of Christ are working in a man, he is our brother, whether Tractarian or Evangelical, if we could but believe that very simple proposition.

      I remain, yours faithfully,
            F. W. R.

Shortly after the unusual exertion of the lecture on Wordsworth, he suddenly fainted in the street.

           April 4.

During the day, while walking with J. Young, in West Street, on my way to the Training-school, I fainted and fell. My first sensation, on coming to myself, was that of being conscious of voices around me, and I knew instantly that a crowd had gathered, though I had not in that hundredth part of a second opened my eyes. They tell me I leaped to my feet as if shot: I went a few steps into a shop, and fainted quite off into unconsciousness a second time; then came intense pain in the back of the head, which lasted for three hours. However, to avoid making a sensation, I went out to dinner, keeping my engagement; but it saved me nothing, for the fact is duly pilloried in the "Brighton Gazette" this morning, and my bell has rung with inquiries half-a-dozen times already.

This warned him that there was more radical mischief in his weakness and pain than he had thought; and, urged by his physicians, he consented to go to Cheltenham for rest. In April he writes:—

On Monday I go to Cheltenham. Severe and bewildering pain in the cerebellum has for the last few days made work dangerous. Dr. Allen's view exactly corroborates my anticipations: the only difficulty is, that the pain is not in the region of the intellectual organs, but in that of the sensational and affectional. When it moves forward I know that the paroxysm is ending, and then it never attains a sensation more vivid than that as of warm water occupying the interior of the head and forehead. The decline in mental power, and the entire incapacitation at times of some functions, and the severe pain produced by the attempt to exercise them, force me to look at the matter now seriously. In Cheltenham I shall ask Dr. Conolly's opinion, if he be there.

While staying in Cheltenham he rallied; but returning on the third week to Brighton, all the old symptoms reappeared. During his absence several members of his congregation, with thoughtful generosity, subscribed to enable him to engage a curate. He gratefully accepted their kindness, and nominated a gentleman known to them, and a personal friend of his own, the Rev. Ernest Tower.

May 17, 1853.

Mr. Tower has accepted my curacy, and both his father and mother, whose letters I have seen, are pleased. He is a gentleman thoroughly in earnest, hard-working, and attached to me. Our spheres and powers lie in different directions, which will prevent the possibility of collision; and as he will take the afternoon sermon, I shall have leisure for more pastoral work, at the prospect of which I rejoice; for I cannot say how humiliated I feel at degenerating into the popular preacher of a fashionable watering-place. In addition to this, he has strong health; so that I shall not have compunction in delegating work to him when I am unfit for it.

These pleasant hopes were disappointed. The Vicar of Brighton, in whose hands the power of a veto lay, exercised his legal right in the most legal manner. Owing to reasons which appear in the correspondence given in the next chapter, he refused to confirm Mr. Robertson's nomination of Mr. Tower. This was on

Trinity Sunday, the 22nd of May. On the 29th, Mr. Robertson preached without the help he had so long desired; and on the following Sunday, the 5th of June, his voice was heard for the last time in Trinity Chapel. His sermon in the morning was for the Orphan Asylum; the subject was the parable of the Barren Fig-tree, — " Then said he to the dresser of his vineyard, ' Behold, these three years I come seeking fruit on this fig-tree, and find none : cut it down ; why cumbereth it the ground ? ' " By a strange and sad coincidence, his afternoon lecture was on part of the last chapter of the Second Epistle to the Corinthians. The closing sermon of a long course of lectures was also the close of his career. With what a sorrowful force came back upon the memories of his congregation the words which he had read as part of his last text, — " Finally, brethren, farewell ! " No one who wishes to penetrate, as far as possible, into the solitary manliness and endurance of his life during the last month of his pulpit ministra-tions, who would understand the suffering and the strength of his nature, the mingling of meekness and noble pride, of self-surrender and high self-confidence, of quiet faith and of an almost triumphant ecstasy of faith, should omit to read the notes of the last three lectures which he delivered on the Second Epistle to the Corinthians.

I remember seeing on the manuscript of one of these, on " The Thorn in the Flesh," the mark of a tear. It had fallen as he wrote alone in his room.

Self-contained, master of himself, when he could weep in the solitude of his study it was full time that he should be freed from his long sorrow. And God blessed him with Death, the Releaser. In three months after he had spoken of the pain of St. Paul, he entered into the painless land.*

LETTERS FROM JANUARY 5 TO MAY 18, 1853.

LVIII.

January 5, 1853.

Last evening I began Benvenuto Cellini's "Life," which I had never read before. What a very strange one, and what strange times it paints! The murder of a man who had slain Cellini's brother in self-defence is related with the utmost coolness, as well as the way in which Pope Clement VII. connived at it. Certainly, an artist's life does not appear one conducing to moral excellence; Cellini was a most ungovernable, vain, passionate man, unrestrained by any rule except his own feelings; yet he seems to have been an intimate friend of Michael Angelo, — a right noble man. If Cellini is to be believed, he killed the Constable Bourbon with his own hand, and almost singly defended the Castle of St. Angelo, besides a number of other wonders, any one of which would be sufficient to make a life famous. His profligacy, too, seems to have been without measure. Such books do not amuse me as they do most people. They set me thinking, and most painfully; bewildering, and entangling the skein of life and human destinies hopelessly. In the midst of it all religion comes in from time to time, — and the names of God and Christ as objects of supposed and, I conceive, sincere worship, jarring, however, upon my sense of

* I have printed at the end of this chapter the letters of 1853 up to the month of June. The remaining letters attached to the following chapter were written, after he had given up public life, during the months of June, July, and August.

fitness, like the Messiah between two thieves, as if He had been their accomplice. What is one to make of it all, and how judge of this strange world, which becomes to me more unintelligible every day?

No reply from M——. I shall be glad to go, not only for the sake of the solitude, but also for the exercise, for I begin to feel it once more indispensable, and without delay, — for mental restlessness and powerlessness increase to a painful extent. I cannot read for ten minutes consecutively, much less think.

LIX.

I have just finished Maurice's three sermons on the Crystal Palace question, recently published. As usual, they are the offspring of a capacious mind and large heart. In the main his view is the same as mine, though the statement differs somewhat, as the idiosyncrasies of the two minds differ, and he has brought more thought and more historical learning to the subject by far. Like all he writes, they are exceedingly suggestive, and likely to do more good, I should fancy, in the study than from the pulpit, were it not that these were addressed to a Lincoln's-Inn congregation, which may be supposed to have in it minds trained to habits of consecutive attention. There is matter for thought for hours in these sermons, but most people would read on from sentence to sentence, and when they turned over the last page and found *finis*, be tempted to exclaim, "But what does he mean? and what is proved?"

LX.

I have just finished writing a sermon for the morning. It is an old subject, from notes, with fresh language, and several fresh thoughts. Somehow I cannot originate thought and subjects now as I used. Perhaps it arises from feeling that enthusiasm, and affection, and trust, and perhaps respect, towards me have cooled, partly from my own fault, partly from the malicious misrepresentations of the Evangelicals, as well as of others. So far as this has chilled the spring of energy, there is something wrong; for energy ought not to arise out of self-respect or the assurance of being heard with sympathy. Yet it is not all wrong even in this respect, for some natures cannot do without sympathy, public or private, — though perhaps pride, or some other peculiarity, makes them haughtily refuse all common and even the fair methods of securing what the Evangelical books call "acceptance," and what old Aristotle lays down as one of the first things to be acquired, and indispensable to the success of one who addresses masses, — namely, the "good-will of the audience," that is, a personal feeling of well-disposedness towards the speaker who is to convince or teach them.

* * * * *

I am proceeding with Cellini's "Life." What a wonderful picture of human life, and human art, and human society! The *naïve* and inordinate vanity of the man is astonishing, and refutes the foolish popular notion that real talent is never vain, and real courage never boastful. Falstaff's braggadocio is modest in comparison of his. Conceive a man gravely telling you that after the vision in his prison a glory encircled his head through life, — visible on his shadow, especially on the dewy grass at morning, and which he possessed the power of showing to a chosen few. And then the religiosity and hymn-writing of a man who records, in admiration, the murder in revenge of three separate persons who had slightly offended him. Very curious, too, is his account of the unblushing rapacity, violence, and profligacy of the Popes Clement and Paul III., to say nothing of the villany of the cardinals, bishops, and Dukes of Ferrara. It was a curious time when men had to redress their own wrongs, and goldsmiths were compelled to be accomplished swordsmen if they would live one day in safety. Fancy Mr.

Lewis armed *cap-a-pie*, or a tailor coming to measure you with a sword on his thigh! Yet à dusky clouded sense of right, honor, and religion runs through the book: *bizarre* enough, it is true, and suggestive of many reflections. Society progresses,— do men? Benvenuto gratified every passion, slashed and slew his way through life. London jewellers wear no swords, and get rich by bankruptcies; is the gain very great, are we not less of men than in those days?

It is a wonderfully graphic life. That power of painting what was seen and what appeared, instead of our modern habit of reflecting and philosophizing upon it, brings the whole scene before the eyes. How living and real, as if of yesterday, the portraits of Francis I., Madame d'Estampes, Titian! And how curious, as compared with Rousseau and Tasso, is Cellini's perpetual discovery of conspiracies against himself, and of the implacable enmities of popes, dukes, ladies! The imaginativeness of a brain, which had in it a fibre of insanity, near which genius often lies, would, I suppose, account for two thirds of this,— and his extraordinary irascibility was but another form of it. An innkeeper whose horse he has overridden, keeps his saddle and bridle in retaliation, and Cellina sets off and buries his dagger in the spine of his neck. Another man affronts him slightly, and he resolves to cut off his arm: then his mad escape from prison, with the ingenuity of a maniac; the descent by sheets, curiously procured, cut in strips, and the desperate fall and fractured leg; all to escape from a Pope, who was trying to murder him in the most incredible ways,— it is very curious.

LXI.

A letter arrived from —— to-day. I did not like the expression in the one you sent me, where she speaks of the sacrifice made for ——, and the strengthening effect of sacrifice on the character. It is a bad habit of sentiment to fall into. People who make real sacrifices are never able to calculate, self-complacently, the good the said sacrifices are doing them; just as people who really grieve are unable at the time to philosophize about the good effects of grief. "Now, no chastening for the present seemeth to be joyous but grievous." That is true philosophy. In the lips of one struggling might and main to strengthen character, and living a life of the Cross and of sacrifice, such a sentence as I have quoted might be real; as it is, it is simply unreal, — a sentence got by heart, and I think very dangerous. Nothing is more dangerous than the command of a pen which can write correct sentiments, such as might befit a martyr or an angel. And the danger is, that the confusion between a commonplace life and that of an angel or a martyr is hopeless. For when the same sublimities proceed from the lips and pens of both, who is to convince us that we are not beatified martyrs and holy angels? Such a sentence as this would have been more real, though somewhat sentimental still: "How dare I talk of Sacrifice! and how little of it is there in my life, — one perpetual succession of enjoyments!" It has often struck me that Christ never suffered these sentimentalisms to pass without a matter-of-fact testing of what they were worth and what they meant. It is a dangerous facility of fine writing, which — I say it in deep reverence to Him — Christ would have tested by some of those apparently harsh replies which abound in his life, such as to one professing great anxiety to be with Him, saying he wished it and not doing it, "Foxes have holes, and the birds of the air have nests, but the Son of Man hath not where to lay His head."

* * * * *

I only took the morning duty yesterday, being too tired for the second. As I sat inactive in the afternoon listening to Mr. Langdon, and gazing on the dense crowd before me, I felt humbled exceedingly to think I had to address those numbers every week twice, and that their spiritual life depended, for those hours at least, speaking humanly, on me. How wonderful the opportunity, and how heavy the responsibility! In the crush and rush and hurry of work, and the personal anxieties connected with it, such thoughts do not come, except rarely; but when out of harness, and looking, in the dusky light of evening, into the almost solemn darkness, the feeling came painfully. Such feelings, unhappily, evaporate in the dust of life.

LXII.

The last hour has been spent in examining a pile of eighteen letters waiting my arrival,—some long, none important, two anonymous,—one of them from a young lady defending fashionable society against my tirades; these last I feel are worse than useless, and very impolitic. Nevertheless, more and more, a life of amusement and visiting seems to me in irreconcilable antagonism to Christianity, and more destructive to the higher spirit than even the mercantile life in its worst form; and yet I do not know; who shall say which is the national spirit more surely, inevitably tending to decay, — that of the cities of the plain, or that of Tyre and Sidon?

* * * * *

The austerity that comes *after* life's experience is more healthy, because more natural, than that which begins it. When it begins life it is the pouring of the new wine into the old weak wine-skins, which burst; and the young heart, cheated out of its youth, indemnifies itself by an attempt to realize the feelings which were denied it by a double measure of indulgence in age. An unlovely spectacle! Can anything be more melancholy than the spectacle of one who is trying to be young, and unable to descend gracefully and with dignity into the vale of years? There is a fine tomb of, I think, Turenne,* at Strasbourg. An open grave lies before

.* Query, Maréchal Saxe.

him; Death at his side, touching him with his dart; and the warrior descends, with a lofty step and saddened brow, but a conqueror still, because the act is so evidently his own and embraced by his own will, into the sepulchre. I remember it impressed me much with its moral force, and it has little or nothing in it of French theatricality and attitudinizing.

LXIII.

A long dreary vista of many months of pain opens out before me. Was that a good omen, — just as I wrote those words a sudden gleam of sunshine burst out of this gloomy day upon my paper? Benvenuto Cellini would have taken it for a special prediction vouchsafed from heaven, yet it would have made him not a whit the better man. What I miss exceedingly is any religious aspiration through all his book. Convictions of Heaven's personal favor and favoritism are expressed in abundance, but I do not think those religious, in the true sense of the word. In a lower sense, perhaps, they are; at least, a feeling of Divine and personal sympathy is indispensable to religion, — perhaps one of its bases; but the other basis — a belief in and aspiration after what is high, beautiful, and good — is the more solid and the less easily misused basis of the two; and this you do not find in Cellini's art as in Michael Angelo's, Canova's, Beethoven's, — no effort at expressing a something unearthly, which is the true province of imagination.

I think it would be an interesting thing to work out that thought: How far Religion has those two sides, — the sense of Personality, including sympathy, and the sense of an abstract Beauty, and Right and Good, — the one, if alone, producing superstition and fanaticism, or else the mysticism of the Guyon school; the other, if alone, producing mere ethics or mere statesmanship.

LXIV.

This morning I arrived here on a visit to Lady Byron, and have been in the house all day, having had no time yet to go out to see the country, which I am told is interesting, with rich woods and fine commons. Lady Byron showed me a picture of Lady Lovelace, taken at seventeen. How different from what she was when I knew her, — unquestionably handsome, and with an air of sad thoughtfulness which then characterized her! Startling lessons these, in which two or three portraits bring a whole life before you, and show the fearful changes in the outward being. "Our little life is rounded with a sleep." Startling, because it reminds how the only thing that remains permanent is character. I have seen, too, to-day, the original MS. of *Beppo*, from which the poem was printed. All such things are curious, and, in certain moods, prolific of much reflection, or rather feeling. The sweep of time, the nearness of the farthest off to that which is nearest, the nothingness of one's own existence in that flood of time, — these are the thoughts which come, and, though very old words, very new every time they present themselves, for they always startle.

The quietude of this place is refreshing, after the inevitable life *en evidence* of Brighton, its hurry, and its glare. I have only been a few hours away, and I feel as if I had got back to the home-life of life, and am myself again, with no weight of weary duty hanging over me, and no necessity of addressing a crowd of critics who are supposed to be before me to be taught; and yet within three days I shall be there again, in my old place, and at my old work. I wonder how you will like those sermons I sent you on the Virgin; the wiseacres at Brighton called the first Popery.

Coming in the train to-day, I read in the "Edinburgh" a review of Mrs. Jameson's "Legends of the Madonna," and was startled to find that it expressed, almost in the same words, what I had said the last two Sundays. Now, as I had held the same views long, and even preached them years ago, it puzzled me how the identity could have arisen. At last I recollected that three years ago, while Mrs. Jameson was preparing her work, she asked my opinion on the theology of Virgin-worship, which I gave to her, and which I perfectly remember seemed new to her. It has worked in her mind ever since, and she has published almost my words, perhaps unconscious of whence they came. That this must be so is evident to me from the reflection that, when the mind is full of any subject, it is impossible for the most casual remark to fall upon it without impression and without fructifying. The "Edinburgh" gives her credit for much originality in this view. I am pretty sure of its true origin, and I am not aware that I got it from any source except my own reflection. It would be awkward if ever I were inclined to publish those sermons, for it would be hard to prove that plagiarism was not on my part, and it would seem ungenerous to charge it upon her.

Tell me what you think of the two sermons* on one subject. They have excited here a good deal of ignorant gossip and pious horror; people shaking their wise heads, and ominously predicting that I am on my way to Rome. How many ages would it take to explain what Shakespeare meant by "the soul of goodness in things evil"? and how long would it need to prove, that to say an error rests upon a truth is not quite the same thing as saying that an error is truth.

I consider these two as an instalment towards an intention, long indulged, of going through some of the main doctrines of Romanism, which I consider to be erroneous, and showing what the corresponding truth is, which the error meant to say. I do not mean to do this in a way that would satisfy the learned, but only popularly. I shall leave out all recondite searchings into Councils and dogmas, and try the matter by the test of common sense, and what may be called the

* Second Series, pp. 261, 277.

spiritual sense, which we surely all possess, more or less,—the best in the highest degree. Such a publication might at least stir up deeper minds to try the same plan with more success.

LXV.

Your question on the subject is not full enough for me to be sure that I am replying to what you want to know. A person can believe in a fact or a being whose nature he cannot comprehend,—as, for instance, in God, or in vegetation, or life,—but no one can believe a proposition the terms of which are unknown to him. For example, "Three persons are one God." Unless he knows what "person" means, he cannot believe that, because he attaches no meaning whatever, or else a false one, to the assertion. And it is preposterous to say he must believe it as a mystery, because the Church says it; for all that he does in that case is to suspend his judgment on a subject of which he knows nothing, and to say, "The Church knows all about it, but I have not the smallest conception what it is she knows." So, for instance, a mathematician says to me, an ignoramus, "The velocities of planets vary inversely as the squares of their distances. Presumptuous sceptic! don't you believe that?" "Well," I reply, "I dare say you are right,—nay, I believe you are; but I cannot say I believe that long sentence, because I do not understand what it means." "Dolt! idiot! believe without understanding." "Well, wise sir, I will. 'The inverse squares of the planets,'—no, how is it? 'The velocities of planets vary inversely,' &c." "Quite right,—good and orthodox scholar." "Now, do *you* believe in Abracadabra?" "Sir, do you?" "Yes." "Then, so do I." "But what is Abracadabra?" "Never mind that,—believe."

All that is simple nonsense. No man can believe that the earth goes round the sun, unless he knows what that proposition is, and what is the meaning of "earth," "round the sun";

but once knowing this, he may believe it, though it is contrary to the evidence of his senses, and though he does not understand how or why it is.

Apropos of believing in things which we do not understand, a Tractarian was in Trinity when I preached on Mariolatry. "I did not agree," said he afterwards, "with Robertson. Woman,—woman! I do not understand what woman is." I sent him a message, to say that I have been exactly in the same predicament all my life.

Just returned from Earnley. I found the shooting experiment useless, in consequence of the hard frost having frozen up all the streams; so, after two days' hard walking, in which I saw five snipes, shot two, and two plover, I thought that even Nimrod's ghost would absolve me from faintheartedness if I gave up the attempt as hopeless. However, I spent an exceedingly pleasant evening with Mr. L——, and drank a glass or two of Mrs. L——'s orange-wine with a good grace. He is possessed of intelligence quite uncommon in that line of life,—I mean the agricultural,—and is reckoned the best farmer in the neighborhood. I should have learned something if I could have, with decency and the excuse of sport, staid longer. As it was, I dived into the mysteries of "shoulder-drains," "wedge-drains," and "tile-drains." He has been for years a free-trader, but is very anxious for the repeal of the malt-tax. He says that if you were to offer him a return of 500*l.* of rent, and as an equivalent the repeal of the malt-tax were proposed, he would sacrifice the rent without hesitation. He gave me a very lucid account of his view of Sir R. Peel's currency measure some years ago, which he said was a loss of 5*s.* in the pound to the farmer. According to him, the farmers have been very ill used, but he is very cheerful about it. I said,—"But the brewers say the repeal of the malt-tax would be unfelt by the consumers; consequently more beer would not be purchased, and the farmers would gain nothing. Is that true?" He replied that some years ago, when the duty on salt existed, there were salt-basins all along this coast, — Bognor, Selsea, and two other places between this and Portsmouth. But when the tax was taken off, no one thought it worth while to make salt. "How was that?" "Why, the makers ran (smuggled) a large proportion, and so managed to gain all the tax in addition to the profit." "Do you mean that that is the reason why the maltsters now are against the repeal, because they pocket a part of the tax?" "I know they do," said he.

He is a good churchman, makes all his laborers go regularly, and is firmly but modestly opposed to Calvinism and Tractarianism. Before the present incumbent, there was one who wrote him a note, very civilly expostulating with him for not turning to the altar, and even turning from it to the light to read his prayer-book, and if he would not do it on principle, to do it for his sake. Mr. L—— replied, quietly, that if he did not do it for the honor of the Creator, he certainly would not for His creature. But not knowing the matter *à fond*, and conscious that it was with him a vague feeling, he asked a neighboring clergyman where he could gain information on all such subjects. "I do not like," said he, "to know nothing, and the clergyman to know all." The book prescribed was Milner's "Church History," and he spent the winter in reading that long book right through, and, as his memory is good, has forgotten nothing of it.

The house is a capital one, — too good, he says, for a farm-house, — with cellars, which he turns into a dairy. I slept in a good comfortable room and capital bed, and nothing could exceed his efforts to be hospitable in the hearty old English way. The farm is liable to overflowing floods, which is considered in the terms of the lease, — low in consequence. He told me of his dismay in seeing the tide once come pouring over the barrier, which it at last swept away, and flooded the whole farm, regular billows going over his sown land up to the house. It went down, and, though the barrier was gone, did not rise the next tide beyond its accustomed height. For three years after such a flood the land is injured, and all the grass poisoned.

The farming is, even to an ignoramus, visibly admirable; draining going on in every direction; hedges, or rather fences, unbroken; no useless expense; living plain and simple; no foreign wines: "I like them, but they are not fit for us farmers in these days." Beer, and home-made wines, costing sixpence per bottle, and cherry-rum, almost indistinguishable from cherry-brandy, but saving very many shillings per gallon: these were the beverages of that hospitable home. I wonder what an Irish squireen would say, or would once have said, to this.

I walked all day yesterday and to-day on the thick snow and half-frozen streams alone, with little enjoyment, haunted by miserable thoughts, dispirited, hopeless, — feeling the bleak sunshine and the distant bellowing of the sea as if they were the visible type and audible echo of life, with its disappointments and its shocks! It was a relief to be alone. It was strange, but L——'s graphic account of the desolate spectacle of the flooding tide which he had stood to witness seemed to me as if it were the wraith of the feelings I had experienced; and in the bewilderment the two got mixed, and I could not at certain moments distinguish which was the dream and which the reality, or be certain that he was not narrating objectively what I had already seen or felt in ecstasy or vision. I shall never forget those strange days: the sweep of desolate plain, the glaring snow, the bleak sunshine without wind, the frozen streams, — the rushes without the usual life of birds springing from them, which one expects, — the sea-roar, the lifelessness of all, — the stillness which was not relief, and the sounds which were not expression, all combined to image that "Death in life, the days that are no more."

Mr. ——'s irreverence about the Fire is very like that school of Evangelicalism. I must do them the justice to say that that is not the fault of them all: Mr. —— here, for instance, is solemn enough; Mr. P——e told me of his being asked out to wine at college, and replying, with sepulchral solemnity, "I am *serious*." That false notion of a peculiar favoritism which they have with God, unshared by others, gives them that familiarity. The view which I believe to be the true one of baptism, declaring Sonship the right of all, "mine, because I am a man," is the only thought which I think an effectual antidote.

The letter I received from *that* lady is in earnest, so far as it goes; only that fatal facility of strong words expresses feeling which will seek for itself no other expression. Those resolves to study, to be serious, religious, &c., are such as might have been made at John the Baptist's baptism,— a solemn call to a new life; and followed by serious and earnest effort, they would in such a case have been well, but uttered at the outset of a London season, they will pass off in the first polka, and do much more harm than if they had never been made. She believes or means what she says, but the very vehemence of the expression injures her, for really it expresses the penitence of a St. Peter, and would not be below the mark if it were meant to describe the bitter tears with which he bewailed his crime; but when such language is used for trifles, there remains nothing stronger for the awful crises of human life. It is like Draco's code,— death for larceny, and there remains for parricide or treason only death.

LXVI.

Last night I spent at home; I meant to dedicate the time to writing, but I was in a mood too dark and hopeless to venture. The exhaustion of Sunday remained; I tried light reading in vain. At last Charley came in from school, and I made him do his Latin exercise before me; all the while I kept my eyes fixed on that engraving of the head of Christ by Leonardo da Vinci, which I have had framed, and felt the calm majesty of the countenance by degrees exerting an influence over me, which was sedative. Then I made him read over, slowly, the Beatitudes, and tried to fix my mind and heart upon them, and believe them; explaining them to him afterwards, and to myself as I went on. "Blessed are" — not the successful, but "the poor in spirit." "Blessed," not the rich, nor the admired, nor the fashionable, nor the happy, but "the meek, and the pure in heart, and the merciful." They fell upon my heart like music. Then I thought I would just read a little of Golding Bird's volume of "Natural Philosophy," in order to brace the mind and add tone to harmony; but the effort had been too great, and after reading some twenty or thirty pages, I fell asleep, and woke again.

To-day I have spent in the Town Hall, in the midst of a tumultuous meeting. We are trying to get the Health of Towns Act introduced into Brighton. Demagogues, whose interest will be injured by it, are stirring up the working classes against it. It was an odd sight,— as the mob always is.

> Thou many-headed monster thing,
> O who would wish to be thy king?

At the root of the whole matter, as usual, lay selfishness and ignorance. One respectable man said to me, in reply to my observation that modern science had discovered the cause of epidemics, &c., in want of cleanliness, undrained houses, &c. "Why, sir, if these are injurious in 1853, I want to know why they were not injurious in 1800?" "Suppose," said I, "they were, and suppose in former ages, when people wisely attributed the plague to the poisoning of wells by doctors, there were some other very simple reason which they really did not know?" The truth is, the knowledge of this enlightened age is the knowledge of a few,—the many are as dark as they were ages back.

I enclose one sheet of a letter from Lady Byron, containing strictures upon my "Lecture on Wordsworth." They are erroneous, because she misunderstands my meaning, which I had not sufficiently developed. I maintain that the localizing of Deity of which he speaks was only that which an affectionate imagination does in reference to the presence of any loved person; an act which has only reference to his or her own mode of conceiving that presence,—as when a relic or keepsake is preserved, or a chair felt to be sacred. An enlarged mind in such a case localizes safely, because it is in no danger of confounding its own modes of viewing and realizing with an actual presence there. It knows that there is a presence, but only suggested, not inherent. A limited intellect confuses its own necessary helps with an actual something external to itself, and the spirit of the loved one is supposed to be *there*. So in Wordsworth's High Churchism, I maintain it was in him only the poet's creative power. He felt a relief in associating God, the personal, with definite places and acts; but Wordsworth never merged God's indefinite in those conceptions: vulgar High Churchism does.

What Lady Byron says of the apparent contradiction to my views of the progress from Judaism to Christianity, in Wordsworth's progress, viz. that the former was from the localized to the illimitable, the latter the converse, is only true in appearance. All human education does not follow the same exact course; nay, it may begin in one case at the opposite extreme from what it does in the other. The great question is, "Do they end in the same at last?" I think Wordsworth's mind at first lacked the conception of personality. It was added afterwards; and if this reverse method of procedure were unlawful, how could a man who sets out with pantheism ever come to truth? He cannot follow the Jewish order, which I admit is the more natural one, as existing in the order of thought by which childhood passes into manhood.

* * * * *

The historian I mainly meant in speaking of national decline was Arnold: But do not misunderstand me. I do not say I respect long ancestry much; I only say the *prestige* is a valuable one, and more spiritual than the power of wealth; and also that frequently having a character to support insures a character, so that there are certainly virtues which are essentially aristocratic. But when it is remembered that the purer the blood is, and the less mixed, the more certain is the deterioration physically and morally, and also that the regeneration of a people never yet came from its aristocracy, there can be no doubt that while our sympathies cling to the past, and while we feel that, in the past, hereditary rank has done a great part, it is impossible to hide the fact that the passing away of it is not an unmixed cause of regret. Blood, so far as it represents real worth, is much to be desired for its *prestige;* but when the *prestige* is gone, blood, with its feebleness and faults, is not to me an object of respect at all, — at least, I mean in the individual cases.

> What can ennoble sots, or fools, or cowards?
> Alas! not all the blood of all the Howards!

It is a thing that has been, that will never be again, — a thing that once did a work, and now has no more work to do. I honor old Greece, and the old Greek work; but I have not the smallest respect for a modern Peloponnesian or Athenian, though he had in his veins the unblemished descent of Aristides, or Solon, or Lycurgus.

LXVII.

To-day I walked to Lewes with H—— over the Downs, and home by the road. The walk to Lewes was a stiff one, for the hills were wet from the scarcely-melted snow, and on the north sides they were hard with frost, so that we slipped about considerably. We did it, however, all the way at a racing pace,—there and back in three hours and a half. I took a hot bath in my own room directly on my arrival, and feel considerably refreshed,—the brain clearer, and at this moment all my nature sinking into a natural and healthy weariness such as has not come to me for a long time. It is wonderful how views of life depend upon exercise and right management of the physical constitution. Nor is this, rightly looked at, any cause for perplexity, though it seems so at first; for though you might be inclined to view it as a degradation of our higher nature to find it so dependent upon the lower, and hope and faith and energy resultant from a walk, or early hours,—yet, in fact, it is only a proof that all the laws of our manifold being are sacred, and that disobedience to them is punished by God. And the punishment in one department of our nature of the transgressions committed in the other,—as, for instance, when mental gloom comes from uncleanliness or physical inertia, and, on the other hand, where ill-health ensues from envy or protracted doubt,—is but one of many instances of the law of vicarious suffering. We are, as it were, two, and one suffers by what the other does.

LXVIII.

As to the "History of England," Lingard's is very good; dry, however, and on all Roman Catholic questions not to be depended upon. It appears to me that the History of England is a subject too enormous to attempt to teach a child. I would rather select some salient points; for example, the reign of Alfred,—then the Norman Conquest. Thierry might be extracted for this with Lingard. The times intermediate between this and Henry VIII. I would teach by some abridgment; for his reign I would take Lingard, and Blunt on the Reformation. Mary, in Miss Strickland, who leans however, unduly to her, as you will see by the "Westminster," when I send it. Elizabeth's is very important,— Lingard; for the Charles's reigns, Guizot, and Mackintosh, and Fox, though the two latter might be dispensed with. Then Macaulay for the Revolution. In this, or some such way, a course of English history might be gone through, in a calculated number of months, and mastered. The intervals might be filled in in after years. But, when taken as a whole, English history becomes to most minds either a string of dates and names, with no principle of national life traced out, or else a dreary continent of mud. For French history, I would content myself with Sir James Stephen's lectures and Sismondi's history, abridged by himself in three volumes; but I would not be induced to teach more until these were mastered.

In Oxford four years are spent in preparing about fourteen books only for examination; but this is only a partial representation of the matter, for those fourteen books have been the subject of school-work for years. These are made textbooks, read, reread, digested, worked, got up, until they become part and parcel of the mind; about four histories, three or four philosophical works, four poets, and two or three miscellaneous works. These are the choice master-works of two languages, and whoever has mastered them is a scholar indeed. By C——'s letter to you I see she is reading Southey's "Peninsular War," and meditating one or two other great works. At Oxford, Southey's "Peninsular War" would take six months to study, pen in hand, getting up the details of policy, battles, laws, geography, &c. It is better not to read at all than to run through such a book. I have got a small popular book on chemistry, which I am reading now, of 160 pages. I have read little else for a fortnight; but then, I could bear an examination on every law and principle it lays down. Fownes's "Manual of Chemistry," a small 8vo, will take me six months I calculate; but then, as a medical man said to me to-day, if you study it in the way you are doing, you will know by that time more chemistry than nine out of ten of the medical men in this town. I never knew but one or two fast readers, and readers of many books, whose knowledge was worth anything. Miss Martineau says of herself that she is the slowest of readers, sometimes a page in an hour; but then what she reads she makes her own. Do impress this on E——. Girls read too much and think too little. I will answer for it that there are few girls of eighteen who have not read more books than I have; and as to religious books, I could count upon my fingers in two minutes all I ever read,—but they are mine. Sir Erskine Perry said the other day that, a fortnight ago, in a conversation with Comte,—one of the most profound thinkers in Europe,—Comte told him that he had read an incredibly small number of books these last twenty years,—I forget how many,—and scarcely ever a review; but then what Comte reads lies there fructifying, and comes out a living tree, with leaves and fruit. That multifarious reading weakens the mind more than doing nothing, for it becomes a necessity at last like smoking, and is an excuse for the mind to lie dormant, whilst thought is poured in and runs through, a clear stream, over unproductive gravel, on which not even mosses grow. It is the idlest of all idlenesses, and leaves more of impotency than any other. I do not give myself as a specimen, for my nervous energies are shattered by stump oratory, its excitements and reactions; but I know what reading is, for I could read once, and did. I read hard, or not at all,—never skimming,—never turning aside to merely inviting books; and Plato, Aristotle, Butler, Thucydides, Sterne, Jonathan Edwards, have passed like the iron atoms of the blood into my mental constitution. My work is done. I know and feel it; but what I have appropriated remains; and if I had not appropriated it so, there would be no soil now or hereafter to grow anything on even for appearance.

LXIX.

An evening of failure. In vain have I tried to work or think. The only resource at last is to fall back on an old sermon. This mental powerlessness is becoming fast an alarming thing; memory and grasp are both going; and with an incessant call for fresh thought, this feeling is a more than ordinarily painful one.

I have done all I can to throw off this impotency of mind and will, and this growing coldness of a species of despair, by long walks, cold baths, and complete change of study, — by taking up chemistry and natural philosophy again. Such studies bring a different class of faculties into play from those exercised in my own work, and so rest the overtasked ones; but as yet I feel no benefit.

Mrs. V—— read to me ——'s letter about the Wordsworth lecture. Yes, indeed, if I had not been a parson! but what Mr. —— speaks of as the alternative in this case, the being heard of in the world, would be a poor thing to have won. What I long for is work that I can do in love, without meeting the rancor and the bitterness and the malignant slanders which I rouse on every side. It is a bitter thought that this is the only visible result of efforts that have been long wearying life.

How rare is it to have a friend who will defend you throughly and boldly! Mr. —— missed an opportunity of doing this for me, and has not the courage to do it now as he ought to do; leaving me, in consequence, defenceless against a slander, though I put the proof into his hands. How indispensable strength is for high goodness, — strength, moral or intellectual, — neither depending necessarily on physical strength!

Yesterday I took a walk beyond Hove with Mr. V——. In the cross-road between the Worthing Road and the Upper

Road we found a crowd behind a hedge, and shoals of women flocking from Brighton towards the place. On inquiry, we found that it was the spot where a child was murdered, or rather its body hidden two days ago by its mother, a servant-girl. The child was six years old, and it is supposed that she murdered it in order to be unencumbered, and to be able to go out to Australia. It is very inexplicable to me how such things exercise an attraction over people, and what can induce them to take long excursions to see a *spot*, where nothing but the spot is to be seen. How utterly vain it is, with such an instinct in human nature, to attempt to eradicate the High-Church tendency, the disposition to localize, as I said in my lecture! If they cannot guide the feeling and direct it rightly, all attempts to merely thwart it will be vain.

I have been spending my time in laborious idleness,— every thought I think, and every line I write or read costing pain, sometimes acute and sometimes dull, of brain. I shall not be able to go on much longer if this continues; whole tracts of brain seem to be losing their faculty, and becoming quite torpid and impotent,— memory being the most observable and the most tormenting. All originating power I have ceased to try to exercise, on principle, lest it should go entirely. I seem to myself already in sight of that goal which a London physician, an American, told me I should reach in due time,— organic collapse of the brain. I have been reading a little chemistry, by way of change, and am beginning regular experiments in it; but then this I cannot work at except for a quarter of an hour at a time.

A hideous accident occurred to-day at the station. At 7, A. M., a loud explosion shook my house. Some persons took it for an earthquake. Shortly after I learned that a boiler had burst, and that much damage was done. I went to the station, and found an enormous portion of the roof on

ACCIDENT AT THE RAILWAY STATION. 211

the Portsmouth line had been blown away, and all the windows of the station, as well as many in the road above, broken in. I saw three human bodies reduced to one hideous bleeding mass of fragments,—a scalp here, a shoulder there, and a leg or hand in another place; one was recognizable, but his face was scalded like a Red Indian in color, and all the skull stove in, one arm blown off, and the limb shattered; the other two were torn to shreds. A leg was blown over the houses into Guildford Street, and through the windows where two people were at breakfast; another, on the other side, towards St. Peter's Church, into a garden. I will not attempt to describe the horrible scene minutely, for I never saw anything so humiliating to our humanity; nothing but a "knacker's yard" could give a conception of it. I thought at once of a French invasion, and of those lines in the "Siege of Corinth": —

Alp turned him from the sickening sight, &c.,

just after he had seen the lean dogs beneath the wall

Hold o'er the dead their carnival.

It was a strange contrast to come back again into the busy town, and see people unconcernedly walking about within a hundred yards of so much horror! but I felt there was nothing in such a sight to *create* one religious emotion or resolve, though it might evoke it if it were in the heart already. Of themselves such things only tend to harden and degrade, I am quite sure; for how can horror, or the thought of death brought near, make goodness beautiful or God lovable? I see in them no natural tendency whatever to convert the heart to God; and I can understand how the dissecting-room and the field of battle may brutalize low natures, at the same time that they may elevate high ones. Pray read over again, with reference to this thought, Wordsworth's "Happy Warrior."

LXX.

I have spent this evening in reading thoughtfully and meditating on Neander's "Doctrine of St. John," imbuing my mind with a tone of thought for Sunday next. I find that to be the only way in which my mind works. I cannot copy, nor can I now work out a seed of thought, developing it for myself. I cannot light my own fire; but whenever I get my fire lighted from another life, I can carry the living flame as my own into other subjects which become illuminated in the flame. Mechanical composition of any kind is out of my power, — always was. It is wonderful how powerless I am, except as working from life. Even memory seems extinguished when the heart's life is not in play; and any inspiration brings out its invisible traces again, as fire brings out the colors of sympathetic inks on paper. Unhappily, of late, such life cannot be as once, — seemingly, at least, — self-kindled. I need a foreign influence to imbue my mind with some other great mind, till the creative power rises in the glow. All, therefore, that I can voluntarily effect is to bring myself intentionally and purposely within the sphere of such influences as can kindle; only they become fewer every month; and their power to inspire is more uncertain and more dependent upon outward circumstances and seeming chance.

Did I tell you of a practical solution in part of the question as to what the influence of pictures may be religiously? I took the "Leonardo" up to my room some weeks ago, on a Sunday night. The next morning I awoke tired, and felt inclined to dawdle away my time in bed; but that calm, dignified look, bent down from my mantelpiece, absolutely rebuked me, and made it impossible. It is true, the impression would have worn off before a second experiment could have been fairly tried.

Rodney House, Cheltenham: April 15.

I am truly glad you like Humboldt's letters so much. How necessary for appreciation of a book, scene, picture, society, is a certain previous adaptation of the frame of mind! Do you remember how little you cared for that book the first time of reading it in a smaller form? Experience, added light, and the aspect given by events which no purpose or control could have arranged, have given it now fresh meaning and made it a new book.

The difference which you remark between the moral effects of those two places is curious. The contemplative *genius loci* of the one I can comprehend, though it always impelled me to action, exercise, and excursions; but the activity-exciting spirit of the other place I less readily can conceive. There is a certain sombreness there which rather invites to sadness, unless you rush to action in self-defence; and perhaps the air of civilization reminds you there that you are in a world where the law is, Be busy about something. Now in a state of savagery or anywhere that the march of contrivance and the teeming numbers of population urging to industry are shut out, life can more readily become a dream, — a melancholy, but tender, and not rude dream.

Here in this place I find much altered: most of my intimate acquaintances are gone, married, buried, or estranged.

LXXI.

Cheltenham.

Light reading and visiting old acquaintances have been my sole occupation here. I have finished "Ruth" and "Villette," and several of Sir Walter Scott's, and am much struck by the marked difference between the fiction of his day and ours; the effect produced is very opposite. From those of Scott you rise with a vigorous, healthy tone of feeling; from the others, with that sense of exhaustion and a weakness which comes from feeling stirred up to end in nothing. Scott's narratives run smoothly on with a profusion of information respecting the outer life of the days which he describes, — the manners, customs, dress, modes of thought, and general feeling; but you have no glances into the inner life, — no throes and convulsions of conscience, — no conflicts of Duty with Inclination, — no mysteries of a soul treading wilfully, or compelled by circumstances, the dangerous, narrow borderland between right and wrong. Partly this is accounted for by the fact that in his stirring times life was an outer thing, and men were not forced into those mysterious problems which are pressing for solution now; and partly by another fact, that women have since then taken the lead in the world of literature, and imparted to fiction a new character. They are trying to *aborder* questions which men had looked upon as settled; and this might have been expected, from their being less able to understand or recognize the authority of statute law and conventional moralities than men, and much less disposed to acknowledge their eternal obligation, and also much more quick to feel the stirring laws of nature, — mysterious, dim, but yet, in their way, even more sacred. The result of this has been that questions which men would rather have left unexamined, or else approached with coarseness, are now the staple subjects of our modern fiction, — "Jane Eyre," "Villette," "Ruth," and many things in Margaret Fuller's writings; these, with the works of several American writers, as Hawthorne, in whom, though men, the woman-movement has worked deeply, are the most remarkable of our modern novels, and characterize the commencement of an epoch. That great question, how far conventional law is to stifle the workings of inclination, and how far inclination — supposing it to be sacred and from our higher nature — is justified in bidding it defiance, what a wide field that opens! It is a perilous question, and opens a door for boundless evil as well as good.

The French writers have said, as usual, with the full license of a nation to whom Duty has no meaning, that the door is to be wide as hell; "Evil, be thou my good," seems to be the watchword of those that I have read. If they are right, God is a Being whose existence is as superfluous as a devil's. A sense of horrible materialism steals over me in reading their attempts to solve the problem, and the laws of materialism seem the only ones left to guide man. The " constitution of man " must replace the prophets, and a study of the cerebral laws of organization sweep away the sanctions both of the Law and the Gospel. Mesmerism and Electro-biology must take the place of the New Testament, and *les beaux sentiments* become our compass instead of the Book of Life. Happily, the English novelists have approached the question with purer instincts and a more severely moral tone, — witness "Jane Eyre" and "Ruth"; and yet they do open the question, and I rejoice to see it opened: yes, and more, — opened by women; for I despair of men ever doing it with justice. The new divorce law, as proposed, refuses to the woman the right to divorce her husband, let his crimes be what they may, unless he adds brutal ill-treatment of her to crime. What hope is there from such a social state of feeling?

The worst, however, of the new tone in novel-writing is that it sets one thinking in a way that can find no vent in action, and makes one dissatisfied with existing errors and institutions, without the slightest possibility of altering them; nay, or even knowing what alteration to desire. The result of this becoming general, may, perhaps, produce a restlessness, which will issue in improvement; meantime, each must be content to bear his share of the unsatisfied restlessness which is hereafter to find such issue.

I am not well: I am suffering much, but it is of no use to talk about it. Nothing can be done except by attacking symptoms, and that is useless. The causes are irremediable, and they must go on working to their consummation.

LXXII.

Cheltenham.

To-morrow, by the early express, I return to work. I wish I could take another fortnight, for this rest has only done partial good. The chief good it has done me is in having showed me much more of stanch affection, unchilled through six years' absence, than I supposed was to be found in this light place. Certainly I have been surprised to find how warmly and truly many have cherished the remembrance of me. Five men here I have found steady as steel to the magnet; and that, out of so few who remain, is a large number, — all laymen.

It is not necessary to say that absence from Brighton is now impossible for some months to come; by August I shall be thoroughly tired again, I fear, — nay, if I were to search for a word to exactly express what I feel now, mentally and physically, I should select "shattered." In a literary point of view, I find Sir Walter Scott the most healthful restorative of any. There was no morbid spot in that strong, manly heart and nature.

Brighton.

What a valuable gift it is to be able to take up the thread of thought as if it had never been broken! Scott had it. He would dictate two novels and to two amanuenses at once. With me a broken flow of thought will not gush again. I began with my mind full of thoughts. Now, after a long interruption, I feel exhausted and dissipated: the thing is gone from me, as the simple writers of early days expressed it. Moreover, the splitting headache has come back again: it returned on Saturday, as soon as I began to work; and on Sunday I could scarcely see for pain. I only took the morning pulpit, and preached an old Cheltenham sermon. All the evening I spent lying on the ground, my head resting on a chair.

I have been reading "My Novel," — the first volume only

as yet, — the only work in the form of a tale I ever read which succeeded in introducing moral and political discussion, and even making the work practical by their introduction, without being tedious, tempting the reader to skip the politics and take the story; even "Coningsby" failed in this. "My Novel" weaves the tale and the doctrines inseparably together, and in a really masterly way. The discussion of the Parson and Riccabocca with Linney respecting the pamphlet with the motto "Knowledge is power," is very clever and interesting. The book breathes a sound, healthy tone of feeling, very different from Bulwer Lytton's earlier works. For instance, in page 204: "He had been brought up from his cradle in simple love and reverence for the Divine Father and the tender Saviour, — Whose life, beyond all record of human goodness, — Whose death, beyond all epics of mortal heroism, no being whose infancy has been taught to supplicate the Merciful and adore the Holy, — yea, even though his later life may be entangled amid the storms of dissolute pyrrhonism, — can ever hear reviled and scoffed without a shock to the conscience and a revolt to the heart."

Bulwer's mental career is a very peculiar one. Generally minds exhaust themselves, — the wines first, the lees afterwards; witness Sir Walter Scott after many years. But his was a strong nature. Commonly the indications of running dry, or repeating old views and character under new forms, show themselves after one or two works: in the lady novelists this is very conspicuously so, — so, too, in Hawthorne; in the voluminous James, of course. But here is Bulwer coming out with his last two novels as fresh and different from each other, and as racy and original, as if he had never written anything before.

LXXIII.

MY DEAR ——: — I have read gratefully your most eloquent letter: but for the life of me I cannot make out the exact practical upshot of it. Beyond the direction to consult a "finger-post physician," I read it through again and again for guidance in vain.

Well, as to that, I have not been so foolish as not to have done it long ago. I paid three guineas foolishly, to three leading London physicians for an opinion. The first (——) prescribed, I forget what,—some hash or other; the second threatened "organic collapse of the brain," and refused to prescribe anything save entire and total cessation from the pulpit for life. The third (——) recommended *lettuce!*

Here Taylor recommended opiates. Allen Whitehouse, a man I have profound confidence in, says that all medicaments in my case are charlatanry. In Cheltenham, the only man I would trust in this particular case was away. A personal friend, a homœopathic physician, amused himself with giving me microscopic points of aconite, to my benevolent enjoyment of his credulity. They can do nothing, and they all tell me so; only they disagree as to the amount of danger. One hinted idiotcy. Others advised relaxed toil. Now, as I *cannot* toil, and do so no longer, this advice is in vain.

A curious circumstance occurred yesterday. A member of the Trinity congregation, a chemist, fancied galvanism would do me good, and kindly offered his battery for my use one hour a day. I called to thank him and decline the offer. But in conversation he persuaded me just to go and look at his apparatus. I took the ends of the wire, completed the circuit, and experienced the usual pleasurable tingling. Then holding it in one hand, and he holding the other wire in his, he touched the back of my head and neck, where I have lately felt pain and numbness. Not a sensation did it elicit, though the spot which is generally, he says, most sensitive. Then he touched my forehead. It was but for a second. Instantly a crashing pain shot through as if my skull was stove in, and a bolt of fire were burning through and through. I sprang to my feet, stood for a second or two wild with pain, and then sank down, and should have had another lady-like-swoon, if he had not run to the shop and fetched some poignant aromatic. He seemed much astonished, frightened, and perplexed at what had taken place. I was not surprised. I knew that something was wrong there. Allen thinks nothing organically, as yet (I have not told him this); but the sensations are very strange and startling which I experience in twenty-four hours. It has nothing to do with "tic," which always attacks the chest, &c., &c. The worst sensation now is numbness in the neck.

You will perhaps think me a hypochondriac. But a man who knits his teeth together in solitude for hours, without a groan, in torture, and is guilty of nothing effeminate except fainting, and upon whose life a sentence of death for to-morrow would scarcely bring any other words than *Nunc dimittis*, is hardly hypochondriacal. Nevertheless, it is my conviction that my work is done. I do not mean my life; that may drag on for many years to come; but all that makes life worth the having, and which certainly I had once, — *power*. What would you have me do? I go through as little work as possible, nor could I diminish except by totally giving up. Give up I cannot, because I cannot afford it; among other reasons, my generous congregation have munificently put funds at my disposal which will enable me to provide a curate's assistance for two years, — so that is a great step, and I have thought it right to accept their offer. But I acknowledge that the sensations of brain by day and night now are so new, strange, and unnatural, that I feel they have only contrived, by their kindness, to keep among them a worn-out Chelsea pensioner, with leave to wear a red-coat and play at shouldering arms.

You mistook me in thinking I did not sympathize. A few years ago, when I felt less, you would have been more satisfied when the eyes showed moisture, the voice emotion, and when I had a gentler manner and a more ready show of responding to what was expected. Now, a certain amount of iron has got into my blood; and a sardonic sentence often conceals the fact that I wince to the very quick from something that has gone home.

> O, many a shaft at random sent
> Finds mark the archer little meant!

I no longer wear my heart upon my sleeve, "for daws to peck at." But there is not a conversation, there is not a book I read, there is not a visit I pay, that does not cut deep traces in the "Calais" of my heart.

LXXIV.

I answer some of your questions: 1 Cor. ix. 27. "Cast away." The meaning is,—Lest after having preached to others the doctrine of self-abridgment of indulgences in things lawful, I myself should fail when put to the test; literally, should be that which will not stand proof. The advice to abstain from things lawful, he gave them in the eighth chapter, — see verses 9 and 13; then, in chapter ix., he shows that he had only done what he advised; he had a right to a wife (verse 5), and a right to be supported by pay; but he had abridged himself of both these rights (though every principle of the Old Testament, chapter ix. 8, . . . 13, 14, established his right), simply in order to be beyond suspicion and gain the more to Christ. Read the two chapters viii. and ix. as one argument, and the whole will become intelligible. "If there be any virtue:"—"if," &c., is not an oddly-constructed phrase; it is purely classical Greek. It means whatever is virtuous, praiseworthy, &c., think upon such things. An old poet writes, "nor if old Anacreon wrote aught sportively has time destroyed it." He does not mean to hazard a doubt, but simply to say, whatever Anacreon wrote is undestroyed. It is a Greek idiom, and only sounds curious in English.

You would not like ——'s preaching. It is not what it

was once, — concise, sinewy, masculine, and clear as crystal, defying any listener to suspend attention. He has degenerated into verbiage; and in the last sermon I heard, he took ten minutes to say what three sentences might have settled. He has lost his power, which was once the greatest I ever knew. The sentimental people of his congregation attribute it to an increase in spirituality; but it is, in truth, a falling-off of energy of grasp. I heard four sermons from him with scarcely four thoughts, and much absolutely false logic. But how can a man preach for ten years without exhausting himself, or else pandering to popularity? Talk, talk, talk forever, and no retreat to fructifying silence!

That is a well-put criticism you quote respecting Currer Bell. Her talk is of duty, her sympathies lie with passion. And the dangers of that style of composition are great; but she never blinks the question of right and wrong, and her right is of a stern order, though her wrong may be very tempting. In point of power she is a giant to the authoress of "Ruth," but her book is less sweet and human.

Poor ——! how bounded every life seems, judged as we judge; yet the results are forever; and, as it has been again and again declared, the deepest philosophy in the universe is repeated in every cubic inch, and all the laws of the ocean in a cup of tea, — why not be satisfied, then, with the cup of tea whose sphere is not absolutely illimitable?

LXXV.

I have found pain a humbling thing, and, what surprises me, certainly not a souring one. Many and many an hour have I spent lately incapable of even conceiving enjoyment or pleasure, and feeling as if youth and hope were settling down into premature decrepitude, my very limbs having shrunk to the dimensions of Shakespeare's lean and slippered pantaloon; and yet I am grateful to say that not for years has the feeling been so true or mixed with so little bitterness. "Not as I will."

On Sunday, after service, a lady came up to me whom I had known in the very outset of my ministry. She talked with me of the past; and then said, with tears, "But, O, you are so changed in mind, it is quite heart-aching to hear you preach: it was no longer the bright, happy Mr. Robertson." The truth is, I had been preaching on St. Paul's thorn in the flesh, and this would partly account for what she remarked. Yet conversation with her brought back those days at Winchester strongly, and I felt that she was right, and that the shadows of life had settled down. Yet is not this the common experience for the first four-fifths of life at least?

> Knowledge comes, but Wisdom lingers, and he bears a laden breast,
> Full of sad experience moving towards the stillness of his rest.

LXXVI.

I must acknowledge the truth of what you say, in the main, that I do not admire any one who is not in robust health. Of course I must bate a little exaggeration in the form of statement; but I acknowledge that I think health more beautiful than ill-health, and a normal state more pleasant than an abnormal. There may be some apparent exceptions to the rule, as in the case of recovery from illness there is a certain delicacy which is very attractive; but then it is the first flush of health that gives the beauty, just like that which makes spring more interesting than summer. Still it is not merely delicacy that is beautiful, but delicacy pervaded by health and conquered by it, — life in its first, fresh rising, like a new childhood; but I acknowledge that I cannot acquire the sickly taste of admiring the delicacy of ill-health. Beauty, in my eyes, depends much upon association; and delicacy that calls up one's knowledge of morbid anatomy, and suggests the thought of disordered functions, and abnormal states, and physicians' attendance, never affects me with a sense of beauty. This may be an unfashionable view, but I am certain it is a sound and healthy one, fresh from Nature's heart. The other taste is of the same family as that which makes the Chinese admire feet quashed into smallness. I admire refinement in a female form; but the moment that it appears as the result of ill-health, I reject it as a counterfeit. For this reason I cannot even admire the hectic of consumption; it puts me in mind at once of glaring eyes and panting breath, and I see what will be. I have a fastidiousness of taste in this respect, almost painful, and I acknowledge that I admire the beauty which God made — health — immeasurably above the counterfeit which man procures. A country girl, modest and neat, is not my *beau idéal* of beauty; but I admire her far more than a pale, languid girl of fashion, just as I like brown bread better than bled-white veal; but I think you are much mistaken if you mean by delicacy that I do not admire refinement. I cannot admire anything that reminds one of the "mould above the rose," and forces upon one the question, whether an allopathic or homœopathic druggist could best get rid of that delicate look. I delight not in anything unnatural or diseased. Lord Byron has well described this unhealthy taste about beauty, in his description of the Spanish ladies, as compared with the "languid, wan, and weak" forms of others.

I rejoice that you like Wordsworth's "Life." Badly and coldly as it is written, the extracts from his own letters give some insight into his inner life. And it seems to me, in reading lives, the question too often is, whether it be one which in all respects answers our ideal of a life; whereas the question ought to be, whether it has strongly exhibited some side or other of our manifold and many-sided life. I am satisfied with One life, — with One ideal, and I read all others to understand that, by illustration or contrasts of their whole to parts of it. Now Wordsworth throws some light on its purely contemplative side. The life of Action and Sacrifice is wanting, but I can find those in various forms,—in Wellington's life, or women's, &c.

My life for the last few weeks has been one of perpetual pain,—forced to work, and forced to mix with people, and to talk, when it has taken me actually, only two days ago, an hour and a quarter to crawl, by back streets, from Kemp Town, in suffering all the way; and now at this moment languor makes me stop in writing after every third line. If my congregation had not come forward so generously, and if I had not received so many letters full of kindness, containing expressions of pain and regret about my looks, &c., I should, I verily think, have given up work entirely, so hardly does it press upon me, and so much that is painful have I had to submit to. But their warmth has settled the question and left me no alternative, and I must work on as long as I have strength for it.

CHAPTER IV.

JUNE, JULY, AUGUST, 1853.

Mr. Robertson leaves Trinity Chapel forever. — The Controversy with the Vicar of Brighton. — The last sad Months. — His Death and Burial.

THE last few months of Mr. Robertson's life were not passed in peace. A blow was dealt him by one to whom his courtesy had been invariable, and dealt him at a time when its stroke was fatal. The Rev. H. M. Wagner, the Vicar of Brighton, refused, from personal *pique* against Mr. Tower, to allow of his nomination as curate to Trinity Chapel, unless under conditions which Mr. Robertson refused even to propose to Mr. Tower. There was nothing for Mr. Robertson to do but submit; but that submission hastened his death. It was imperative that he should have rest. In his letter to the Vicar he urged not only his friend's cause, but the opinion of the doctors, that without help his own health must finally give way. The Vicar replied that his objection was conscientious and final; and yet this objection rested on the single circumstance that two years before Mr. Tower had resisted the Vicar's will, not on a religious, but on a financial question. "You will agree with me," writes Mr. Robertson in his published letter to the Committee, "that this conduct leaves me without an alternative. I will not trust myself to characterize it as I feel it, for strong sense of wrong makes a man prone to use strong words. It is enough to say quietly, using the mildest terms which are consistent with truth, that by a discourteous and ungenerous exercise of legal power, and by the rude manner in which I was personally treated, and of which I have said nothing in this letter, the Vicar has put it out of my power to offer another nominee, or to accept any favors at his hands. I owe this both to my friend's character and to myself. There remains for me nothing but to go on with my work single-handed as long as I am able."

Undeterred by the tone of this letter, Mr. Wagner wrote to ask Mr. Robertson to name another curate. This proposition was the last stroke. It was answered by the following dignified and forcible refusal.

60 Montpelier Road: June 22, 1853.

REVEREND SIR:—I have to acknowledge the receipt of your note of the 18th instant, in which you recommend me to present another nominee for your approval, and offer to find some one to supply his place till appointed.

I regret that I cannot reciprocate the bland tone of this last communication; for I confess that patronizing offers of favor seem to me out of place, when that which is asked for, and still peremptorily refused, is the redress of a wrong. And I regret to find that you view the matter between us, your own part in it in particular, in a much more light and easy way than that in which any one else will see it. Suffer me to be explicit; for the forbearance of my first letter having been unappreciated, I am compelled to speak English that cannot be misunderstood.

I cannot offer another nominee; nor is it in my power to accept at your hands the favor of any aid such as you offer.

I will examine, first, the objection against Mr. Tower, and how far it is possible for me to pass smoothly by the rejection of my friend, and receive a favor from his rejector.

The charge, as I collect it from your words, assumes two shapes: —

1. Unbecoming behavior in interfering with the affairs of the Lewes Deanery Branch of the Society for Promoting Christian Knowledge, — a society established in your parish.

2. Unbecoming conduct towards yourself.

With respect to the first, it must be remembered that, though Brighton be the head-quarters of the Branch Society, and the Vicar of Brighton at present chairman, it is not a Brighton Society, but one belonging to the whole Deanery of Lewes, and that, as a clergyman of the Deanery, and member of the Committee, Mr. Tower had an equal right with yourself to move any measure he thought right. It is as incorrect to imply that he interfered with a parochial society, or the prerogatives of the Vicar of Brighton, as it is unjust to insinuate that, as a curate, he took too much upon him. The country clergy *gave* him — he did not *assume* — a leading part in the discussion, because he was furnished with considerable information from the Parent Society.

Secondly. With respect to Mr. Tower's personal conduct to yourself. An overwhelming majority of the Committee, — all, indeed, I believe, except those who are bound by some personal tie to yourself, and, therefore, perhaps naturally, feel with you, — are prepared to assert that Mr. Tower's conduct on those occasions was that of a Christian and a gentleman. If necessary, I shall call for that testimony. I *could* call for more, but I have no wish for recrimination.

For the question is not, after all, whether Mr. Tower spoke warmly to you, or you to him, nor whether Mr. Tower was right or wrong in the course which he, at least, pursued conscientiously; but the question is, whether that course was sufficient ground for permanent unforgivingness on your part, and whether such offences as a personal difference with yourself, and interference in a favorite society of your own, admitting them to have existed to their fullest extent, are just grounds for the rejection of one whom you yourself admit to be in conduct and doctrine an exemplary Christian minister. No bishop would exclude from his diocese on such grounds; if he did, all England would ring with the news of the transaction.

I will now advert, with much regret, to your treatment of myself, which will account for my inability to adopt suddenly the suave tone of your last communication. I fix on a single instance.

On Trinity Sunday, during our first accidental interview between services, I told you several times that I was desirous of postponing the subject of the curacy till the morrow, and anxious to return home, as I had to prepare for the duties of the afternoon pulpit, and was much pressed for time. In spite of this, within half an hour you abruptly and unnecessarily invaded a privacy which you knew I had such anxious reasons to keep calm and sacred from interruption; and with yourself you forced upon me as a witness a gentleman personally unknown to me. The witness system, in a conversation between gentlemen, used by you to me even more offensively on a previous occasion, is in itself a very objectionable proceeding. It is scarcely necessary to say that the interruption incapacitated me from addressing my congregation on the intended subject.

I select this fact, not because it is the only instance, by many, of your discourtesy, but because your own witness was present. These are not supposed to be the manners of civilized society; nor can the grievance of them be obliterated by a few smooth lines, not of apology, but of patronage. It is curious to see with what marvellously different degrees of tenacity men retain the recollection of their own discourtesy to others; and that of others towards them. At the end of a couple of weeks, all that you said and did to me seems to have vanished from your mind; — at the end of two years, Mr. Tower's so-called transgression against yourself is as indelible as ever.

I much regret that it is my duty to write thus plainly, because I foresee that the publication of this letter may be necessary, — the right of doing which I reserve to myself; more especially as your uncalled-for offer to supply my pulpit may give a fallacious aspect to the whole affair, unless I very distinctly show what the question at issue is, and what it is not.

I can offer no other nominee, because I cannot admit your right of rejection on personal grounds. I am informed that you have a legal right; but I believe the whole world will deny your moral right. I know that, as you have stated, you are irresponsible by law, and can reject without assigning a reason. But irresponsibility is one thing in despotic Russia, and another thing in free England. No man can be irresponsible to public judgment in the exercise of a solemn public trust.

Nor can I subject another friend to the chance of your discovering, as in Mr. Macleane's case, a ground of objection in the circumstance of his taking pupils; or, as in Mr. Tower's case, in the fact of his having had the misfortune to vote against you an indefinite number of years ago. Lastly, I will not subject any gentleman again to the indignity of being asked for guarantees for conduct, or willingness to support, blindfold, the particular societies which you choose to name.

I have the honor to be, Reverend Sir,
Your obedient servant,
FRED. W. ROBERTSON.

Mr. Wagner won his legal victory. Mr. Robertson gave up the contest, and went home to die. He could bear no more. The endless committee meetings and correspondence harassed a frame already worn out, and all chance of recovery became hopeless.

I am really and seriously unwell (he writes); more so, I

think, than even the doctors say; for the prostration of every kind of power has been too complete and too permanent to mean nothing, as there is no distinct cause. Do not put it down to hypochondria. I can endure any pain, and am not afraid of any future; but the entire inability to do any work, physical or mental, without exhaustion which is intolerable, appals me. To such suffering as I have borne for months death would be a very welcome relief.

No defence worthy of the name was put forward by Mr. Wagner. No one can say that he knew what he was doing, or had any idea of what Mr. Robertson would suffer; it was incapability, not animosity, of feeling. He did not know that his brother minister was dying, but he did believe that his own dignity had been hurt; and, alas! he could not see that there are times when the resentment of a personal injury is a public injustice, and the exercise of a legal right a moral wrong.

Nevertheless, as if these excuses had not existed, the indignation in Brighton was extreme. To so great a height, indeed, did it rise, that assuredly, had he known of it, Mr. Robertson would have endeavored to check its violence; but he was closely confined to his room, — forbidden either to read the papers or to see his friends. It was all over for him, — happily enough; the ceaseless contest against underhand slander on one side, and open opposition on the other. Little did he now care for the gentlest praise or the loudest blame. It was a curious and sorrowful contrast to turn from Brighton and its excitement on this matter, — from the papers in columns of which appeared letter after letter, some violent, some satirical, and few moderate, — from the angry discussions in public and in private, every one almost taking one side or another, — to turn from these things and enter the stillness of the sick-room, where the unwilling cause of all this lay, his life ebbing slowly from him in bitter and unremitting pain.

The only history which can be given of the last two sad months of his life is from his own pen, in the following short and hurried letters. Nothing can be more pitiable to look at than the handwriting. Few men wrote so clear and fair a hand. But the last ten or twelve of these records would seem to have been written by one who had just been delivered from the rack. Every stroke of the pen zigzags with the feebleness of pain: —

June 20.

I received your letter this morning with many thanks. I am unfit to write, though a trifle better. I have scarcely manhood enough to hold a pen. I was forbidden to do any duty yesterday, and spent the day in listlessness and semi-dozing. The Confirmation candidates must be prepared, and it is my duty. They may be empty, unmeaning girls, — but so most girls are, — and among people of this character the chief part of ministerial work lies, for the simple reason that others are the exception: and if we are only to teach and preach to those who have much meaning in them, I fear schools and churches must be shut up. If I prepare them now, I may get away with a better grace in August; if not, I must either return a little after that time, or leave this important part of my duty at sixes and sevens, with a fair cause for grumbling on the part of parents, and for running all over the town to different clergymen to prepare them, subject to the question in each case, "Why does not your own minister prepare them?" Now it is foolish to defy public opinion. Prime Ministers cannot do it: the only man who can is the man who has neither profession nor public duty. Every one else has to pay a certain price for his office, from the throne to the parish-constable, and he must either submit to those restrictions and penalties, however galling, which are shared by all, or else give up his office.

I do dislike Brighton, but it is my present sphere, and I must make the best of it. The ministry is nowhere a bed of roses; and if there were so delectable a spot, it is not open for me to change to instead of this. It is a wise man's duty to try to work within his limitations in the best way he can, and grumble as little as possible: or else cut himself asunder at once from all restrictions and obligations, by giving up his sphere of work entirely. What makes it, too, all the more difficult in my case is, that I am a marked man: and whether it be notoriety or popularity, no one on whom others' eyes are fixed in affection, or in malicious watchfulness for a false step, can emancipate himself from the necessity of caution, or take his own will for his law, when Will merely means unbridled course of inclination. Duty must cut public opinion boldly against the grain, if necessary; but if any one assumes for inclination the same rights, and does what he likes because he likes, in defiance of public opinion, he must first secure the indemnity accorded to unfeigned eccentricity, or else must pay the penalty without murmuring. Now I acknowledge I am not invulnerable to slanders, — I know no one who is, — nor am I a man to whom the world will accord impunity. Even in to-day's *Gazette* there is a long, vulgar, dull lampoon upon my views, which, wretched and ignorant as it is, is yet irritating.

July 2.

Thank you for your kind invitation to go to your house, but I had hoped to be well enough to go through the Confirmation work. Since then I do not think you have any idea how ill I have been. Even yesterday it took me fifty-five minutes, with rests, to walk to the Vales; I could not walk back. A tradesman, unknown, came out and offered me a seat in his shop. A poor man offered me his arm; and so my looks cannot have been either fascinating or herculean. Life has been for a month one long pain and languor; the lower extremities were partially paralyzed, so that I drag them after me. At night, sleepless pain; by day, change of powerlessness from two chairs to the sofa, and from the sofa to the ground.

I am not a bit stronger or better, except that I can sit up and write. Recovery is much more tedious than I expected, still I hope to be all right before long. Sometimes, in powerless moments, I am tempted to think that my work is done; I do not mean life, for that will go on long enough, but all work of thought, energy, — all except the mean work of attending to health. At other times things do not look so bad. Anyhow, the lesson that *will* get itself learnt is a good one; and the truest view of life has always seemed to me to be that which shows that we are here not to enjoy but to learn.

July 8.

I send you a letter of Faraday's, published in "The Times," which gave me pleasure, because it assigns, almost in my words, precisely the same origin to table-turning, &c., which I had discovered; because, too, the principle of the test invented by Faraday is exactly the same as that which I applied to Rutter's imaginary discovery, and because his remarks at the end coincide with the opinion which I have so often expressed about the false and ignorant state of the public mind which these endless credulities and restlessnesses betokened. On this I could, and some day will, say much, but I can scarcely get strength to guide my pen. I am sentenced finally to abstinence from duty for six months. The lower extremities, for several days, were in a state of semi-paralysis, but Taylor said:—"We think we can make a cure of you, but you will have hard work; you are thoroughly broken." Nevertheless, I am better, having had four Sundays' rest.

Pray let me have Faraday's letter back again. It did me more good than blisters, morphine, quinine, steel, or anything else which they give me. Sound, genuine, healthy, scientific truth, instead of the sickly craving after mysteries and preternaturalism that marks the idler classes now. It is the same state of feeling as that blamed in Scripture, as "the seeking after wizards that peep and mutter," "seeking after a sign," &c., — a state neither scientific nor religious.

Almost to the last he did not expect to die. No one, however, can feel otherwise than thankful that God mercifully emancipated him, for his brain was mortally injured. The disease was supposed to be abscess in the cerebellum.

He became at times partially paralyzed, and his emaciation was as pitiful as his infantile feebleness. The pain he endured was so intense that even he said, "I would not pass the horrors of last night again for half a lifetime." But worse to him than the pain was the prostration of all mental force, the obliteration of large spaces from the memory, and the loss of all power of attention. He retained, however, to the last his deep delight in the beauty of God's world. He got up once, when scarcely able to move, at four o'clock, and crept to the window "to see the beautiful morning." His hope and trust in his Heavenly Father never failed during this dreadful time. He felt assured of his immortality in Christ. A night or two before he died he dreamt that his two sisters, long since dead, came to crown him. "I saw them," he said, earnestly. Nothing could be more touching than his patience, thoughtfulness for others, and the exquisite and tender gratitude which he showed towards those who attended on him.

Those who had injured him he not only forgave, but

was anxious that all justice should be done them. At the very moment when all around thought that he was dying, he asked, in reference to Mr. Wagner, "Is there anything printed which requires my interference?"

Now and then he rallied, slept a little, and woke, as he said, "bathed in the morning sunshine, and feeling that recovery was possible." At these moments his healthy temperament reasserted itself, and he seems to have wished to live longer.

The following letter was written in the beginning of August; but the rally he mentions was but temporary. The terrible pain baffled every effort of the physicians, and he sank rapidly from day to day: —

August.

I take advantage of the first rally to write a few lines to you to give an account of myself. Yesterday, after a few hours' sleep, I had a sudden and surprising rally; and though I am as weak as water, and can scarcely move a few yards without sighing and sobbing like a baby, I do trust in God I have turned the corner. Such an illness I never had before, and hope never to have again. For twenty-four hours I thought all was over, and Dr. Allen frankly told me he had ceased to be sanguine of my recovery.

2, P. M.

I was obliged to give up writing from exhaustion. I try again. How far the brain is injured God only knows. It is the great *ganglia* or bunches of nerves which are at the roots of the brain that are affected. For many days I have not stirred from my bed, and a hideous-looking ourang-outang I am. Taylor, Whitehouse, Allen,—the latter twice, Taylor once,— every day; and, as if that were not enough, they have sent for Watson from town. He will be here this evening. God has treated me very mercifully. That I have felt in the direst pain and deepest exhaustion,— the house filled with delicacies, presents which I cannot use, however. How different from the lot of Him who would fain "have slaked his morning hunger on green figs!" I have not been allowed to see any one. Lady Byron left a sick-bed ten days ago to come to see me, and I have only once conversed with her for three minutes. Again I am dizzy, and must stop. I am broken as I never was before; but by God's mercy I may recover permanently now, — nay, even rapidly.

August 12.

I have grown worse and worse every day for the last fortnight. From intensity of suffering in the brain, and utter powerlessness and prostration too dreadful to describe, and the acknowledged anxiety of the medical men, I think now that I shall not get over this. His will be done! I write in torture.

These were the last words he ever wrote. Three days afterwards, on Sunday, the 15th of August, at the age of thirty-seven, — in the prime of early manhood, — he died. At his own chapel, that morning, when the rumor went round that there was no hope, and God was besought to hear the prayer for him and all sick persons, many wept bitterly; but the greater part of those who loved and venerated him were stunned beyond the power of weeping. That which they greatly feared had come upon them.

The same night his spirit left them. He had passed through the day without intenser suffering than usual. He was moved from his bed to the sofa, near the open window, where he lay until the evening. But towards ten o'clock a change took place. The pain returned with bitter violence. Feebly crying at intervals, "My God, my Father, — my God, my Father!" he lived for two hours in a mortal agony, during which he never lost clear consciousness. His mother, wife, and one friend, with his physician, watched over him with devoted care. At last they sought to relieve him by changing his position. But he could not endure a touch. "I cannot bear it," he said; "let me rest. I must die. Let God do His work." These were his last words. Immediately afterwards, at a few minutes past midnight, all was over.

So lived and so died, leaving behind him a great legacy of thought, a noble gentleman, a Christian minister. To the tenderness of a true woman he joined the strong will and the undaunted courage of a true man. With an intellect at home in all the intricacies of modern thought, he combined the simple spirit of a faithful follower of Christ. To daring speculation he united severe and practical labor among men. Living above the world, he did his work in the world. Ardently pursuing after liberty of thought, he never forgot the wise reticence of English conservatism. He preserved, amid a fashionable town, the old virtues of chivalry. In a very lonely and much-tried life he was never false or fearful. Dowered with great gifts of intellect, he was always humble; dowered with those gifts of the heart which are peculiarly perilous to their possessor, he never became their slave. He lived troubled on every side, yet not distressed : perplexed, but not in despair : persecuted, but not forsaken : cast down, but not destroyed : always bearing about in the body the dying of the Lord Jesus, that the life also of Jesus might be made manifest in his body. He died, giving up his spirit with his last words, in faith and resignation to his Father.

He lies in a hollow of the Downs he loved so well. The sound of the sea may be heard there in the distance; and, standing by his grave, it seems a fair and fitting requiem; for if its inquietude was the image of his outward life, its central calm is the image of his deep peace of activity in God. He sleeps well; and we, who are left alone with our love and his great result of work, cannot but rejoice that he has entered on his Father's rest.

HIS FUNERAL.

IT was wished by his surviving relatives that the funeral should be strictly private, but they could not resist the general desire of Brighton to record its sorrow. It was understood also that his congregation was anxious to express the feeling of its loss. The members of the local literary societies, of the Mechanics' Institute, the Athenæum, and the Manchester Unity of Odd Fellows, severally met, voted addresses of condolence to his family, and asked permission to walk in procession after the remains of their friend and teacher. The funeral took place on Monday, the 22d of August. It resembled more a public than a private mourning. All the shops along the way from Montpelier Road to the Extramural Cemetery, as well as many in the most frequented streets of Brighton, were closed. The pavements and balconies were crowded with sorrowing spectators. The principal townsmen assumed mourning. Two thousand persons pressed into the quiet cemetery.

There were united around his tomb, by a common sorrow and a common love, Jews, Unitarians, Roman Catholics, Quakers, and Churchmen; the workingmen, the tradesmen, and the rank and wealth of Brighton. For once — and it was a touching testimony to the reality of his work — all classes and all sects merged their differences in one deep feeling.

They have raised above him a simple and massive monument. On two of its sides there are bronze medallions, — one given by his congregation, the other by the workingmen of Brighton. They record, in touching words, the gratitude of thousands. A careful hand keeps, even in winter, flowers always blooming on his grave. They speak to many, who make their pilgrimage to the spot, of the fair immortality which is given to the faithful Soldier of Jesus Christ.

CHAPTER V.

Robertson's personal Appearance. — Is he to be judged from his Letters or his Sermons? — His passionate Heart and inquiring Intellect. — Necessity of Self-expression. — The Work of his Life. — Results of his Preaching; of his Labor among the Workingmen. — Results of his Life and Teaching as a Clergyman; as the Uniter of Parties; the fearless Speaker; the prudent Christian; the individual Thinker. — Accused of Latitudinarianism and Faithlessness to the Church of England. — The unexampled Circulation of his Sermons. — Recognition of the Value of his Work since his Death. — Subscription at his Funeral. — Bust erected in the Pavilion; in the Bodleian. — Memorial Window at Brazenose. — Farewell.

THE portrait at the beginning of this book gives but a very inadequate idea of Frederick Robertson's personal appearance. It is a photograph taken from a daguerrotype, and it has imparted a set and rigid form to features which were remarkable for their changing play of expression. The high and intellectual brow, strongly marked, suggested a thoughtful and an artistic nature; and the blue, deep-set eyes, full of a beautiful, pure light, flashing often with a bright and eager lightning of excitement or inquiry, told of the strangely-mingled qualities which lay within, — will, tenderness, and courage. The instinctive cheerfulness and sensitiveness of his temperament appeared in a mouth, the smile of which was as radiant as its mobile obedience to every change of emotion was wonderful. The same flexibility, brightness, and charm of character were expressed in his slight elastic form, which, capable of great activity and endurance, seemed to be always inspired with the fire of the thought which possessed him at the time.

The personal advantages with which he was endowed added to his effectiveness in the pulpit. Sometimes, however, they seemed to subtract from it. The very refined face and air, the peculiar — sometimes startling — modulations of the voice, the apparently studied manner, made many, who for the first time heard him preach, condemn him as an "exquisite," and fancy that he affected the theatrical graces of a popular preacher. It is impossible to conceive anything more abhorrent to his nature. For instance, he was accustomed, when commencing his closing address with the words "My Christian brothers," to lean forward and allow his right hand to hang carelessly over the desk. On seeing this characteristic attitude reproduced in one of the portraits made of him when at Brighton, he said to a friend, "Surely I am never guilty of that?" On being told that it was always adopted, he replied, "It shall never be so again." This anecdote marks the man. So far from using any conscious art, tricks of oratory, or effeminate mannerisms to recommend his preaching, he sternly checked the flow of his eloquence when it tended towards redundancy, and refrained even from instinctive gesture. So far from seeking popular admiration, he would have gladly accepted obscure work in an East-end parish, among the lowest poor, if circumstances had enabled him to leave Brighton.

It may be asked whether the truest idea of what he was can be gathered from his Letters or from his Sermons. The best reply is, that the Sermons picture what he strove to be, what he was when he felt and acted best, what he would have been had his life been less vexed, his heart less fiery, and his brain less attacked by disease. Of the Letters, some represent him in his happiest and most intellectual moments; others in times of physical weariness, when both intellect and heart were pained with trouble, and beset with questions too hard for him to solve completely; and a few, as in those written from the Tyrol, when his whole being was convulsed in the crisis of a great religious change. They relate his inward trials; his sermons bear witness to his contest and his victory. Only when both are read and balanced one against the other, can an adequate idea be formed of what he was. On account of the overstrained self-depreciation which sometimes possessed him, especially after the intellectual excitement of Sunday, it is not possible to take his own estimation of himself in his letters as representing the whole truth.

No man ought to be judged by a record of his own inner life, — no man ought to be judged entirely out of his own mouth. Far from being too lenient, men of Mr. Robertson's temper are too severe upon themselves. They write in deep pain, from the impulse of the moment; and then, when they have got rid of the pain by its expression, pass out of their study into an out-door life of such activity and vigor, that no one would imagine that an hour before they had been writing as if they were useless in their generation, and their existence a burden too galling to be borne.

On reading his correspondence, some may accuse him of indicating too strongly his loneliness and passionate desire of sympathy; they may call his fancies diseased, his complaints unmanly, and his transient doubts unchristian. But his faithlessness was but momentary: only the man who can become at one with Frederick Robertson's strange and manifold character, and can realize as he did the agony and sin of the world, — only the man who can feel the deepest pain, and the highest joy, as Robertson could have felt them, — has either the right or the capability of judging him. Doubts did pass across his mind, but they passed over it as clouds across the sun. The glowing heart which lay behind soon dissipated them by its warmth.

With regard to his passionate desires and his complaint, they were human, and would have been humanly wrong in him only if he had allowed them to gain predominance over his will, righteously bent all through his life, not on their extinction, but on their subjugation. The untroubled heart is not the deepest, the stern heart not the noblest, the heart which crushes all expression of its pain not that which can produce the most delicate sympathy, the most manifold teaching, or speak so as to give the greatest consolation. Had not Robertson often suffered, and suffered so much as to be unable sometimes not to suppress a cry, his sermons would never have been the deep source of comfort and of inspiration which they have proved to thousands. The very knowledge that one who worked out the voyage of his life so truly and so firmly, could so suffer and so declare his suffering, is calculated to console and strengthen many who endure partially his pain and loneliness, but who have not, as yet, resisted so victoriously; whose temperament is morbid, but who have not, as yet, subdued it to the loving and healthy cheerfulness of his Christian action.

Nor can those who should thus accuse him ever have conceived what that character is which *must* express itself, or ever have realized that there are times when expression is necessary if life is to continue. Such a necessity belongs almost always to the poetic temperament, and appears nowhere so much as in the Psalms. They are full of David's complaints against his destiny. They tell of his long and lonely nights, his tears, his sufferings at the hands of men, his doubts of Eternal Justice ; and it is through the relief afforded by this natural expression of impassioned feeling that he gains calm enough to see into "the way of the Lord," and to close his Psalms of sorrow with words of triumphant trust. It was just so with Frederick Robertson. The expression of his distress neither injured his manliness nor subtracted from his Christian faith. It was the safety-valve by which he freed himself from feeling under too high a pressure not to be dangerous, and brought himself into that balanced state in which active and profitable work is possible. One of the most important things to remark in his life is, that a man may *retain* high-wrought sentiment, passionate feelings, imaginations and longings almost too transcendental, a sensitiveness so extreme as to separate him from almost all sympathy, — and at the same time subdue all so as to do his Father's Will in the minutest as well as the largest duties. But I repeat, without the "timely utterance which gave his thoughts relief," he could not have been strong enough to do the work of his life, — a work distinctive and great, but the results of which do not lie so openly on the surface of society as to be manifest at once to the careless glance of the public. It is necessary, therefore, to close this book with some account of it.

The results of his preaching upon the intellectual men who attended his congregation have already been dwelt on. On those whose tendency was towards scepticism the effect of his sermons was remarkable. "I never hear him," said one, "without some doubt being removed, or some difficulty solved." Young men who had boasted publicly of doubts which were an inward terror to them, could not resist the attractive power of his teaching; and fled to him to disclose the history of their hearts, and to find sympathy and guidance. Nor was his influence less upon that large class whose religion grows primarily out of emotion; for he combined in himself two powers which generally weaken one another, — the power of close and abstract thinking, and the power of deep and intense feeling.

The most visible portion of the labor of his life was among the workingmen. He bound fifteen hundred of them together in a bond of mutual help; he united them — men of a class which is jealous of church interference — in reverence for his character as a minister and as a Christian man, while at the same time he invariably bade them look away from him to his Master.

This is a part of his work the results of which cannot be calculated. No one can tell, who has not had something to do with Mechanics' Institutes, what genius, patience, charity, and width of sympathy were necessary to achieve this. His lectures, and his mode of conducting the controversy with the radical party in the association, have had a wide and beneficial effect upon similar associations in England, not only as an inspiration to the men, but as a warning and a guide to the promoters and committees. The fearless confidence in truth and in human nature with which he met the socialistic difficulties and sceptical opinions among the working classes, has given to clergymen who come into contact with the same classes an example and a lesson for which they have to thank him.

Of all the small band who in 1848, '49, and '50, set themselves to remedy the evils which oppressed the poor mechanic, he has had the greatest influence. At that time he saw more clearly than the others both sides of the question. His conduct was wiser, but not less bold. While in other quarters the breach between rich and poor was at least temporarily widened, in Brighton it was narrowed. By patient explanation to both sides of the temptations and trials which beset the one or the other, and by showing that there *was* a bridge across the social gulf, he drew the divided classes together, and succeeded more than any man of his time in promoting their reconciliation. He was also one of the first and most active, though one of the most unknown, advocates of the rights of laboring men to all the means of acquiring knowledge; and he held up the banner of their rights at an epoch when it was most dangerous to his own peace to do so, and most profitable for them. But his fearlessness in the cause of all freedom and justice gave him the clear insight which sees the right moment to advance, even though, as in 1848, the confusion of battle may be at its height.

As a clergyman, by his clear elucidation of the

truths common to all, but lying beneath widely-differing forms of opinion, he has done much to bring about a spirit of religious union among the various parties of the Church. He has assisted, by his teaching, in the great work of this day, — the preservation of the Church of England as a church, in which all the members vary in views, mode of action, and character of teaching, but are one in faith, one in aim, and one in spirit; for he dreaded that genuine Low Churchism which seeks to force upon all the members of a church a set of limited opinions about illimitable truths.

As a clergyman he has also brought distinctly forward the duty of Fearlessness in speaking. "I desire for myself," he says, "that I may be true and fearless, but still more that I may mix gentleness and love with fearlessness." He was not one who held what are called liberal opinions in the study, but would not bring them into the pulpit. He did not waver between truth to himself and success in the world. He was offered advancement in the Church, if he would abate the strength of his expressions with regard to the Sabbath. He refused the proffer with sternness. Far beyond all the other perils which beset the Church was, he thought, this peril: that men who were set apart to speak the truth and to live above the world should substitute conventional opinions for eternal truths, — should prefer ease to conscience, and worldly honor to that which cometh from God only.

He has taught also by his ministerial life the duty and the practice of that Prudence which fitly balances courage. He was not one of the radicals of English polemics. His was not that spirit, too much in vogue at present among the so-called Liberal party, — the spirit of Carlstadt, and not of Luther; the spirit of men who blame their leaders for not being forward enough, who desire blindly to pull down the whole edifice of "effete opinions," and who, inspired by the ardor and by some of the folly of youth, think that they can at once root up the tares without rooting up the wheat also. Robertson, on the contrary, seems to have clearly seen, or at least to have acted as if he saw, that the question of true outward religious liberty in a national Church was to be solved in the same manner as England had solved the question of solid-set Political Liberty, — by holding on to the old as long as possible, so as to retain all its good; by never embarking in the new till it had become a necessity of the age; by "broadening slowly down from precedent to precedent," and by recognizing the universal truth hidden in that saying, "I have many things to say unto you, but ye cannot bear them now." He clung, for example, to certain theories which seem incongruous with the rest of his views, — which seem strange to many of us now, just because we forget that England and the Church are ten years older since his death. He refused to discuss thoroughly questions which we bring forward prominently. He purposed, for example, writing a book on Inspiration. He refrained; — "the mind of England," said he, "is not ready yet." But if he were alive now, he would write it. I have already said that he would never bring forward in the pulpit an opinion which was only fermenting in his mind. He waited till the must became wine. He endeavored, as far as in him lay, without sacrificing truth, not to shock by startling opinions the minds of those who were resting peacefully in an "early heaven and in happy views." He refrained in all things from violating a weak brother's conscience. He would have hated the vaunting way with which some put forward novel views. He would have hated the pharisaical liberalism which says, "God, I thank Thee I am not as other men are, even as this believer in the universality of the Flood, or that in the eternal obligation of the Jewish Sabbath." He would have disliked such a term as "free-handling"; and as strongly as he reprobated the irreverent boldness of those who speak as if they were at home in all the counsels of God, would he have blamed the irreverent license with which some writers have rushed at things held sacred by thousands of our fellow-Christians.

In one respect especially his life has a lesson for the Church of this time. He has shown that a well-marked individuality is possible in the English Church. The great disadvantage of a Church like ours, — with fixed traditions, with a fixed system of operation, with a theological education which is exceedingly conservative, with a manner of looking at general subjects from a fixed clerical point of view, with a bias to shelter and encourage certain definite modes of thinking, — is that under its government clergymen tend to become all of one pattern. It may be said, and with truth, that the advantages of our system more than balance this disadvantage. Nevertheless, it is a disadvantage which is becoming more and more felt by clergymen and recognized by laymen. And one of the strongest impulses which have given rise to the present theological struggle, is the desire of men in holy orders to become more distinctively individual. Robertson anticipated by some years this deep-set feeling. He was Himself, and not a fortuitous concurrence of other men. Owing to his individuality, he retained the freedom of action and the diversity of feeling which men not only in the Church, but in every profession and business, so miserably lose when they dress their minds in the fashion of current opinion, and look at the world, at nature, and at God, through the glass which custom so assiduously smokes.

Robertson preserved his independence of thought. He had a strong idiosyncrasy, and he let it loose within the bounds of law, — a law not imposed upon him from without by another, but freely chosen by himself as the best. He developed, without rejecting the help of others, his own character after his own fashion. He respected his own conscience; believed in his own native force, and in the divine fire within him. He looked first at everything submitted to his judgment as if it were a new thing upon earth, and then permitted the judgments of the past to have their due weight with him. He endeavored to receive, without the intervention of commentators, immediate impressions from the Bible. To these impressions he added the individual life of his own heart, and his knowledge of the life of the great world. He preached these impressions, and with a freedom, independence, variety, and influence which were the legitimate children of his individuality.

That men should, within the necessary limits, follow out their own character, and refuse to submit themselves to the common mould, is the foremost need of the age in which we live; and if the lesson which Robertson's life teaches in this respect can be received, if not by all, at least by his brethren, he will neither have acted nor taught in vain.

Of course, developing his own thoughts and life freely, he was charged by his opponents with faithlessness to the Church, and with latitudinarian opinions. But he rejoiced in finding within the Church of England room to expand his soul, and freedom for his intellect. He discovered the way to escape from the disadvantage I have mentioned, and yet to remain a true son of a Church which he loved and honored to the last. Moreover, he brought many into the Church of England: both Unitarians and Quakers, as well as men of other sects, were admitted by him into her communion. On the other hand, if the latter part of the accusation were true, and he was latitudinarian in opinion, it is at least remarkable that he should have induced in those who heard him profitably, not only a spiritual life, but also a high and punctilious morality. His hearers kept the Law all the better from being freed from the Law. And many a workingman in Brighton, many a business man in London, many a young officer, many a traveller upon the Continent, many a one living in the great world of politics or in the little world of fashion, can trace back to words heard in Trinity Chapel the creation in them of a loftier idea of moral action, and an abiding influence which has made their lives, in all their several spheres, if not religious, at least severely moral.

These are some of the results which have flowed, and will continue to flow, from his work and his life. They have been propagated by means of his published sermons. The extension of these sermons among *all* classes has been almost unexampled. Other sermons have had a larger circulation, but it has been confined within certain circles. These have been read and enjoyed by men of every sect and of every rank. They seem to come home to that human heart which lies beneath all our outward differences. Workingmen and women have spoken of them to me with delight. Clergymen of the most opposed views to his keep them in their bookcases and on their desks. Dissenting preachers speak of them with praise. Men of the business-world have written to say that they have felt in reading them that Christianity was a power and a life, and that its spirit was that of a sound mind. Men whose intellect has been wearied with our pulpit sameness or our pulpit sentiment, light upon them and read them through. All sections of the press — even those of such widely-separated principles as the "Guardian" and the "Westminster Review" — have expressed, even while they disagreed with their views, sympathy with their Christian feeling and noble thought. There has, however, been one conspicuous exception: the "Record" newspaper has been faithful to its nature.

Eleven editions of the first volume of his sermons have been published, nine of the second, and eight of the third.* In themselves, these figures bear testimony to the great acceptability of Mr. Robertson's teaching. But the value of his work has been otherwise recog-

---

* These sermons have reached their ninth edition in America, and the first three volumes have been produced in the Tauchnitz edition of English authors.

nized. At a meeting held immediately after his death, it was resolved to raise a subscription for the purpose of testifying, in some adequate manner, the reverence in which his friends held his worth, and the sympathy which they wished to offer to his family. In less than a fortnight, seven hundred pounds were raised, and placed in the hands of trustees for the benefit of his children. Of this sum Lady Byron contributed three hundred pounds. The two children, who are thus connected with the love and gratitude given to their father, are still alive to cherish his name and to rejoice in his far-spread influence. His daughter is named Ida Florence Geraldine Robertson; and his son, Charles Boyd Robertson, was educated at Harrow, and, through the instrumentality of the late Lord Carlisle, obtained a nomination from Earl Russell to the Foreign Office, which he entered in the January of this year.

Since his death, other public testimonies have been made to his memory. A gentleman who had found by chance upon a friend's table a volume of the sermons, was so touched by their beauty, that he commissioned a sculptor to execute for him a bust of the preacher. He presented this, with peculiar delicacy, to the Pavilion at Brighton, that the town in which Robertson had done the work of his life might have a lasting memorial of his presence. A few years ago, some men of his own college expressed their desire to erect in the chapel of Brazenose a window to his memory. A subscription was set on foot, many outside as well as within Oxford were glad to join in this graceful tribute, and the sun shines now through the letters of his name upon the spot where he dedicated his youth to God. Nor has the

University been unmindful of one whose powers of thinking were trained within its walls: among the marble images of the great men who are honored by a place in the Bodleian, his bust is also to be seen.

But far beyond these outward tributes of respect, a more perennial one than all, is the epistle written by this man of God upon our hearts. That which God had given him, he has left to us. His spirit lives again in others; his thoughts move many whom he never saw, on to noble ends. Unconsciously he blesses, and has blest. Yet not unconsciously now: I rejoice to think that now, at least, he is freed from the dark thought which oppressed his life,—that his ministry was a failure. I rejoice to think that he knows now— in that high Land where he is doing, with all his own vividness of heart, ampler work than his weary spirit could have done on earth—that his apparent defeat here was real Victory; that through him the Spirit of all Goodness has made men more true, more loving, and more pure. His books may perish, his memory fade, his opinions be superseded, as, in God's progressive education of the Universal Church, we learn to see more clearly into Truths whose relations are now obscure; but the Work which he has done upon human hearts is as imperishable as his own Immortality in God.

APPENDIX.

APPENDIX I.

DURING Mr. Robertson's tour in the Tyrol and his sojourn at Heidelberg in 1846, he wrote a series of letters recording daily and minutely all the events of his voyage, and the impressions he received. These letters were written to his wife. With her consent, portions of them were submitted to the Editor's judgment, and they appeared so useful, as elucidating a remarkable period of Mr. Robertson's life, that Mrs. Robertson was requested to permit their insertion. Being a connected account of one particular period of his life, and having more narrative than strictly biographical interest, it was considered best to present them to the public in an Appendix. To this Mrs. Robertson agreed, and she has kindly consented to the publication of the following extracts. In many ways they are extremely interesting. Those who will remember that they were written at a time when, as I have said, he was passing through the great mental and spiritual crisis of his life, will look through them, and not in vain, for hints as to the drift of his thoughts, and the direction in which his spirit was developing itself. They exhibit also his delight in natural scenery, and the delicate way in which he observed it. His reverence and love for Color appear in his descriptions. The rapidity with which he made his "course," the determination and contempt of pain which carried him, in spite of a strained sinew in his ankle, over twenty-six miles of mountain walking, belong to and illustrate his character. It is curious to see, with all his professed love of loneliness, how fresh his interest was in all classes of society; how he enchanted the German counsellor; how he drew round him, with his customary magic of manner, the rough shepherds of the Tyrol; how he charmed while he taught the English congregation at Heidelberg.

The two last letters, in which he expresses his disinclination to resume the work of his profession, need a slight comment. It is plain that that disinclination arose, not so much from dislike to ministerial work in itself, as from his experience of ministerial work *at Cheltenham*. For we find him pleased and happy in his professional labors at Heidelberg. He had been misunderstood, rejected, and pained at Cheltenham; and his was not the stern nature which could receive and carelessly shake off a blow. With his natural incapability of selfish feeling, he believes that his so-called "failure" at Cheltenham was his own fault. He thinks that he is not fit for work among the upper classes. But when I see him, in these letters, at Heidelberg, — emancipated, his own master, drawing round him the very class he believed himself unfit to teach, — attracting, by the atoning influence he always exercised, both Unitarians and Swedenborgians to the Church of England, — bringing young men to his feet, and awaking at once the intellect and the spirit of those who listened to him, — I begin to see *whose* fault it was if his ministry was a failure at Cheltenham; and I am deeply thankful that God did not permit His servant to enter the hidden country parish he desired, but placed him where he should suffer more and bear a sorer cross, but where also he was to be as a beacon set on a hill, whose light, warning, guiding, and inspiring, cannot be hid from men.

Patsch, near Innsbruck, Sept. 18, 1846.

I begin this letter from a small hamlet up high in the mountains near Innsbruck, where I intend to pass the night previous to an attempt to shoot a chamois. I have got a Tyrolese jäger or chasseur with me who knows the country well, and at half past four to-morrow morning we begin our work. But as the chamois are very rare now, and to get at them is exceedingly difficult, I cannot say that I have much hopes of success.

We spent three days in Munich together, in seeing the different collections which it contains of sculpture and painting. There are a few splendid statues and pictures, especially some of Rubens, whom I admire more and more. Certainly his faults are glaring and visible to all; but his genius is that of a giant; and when a man has to play with mountains as if they were balls, you do not expect elegance in his limbs. From Munich to Innsbruck I travelled with a young Frenchman and two Italians, the one a cardinal and the other apparently his secretary. These two spoke neither French nor German. We were much struck by seeing them for nearly an hour occupied in repeating the evening prayers from their breviaries. It seemed as if it would never be over. But the way in which they did it was exactly that of a school-boy humming over his lessons. They corrected one another when a mistake was made, smiled, took snuff, opened the windows, shut them down, had a few words of conversation now and then by way of interlude, — reminding me very strongly how inevitable a tendency there is in all forms, even the best, to lose all the spirit which once animated them, and become like lifeless corpses. No doubt those prayers were once the expression of true and fervid feeling. Now, a very cardinal can scarcely go through them without yawning.

For a stage or two from Munich the country was perfectly flat; but at length it began to put on the features of mountain scenery, till at Partenkirch it became really grand. Our road wound through mountains, till we began to descend the mountain chain which forms one side of the valley of the Inn. It is indeed a glorious prospect. The valley of the Inn is perfectly flat, about two miles broad, studded as far as the eye can reach in both directions with towns and villages, the spires of churches rising conspicuously at the interval of every five or six miles. This beautiful valley is bounded on both sides by alpine chains, rising steeply and often perpendicularly from the very side of the road. One mighty rock in particular we passed, which is called Martin's Wand. It rises a sheer precipice of fifteen hundred feet. It is celebrated for a wonderful escape of the Emperor Maximilian. He was out chamois-hunting, and in his eagerness fell and slipped down to the very verge of this descent. There, as the guide-book says, he hung with his head over, unable to move. He was seen from below, and the people issued from their cottages, headed by their bishop, who offered up prayers for him as for a man at the point of death. At last a desperate outlaw, who was hunting in that direction, perceived him, came down a descent which seemed impracticable, bound crampons to his feet, and led him off safely in a way which was considered miraculous. We came to this spot, or rather just above it, when the sun was already low, and steeping the mountain sides in that peculiar purple tint which in alpine regions is so inexpressibly rich.

In all this glory there is a strange tumult in my bosom for which I cannot assign any cause. Grandeur makes me misanthropic, and soft beauty makes my heart beat with a misery that I cannot describe. In Retsch's illustrations of Goethe's "Faust" there is one plate where angels drop roses upon the demons who are contending for the soul of Faust. Every rose falls like molten metal, burning and blistering where it touches. It is so that loveliness does with me. It scorches when it ought to soothe. After my arrival at Innsbruck I wandered alone by the gush of that wild and roaring river. Everything was still and solemn. Mighty shadows were moving silently across the valley, like so many giant spectres, as the sun went down behind the hills. The outlines of the mountains gradually blended in a sky which became by degrees as black as themselves, and I was left in the grandeur of darkness. I felt, as I generally do on such occasions, strongly, the swift rush of time, — on and on, bearing everything along with it into the Infinite: and here are we, for a moment, powerless nothings, but endued with powers of agony and thought which none but immortals feel. Then I went slowly back to Innsbruck, heard the hum of life again, saw the windows glittering with light, heard the drone of the church bells, and met the crowds coming away from vespers. It all seemed a dream. Next day I devoted to seeing Innsbruck. My first attraction was the cathedral. In it is the statue of the celebrated Hofer. It represents Hofer in Tyrolese costume, with his rifle, decorations, and a standard in his hand, crowned with laurel by the Goddess of Victory. But the court of Austria, in their aristocratic littleness, considered this part of the design too flattering to a peasant, and the monument stands now without the crown and goddess. As if God had not stamped upon Hofer's brow and heart a nobility of which crowns and titles are but the earthly shadow. The nobles of Austria will have their memory with the worms that eat them when Hofer's name is still high among the aristocracy of the universe.

* * * * *

[The remainder of this letter describes the chamois-hunt, but it is here omitted, a description of the same expedition having already been inserted.]

Brunecken, Sept. 23.

I proceed to take up the thread of my history where it last broke off, which was at Innsbruck, after my return from an unsuccessful chamois-hunt. I have now written three times; once from Frankfort, once by Mrs. Dalzell, and once from Innsbruck. I hope you got them all. On Monday last, the 21st, I set off on a pedestrian excursion on foot alone.

I trudged on, very briskly at first, for the sun shone beautifully. Three hours from Innsbruck I came to Schönberg, from which there is a grand view of three valleys, terminating at this point. At night I slept at Stainach, a small village in the hills, at what in England would be called a pothouse. A motley assemblage was round me in the dining-room, peasants, travellers, servants, all dining at different tables. A figure of the Saviour, half as large as life, looked down on the noisy scene. . . . . The season in which we now are is very beautiful for walking. The fir woods in summer are sombre, from their having but one hue. Now there is a very beautiful contrast. There is the deep green of the older foliage, a delicate light green of this year's growth, and a rich orange of the trees intermixed with them which have now their autumn tint. This orange color is in some places, where it is well sprinkled in irregular patches, superlatively fine. And now I will tell you my general impression of the Tyrol. So far as I have seen as yet, I have been rather disappointed in the people. I have found less simplicity, less politeness, and far less cleanliness than I expected. Religious they certainly are, if crosses and virgins almost at every quarter of a mile be a proof of religion. But I am inclined to believe that all this is looked upon by them in the light of a spell, and has much less influence on their moral conduct than is generally supposed. Moreover, in every inn there is holy water in your bedroom, and in the dining-room, generally, a figure of the Saviour; and at Mittenwald, under the figure, were some most touching sentences on life and death. But I never observed that this had any effect in solemnizing the parties who sit beneath it. They are satisfied with being under protection, and drink, play at cards, smoke, in a way that to us seems incompatible with religious feeling. And this I believe is the very essence of superstition, — to feel great reverence for certain objects, visible or invisible, on account of some mysterious influence with which they are supposed to be endowed, but an influence which all the while has not necessarily any moral effect, or any connection with character. It is quite curious how these chapels beset you at every step, and their number is increased by the erection of one in every place where a fatal accident has taken place. These seem to have been exceedingly frequent, and the rude delineation of the circumstance, a man frozen to death, drowned, buried by an avalanche, &c., is in desolate districts very solemn and affecting. The sound of bells, too, in these Alps is a very peculiar feature.

Cortina, or Ampezzo, September 24. — To-day I had the finest walk of all, indeed the only one that has approached grandeur. The pass of Ampezzo, the shortest between Innsbruck and Venice, is remarkably wild and noble. The shape of the mountains, as well as their height, adds to this grandeur. They are peaked, serrated, and jagged in all directions. After the somewhat tiresome, because unaltering, scenery through which I had gone, this sudden view brought new sensations, and sent the blood thrilling to the heart, and then running about in all directions, not knowing where to go. After getting about half through, it came on to rain, a drenching shower, for two hours. But this scarcely diminished the beauty of the scene, for gleams of sunshine every now and then revealed unseen peaks through the rain, and the clouds drifting in masses round the peaks, now dipping down, and now leaving all bare, formed a picture exceedingly striking. Few things are more interesting than the way in which clouds group themselves in these regions. Sometimes they seem to hold fast to a mountain peak, by a comparatively narrow base, while the rest of the vapory mass soars up and up, widening as it goes, to a height of which you only form a conception by comparing it with the lofty mountain, which does not reach one fourth of the distance.

* * * * * *

Corfara, September 25. — This morning, at an early hour, I turned off from Cortina, which is on the road to Venice, and struck across the hills to this place. Very few English, so far as I can find, have ever come this way. The walk was in some places very grand. I passed castellated pinnacles, covered with snow which fell last night, ruined forests, fir-trees stripped of their bark and cast headlong by avalanches from the heights above, — a castle in ruins, which once belonged to the Bishops of Brixen, and contained the retinue of the commander of this district. Though only thirty years have passed since it was inhabited, it is now in ruins, overgrown with ivy, and huge masses of the ruin lie detached, with several young trees, thirty feet high, growing on them. The more massive a human work is, the more calculated apparently to defy the encroachments of time, the more signally, and I think the more solemnly, at last does it show the triumph of the conqueror. An hour more brought us up another ascent to Pieve d'Andraz, where my companion, who was an actuary of the Landgericht, or Tyrolese Court of Justice, had to stay on his duties. After being parted for a little time, I thought when we met again that he would have kissed me for joy. Just before we arrived at Pième d'Andraz we had a glorious prospect. Monte Civita, with a hundred peaks, lay to my left, at about five miles' distance, closing up the loveliest valley I ever saw, through which a stream runs that divides Italy from the Tyrol. Before me, between two closer peaks, lay Monte Marmoletta, his head clothed in eternal snow, and his waist braced with glaciers; and just to the left the little village of Pième, to which I was going, with its spire and twelve houses. To-morrow, all day, if I can move at least, I will go through the haunts of this people. I am now writing in the stove-room, public-room, or whatever it is to be called, the only sitting-room in the cottage, surrounded by shepherds who have come in wet through, and are discussing their supper and their sour wine, — a new scene of life; but I am more at home with them than in Cheltenham. My guide is supping with me, — an honest, modest Italian, — on some dish whose composition I cannot guess, and dare not ask.

Botzen, September 27: Kaiserkrone Hotel.

I have just finished a letter to you, but still I must begin another, that I may put down my impressions while they are fresh. For I feel strongly that, in this world, things can be felt but once; you cannot recall impressions. You recall only part of them, softened and altered, bearing the same relation to the impression itself that the mellowed Italian does to the original Latin. Pictures, scenery, persons, you can feel them in this world but once. The first time never returns. So I write now, that whatever I have to say may be fresh and living. Memory retains things, but only as a herbarium holds plants; they become colorless and withered after a time, retaining only the shape of what they were, and even that distorted. I closed my last letter at Corfara, after getting in drenched and half frozen to a miserable little inn, resorted to by the shepherds when their day's work is done. Twenty or more sat at tables round me, redolent of garlic, sheep, and tobacco. I make it a duty to feel myself at home in every society, — so I pushed half my supper across to one of them, to his evident surprise, and afterwards spread out my map, when the whole party crowded round me, and I delighted them by pointing out to each his native valley or village. A little after five next morning I threw myself out of bed. The sky was just light enough for me to see that the clouds were gone; and by the time I was dressed, and had packed up my knapsack, the prelude to a brilliant day had begun. I set out with a man to carry my knapsack, for I had a journey before me which all told me was impossible; but, as it was Saturday, I determined to reach Botzen, the nearest town, and not spend Sunday in the cold mountains. Snow had fallen the night before, and our path was slippery, up hill, and steep, and by the time we got to Castleruth, my guide was done up. So I took the knapsack on my own shoulders, and pushed on down a most steep mountain, which fatigued me more than the ascent, and reached Botzen before nine in the evening. The valley through which I passed is a very remarkable one. In it are mountains of dolomite, peculiar from the sharpness and ruggedness of their peaks, being cleft by thousands of deep fissures, perfectly bare, and rising up in all manner of fantastic forms. It was a glorious day all through, and the sun glittered against the white dolomite crags as if they had been silver. A Tyrolese valley on a sunny day, sleeping in the light and rich tints, is exquisitely beautiful. Above Castleruth I paused to look down upon the village below. It lay some miles before me, deep down, but still far higher than Botzen to which I was going. A rich deep autumn tint covered all the undulations and woods and meadows, and the massy peaks, rearing themselves out of it in strange contrast, enhanced the loveliness of the whole. From Castleruth the way was steep, so that it could only be descended by small zigzags, till I came to a bridge thrown by a single arch of wood over the Eisach into the road which I quitted some days ago at Mittenwald. I now re-entered it twelve miles above Botzen. By this time the scenery had somewhat changed its character. Vines, which I had not seen for a fortnight, festooned themselves in rich profusion over trelliswork. Rich yellow pumpkins lay delicious-looking on the ground, and the whole aspect of the country announced that I was near the land of cloudless skies.

At the table-d'hôte here I met with an Englishman, — the first I have seen for many days. He has been fifteen years in Germany, — has married a German lady, and is settled on the Elbe in Bohemia.

September 28.

To-day, instead of going on as I had intended, I made an excursion with Mr. —— to the summit of the Mindola Mountain, the foot of which is about eight miles from hence. We started at half past six A. M., and got back by eight at night. The day, which at first promised to be cloudy, became bright as time passed on; and by the time we were at the top, every distant peak was clear. The view from the top was a noble one. The Valley of the Adige lay stretched before us, nearly as far as Meran to the left, down towards Trent to the right, and in the centre the broad opening of the three valleys with the junction of the Adige and Eisach just above Botzen, which seemed close beneath us. In the distance beyond the valley towered up the dolomite mountains which I passed on Saturday, together with many others which I had not before seen: three lakes lay below me, with villages and innumerable houses spreading the valley and hillsides. My opinion of Tyrolese character is much lowered. Their virtues are primitive, certainly, the virtues of human nature without principle; such as all people have who live scattered, and are not subjected to those allurements which come from the congregation of numbers, from trade and polished life. They are hospitable, simple, honest; but this only so long as they have no temptation to be otherwise. As soon as a valley has become the resort of travellers, and traffic has of course increased, they become as knowing and as extortionate as the inhabitants of any country. They are said to be very religious, and if chapels, crosses, masses, prayers without end constitute religion, certainly they are. But their re-

ligion seems only a spell or charm valuable to keep
them safe from danger; and I call that not religion but
cowardice. There is a picture in the gallery at Munich,
of which you see many engravings throughout the
country, representing a priest and boy attacked by brig-
ands. The priest holds up to their gaze the host, while
the boy raises a lamp to let the light fall full upon it.
The robbers cower down and relax their grasp upon
their victims, awed by the mysterious symbols of religion. This is called the triumph of faith. It conveys
exactly my present notion of the religion of the Tyrolese. I do not call that faith,—it is paltry, abject
cowardice. There are men who would rob and murder; but because a mystery is held before them, which
may strike them dead, they tremble, and give up the
enterprise. It is very necessary to make this distinction, because Newman and his party have introduced a
language now popular, according to which religion consists in awe and veneration. The more of these you
have, the more religious you are. But these are only
religious feelings if they are felt for true objects. A
man who crouches before a crucifix, or trembles before
the sacrament, and does not bow his whole heart in
adoration of the good, the holy, the true, is not religious, but superstitious. They want to show that superstition in itself is good. I say superstition has no
religious element in it at all. It is all cowardice. And
a man who walks into a church with his hat on his
head, breaks images remorselessly to pieces, tosses consecrated bread out of the window, or treads it under foot,
and yet prostrates his heart to goodness and nobleness,
loving, honoring and cultivating all that, is the man in

whom awe and reverence have their right places, though foolish people would call him irreverent.

You cannot conceive how England is detested throughout Germany. The "Allgemeine Zeitung," the leading newspaper, is perpetually attacking us,— our behavior in India, our religious hypocrisy, our slavery to forms and fashions, our commercial policy, &c. A short time ago the "Times" had, in some article, remarked upon the great advantage derived by Germany from the English travellers who pass through it. Upon which the "Zeitung" replied, that if a few innkeepers rejoiced at this, the whole nation mourned. "Only let God deliver us from the infliction of that horrid nation passing through our towns and besetting us like a plague of flies in our diligences, hotels, walks, with their stupid faces, their vulgarity, their everlasting inquisitiveness about hotels and sight-seeing, and utter inability to appreciate anything higher, and it would be a day of jubilee for all Germany." I do not give the words, but that was the purport of the article.

The Baroness gave me a letter to an Augustinian priest living in Meran, the author of the best guide to the Tyrol, who has explored himself every corner of it, in order that I might ascertain from him whether it would be dangerous at this late season of the year to cross the glaciers with crampons on the feet into the Oetz Thal. He received me very courteously in a room most plainly furnished, containing little more than a table covered with books and writing materials, and a few chairs. A bedroom which I saw through an open door, was equally simple, no carpet, no curtains. He told me he thought I might venture with a guide by one path that he pointed out. Accordingly, this morning at six o'clock I set out, the first four hours of my path lying on the high road to Innsbruck. But it soon came on to rain heavily, and I reached this hole of a place by nine o'clock, drenched through once more, the clouds hanging round me so low and dense that it would have been absurd to proceed farther. Ah! well, I suppose I must give up the grand glaciers. Six months hence what will it matter? And, after all, I do the whole of this more as a duty than because I can produce any real emotion of interest in my heart. I hold it a duty to see what can be done by the bracing up of my nervous system, and one mountain is almost as good as another for that. As soon as the fine weather sets in in earnest I turn north, and shall settle in some German place where I can get on a little with the language, for here without books I can do nothing. What I do learn by conversation is but provincialisms and patois.

Innsbruck, Oct. 8.

Here I am again, my pedestrian excursion being over. And now, to take up the thread where it last broke off. I had reached the top of the Stelvio, just after wading ankle-deep through snow and slush, up the most wonderful road in Europe. As usual, I did it fast, accomplishing in six hours and a half what a man in the hotel-book boasted to have done in nine; nay, four miles more, — for he started from Prad, and I had a full hour's work to get to Prad. When I got to the very summit, faint with exertion, the clouds hid the grand view from me; and I went on for an hour more of descent, to a single house on the bleak mountain side, which is at once the custom-house and an hotel, — a massive building, of enormous stones, built to keep off the avalanches, if possible. In this lofty spot I got tolerable accommodation. As I had missed the grand view from the summit, I went back next morning so far to try my chance again, through snow which had fallen in the night as deep as my knee, and on drifts deeper than the hip. But a grand sight awaited me at the top: the sun shining on the magnificent Orteler Spitze, whose peak of snow glittered in brilliant contrast to the bare bleak rocks of his sides, down which, as if in streams, his glaciers, glittering brightly too, descended into the valley. I had a curious series of manœuvres to get rid of an oily, stupid Italian. What a relief it was! I cannot tell you how the love of solitude has grown upon me. I can enjoy these mountains, with their sombre pine woods and their wild sights and sounds, only when I am alone. Rocks and crags crumbling down in a long line of ruin; uprooted trees hurled headlong, bark and branches gone, and their black stumps dotting the mountain far above, where they were before the avalanche or the torrent reached them; wild birds soaring and shrieking as you pass along, disturbed perhaps from their feast on a dead horse; the clouds sailing solemnly in long white lines above, or wreathing themselves like living shrouds round the crags. There is grandeur and wonder in all these things; but the spell is broken if human beings are near you. I spent Sunday at Nanders, — a delightful spot, close to the Pass of Finstermünz. After dinner I strolled down to the Finstermünz Pass, — about an hour's walk, — that I might see as much of it as possible, though I had to walk through it again on Monday on my way. I was disappointed. The Stelvio is more wonderful, and more grand too. It is a narrow cleft in the mountain, through which the river Inn gushes on its way to Innsbruck. The cliffs on each side rise steep and precipitous, leaving only room for the stream and the road by its side. The descent to it from Nanders is very rapid, which adds to the grandeur. The Inn roars and thunders through it, and I took pleasure in watching the fir-tree stumps, which are cut by the woodmen above in certain lengths, and then committed to the stream to be carried down to the valleys. Some pieces stemmed all falls and projecting points gallantly; others sunk for a time, and then you saw them emerging below, conquerors out of trial. Some were stranded, and left high and dry upon the bank, or on rocks in the centre of the stream; others had got out of the current, and were carried round a protecting point into still water, either stationary, or floating slowly back instead of on, as if there had been a destiny before them, and that destiny unfulfilled; while others beside them, not their superiors in activity or strength, were steadily buffeting their way forwards and home. What an image of life! Two days more brought me to Innsbruck, through fine scenery, by the side of the Inn all the way.

Schaffhausen, Oct. 11.

I have taken my path through Switzerland, and pass to-day, Sunday, here. The hotel is about two miles from the town, and just opposite the Falls of the Rhine. I was gloriously disappointed at the first view from this place, as it is higher than the river, and half a mile from the Fall, which looks insignificant. The river turns at right angles by the Fall, and opposite exactly is Weber's hotel. Yesterday, after arriving, I went down to the water's edge, crossed where you see the dotted line, and got exactly beside the Fall, midway between the top and bottom. Here is far the finest view, — the only spot where you can understand and take in its grandeur. You see the mighty river above, a sheet of glass, pouring over the ledge, as if it would overwhelm you. The next moment it flashes past you like lightning, convulsed into a sea of foam, and loses itself below in a cloud of spray, which rises eighty feet at least in height. In this spray an iris, delicately beautiful, was visible, rising out of the very depths below, and arching itself up twenty feet above the highest level of the water. In the centre of the Fall two tall rocks rear themselves out of the froth, the river thundering and foaming down their sides. To the foot of one of these I got the boatmen to row me, through the foam under the Fall, and, after some tossing, landed, climbed up a slippery path to the top, and sat there, the Fall being above and below me, and on both sides; but this view is not equal to the side one. On a near view I felt the full magnificence of the Fall. The blending of the colors was very singular. In places the lights on the descending waters were of a lovely grass-green, while the shadows were warm, almost purple. The full height is seventy feet; but this is lessened by the descent being made partially over a declivity of irregular ledges before the grand leap is taken. The snow mountains of the Bernese Oberland extend themselves in long line opposite the window of the room in which I write. My heart bounds at the unexpected sight, and I am half tempted to set off in that direction to-morrow. The weather has once more become warm and lovely, so different from the bleak weather I had in the Tyrol; and if it were only one week earlier in the year, I certainly should go. The well-known form of the Jungfrau cuts into the clear sky, white and sharp, with that peculiar outline which you only see in this clear atmosphere,—looking, indeed, as if there were no intermediate atmosphere. Last night I sat up long in my bedroom, unable to get to sleep, watching the Fall of the Rhine by moonlight. The pale beams fell beautifully on the white foam, making the dark rocks darker still by contrast. The spray rose up, floating like thinnish silver tissue; and the incessant roar of the falling water, softened by the distance into a murmur like that of a forest shaking in the wind, might have served for a soldier's dirge or a poet's lullaby. It was singularly solemn: stars silent and clear above, looking out of a sky of infinite blue; no wind, no cloud, and the stone statues on the terrace below (something like our own dear terrace at Aix-les-Bains), glittering cold and white, like spectres, gazing on the convulsion of the Rhine beneath them. An English family and myself are alone in this great hotel, yet I have not offered to perform the service for them. I cannot. Even to read prayers seems an effort beyond my power. More and more I feel that I am not a minister, and never can be one. Exercise has not braced my nerves, nor destroyed the phantoms, if they be phantoms, which rise before me. So long as I am awake, I can keep unpleasant thoughts away; but directly I sleep, the power of banishing them is gone. I sleep but little; yet that is no gain, for my half-waking dreams are worst.

Heidelberg, Oct. 13 (Tuesday).

Here I am at last, having exactly carried out all my intentions to the letter; and here I think I shall stay for some weeks at least, as living is tolerably reasonable, and there are but few English. Moreover, the scenery is perhaps the most beautiful which this part of Germany affords. The views in all directions are fine up and down the river, and the ruins of the old Castle are always a delightful place to wander in. I was much tempted to make an excursion in Switzerland, especially the evening before I came away from Schaffhausen. I never saw a scene more lovely than that which presented itself from the terrace before the hotel. The evening was cloudless, the air peculiarly still and clear, and the long range of snow mountains in the Bernese Oberland, Glarus, &c., as distinct almost as the Malvern Hills. A glorious sunset lighted them up with a rich glow, which by degrees subsided into a delicate rose blush, and then a minute after the snow was left opaque and cold. I cannot describe the effect of this singular transition. The paleness of the snow is quite of a livid hue, like the color of a corpse, giving you a very strange sensation, — almost a shudder. The beauty of this spectacle filled me with the wish for enterprise, and I walked into Schaffhausen, two miles from the hotel, to inquire the hours of the diligences to Zurich. However, an old guide who was in the hotel, when I spoke to him of the beauty of the weather, drily shook his head, and said, "Nein; I have been a guide twenty-five years. Take my word for it, it is going to rain." At this moment not a cloud was to be seen; but a little after midnight the rain was falling from a sky without a star, and the dawn broke upon a desolate and dreary prospect of mud and puddles.

* * * * *

Hotel du Prince Charles, Heidelberg: November 11.

I have at last decided upon my course with respect to Christ Church. You were perfectly right, I was most unwise to bare my feelings even to the extent I did. A man who "wears his heart upon his sleeve" must not be surprised if he finds it a temptation "for daws to peck at." That I said as much as I did to any human being I now deeply regret. But I shall go on doing so to the end of the chapter. Sympathy is too exquisitely dear to me to resist the temptation of expecting it; and then I could bite my tongue with vexation, for having babbled out truths too sincere and childlike to be intelligible. But as soon as the fit of misanthropy is passed, that absurd human heart with which I live trusts and confides again, — and so I go on alternately, rich and bankrupt in feeling. Yet, yet, say what I will — when any one soothes me with the semblance of sympathy — I cannot for the life of me help baring my whole bosom in gratitude and trust. A very expensive, perhaps a generous, but certainly a very weak way of giving lessons in anatomy gratis, — vivisection performed by the lecturer upon himself! Mr. —— has mistaken me. He thinks I am disinclined to the work of active good towards my fellow-creatures. God knows it is the only one wish I have on earth to know *how* to do it; and I am sure I set heart and soul to work, till I found that I was at work the wrong way; and I do not see that it is very wise to go on pouring water into reservoirs when you find that there are holes out of which it runs as fast as you pour. The Danaides did that; but the Danaides were in hell. I shall now take my own course, and permit advice from no one. I have given up Christ Church, and now the question is, what is to be the next step? I have two or three plans. The only one I shall mention at present, as the one that I think I shall try first, is, not to give up the ministry, but to make the experiment of working in a country parish, in which I have to deal with the poor only. For the rich I am neither mentally nor morally qualified. There is something either in my manner, language, or tone of thought which they will not brook; and then I have not calmness of nerve or meekness enough to prevent being agitated, and treating this in return with pride and coldness. In this way ministerial work is not likely to get on. But I am not yet *certain* that I could do nothing with the poor. If I had the work to myself, and could carry out my own plans, I have still a lingering hope that I could go on cheerfully, and not unsuccessfully. Will you ask my father if he would kindly be on the look-out for something of this sort, that I may stay in Cheltenham after my return as short a time as possible? I should not like more than a thousand people, at the very utmost. A house would be desirable. I should prefer agricultural poor, and a non-resident rector.

Such things are perpetually offering themselves, and there is no need to be in a hurry. My mind has gone through a complete revolution in many things; I am resolved now to act, and feel, and think alone; your letter and others have completely determined me.

My life goes on here as usual; I am asked out a great deal, almost always in a family way, and have become very intimate with some families. I preach every Sunday. People have come to church who had for long absented themselves. Some Socinians, too, go whenever I preach, so that my absence from England may not be altogether useless; yet I am not, and never shall be, at my ease with the upper classes.

Hotel du Prince Charles, Heidelberg : November 30.

I propose to leave Heidelberg in about a week or ten days from the present time, so that after the receipt of this letter it will not be of any use to write to me. This morning my father's letter arrived, by which I find he is already on the look-out for a curacy. I confess I feel strangely disinclined to work again. A feeling so gloomy and desolate appears to rest upon my heart when I think of the drudgery and apparent fruitlessness of my ministerial career, that I can hardly make up my mind to believe that I am really about to make the attempt again. It will, I fear, be only an attempt; and the last, if it should result in failure. What makes it seem more dreary is, that I have found a home and extraordinary kindness among the congregation here; and in less than two months a warmer union has grown up between us than I have had in Cheltenham after a residence of some years. To-day I mentioned my resolve, and I cannot tell you how I have been touched by the unfeigned regret which has been exhibited. I have had more proofs of my ministry telling here already than during my whole stay in Cheltenham. One family brought over a whole library of Swedenborg's books. They have, it appears, not opened them since I came, and have voluntarily promised not to study them any more. A Socinian confessed that the heart's *want* of the atonement had suggested itself to her strongly. And three young men of high talent, Socinians, come regularly, and listen with the deepest attention. All this is encouraging. It has brightened my stay here much, but it has made the return very painful. I wish I could have so arranged that we could have passed the winter here. However, this is now out of the question, and I must make up my mind calmly and fairly to make the experiment of work once more, if I can. But I shall be able to judge of this better when I get back to England. Since I wrote the above I have been much tried by the unexpected warmth with which the congregation here have testified their regard at my departure. Two young thoughtful Socinians came in tears, and told me it would be the quenching of their spiritual life. A Socinian lady wept bitterly. Two more have been in tears this very evening, warmly urging me to stay. A French gentleman has been equally urgent, and two more families have argued for hours. I may say it to you, the request that I should remain has been unanimous. And yet I feel, on looking over the past, that all this bright sky would be clouded over once more, excited hope would end in failure. They have strangely overrated me, and I know that I could not fulfil their anticipations. Then to feel estrangement again, to see suspicion awaken, misunderstandings arise, and to give up another congregation in bitterness, would be too much to bear. Reluctantly, and with feelings strongly inclined to stay, I have all but decided not to comply with their request. Friday, — I have been again greatly tempted to reconsider the question. There is a congregation earnestly wishing me to remain, not from popular preaching, but because they think they are getting good spiritually and morally. Individuals among them have been roused, and say out plainly that they are anxious not to be deserted in this crisis of their mental history, — that Heidelberg would be no longer the same, in the event of their losing their weekly instruction. Is this a call from God or not? Then, on the other hand, the emolument would be very trifling, — though Heidelberg is cheaper to live in than England. I should lose the time I remain here in English work, though I should gain in mental education. Now balance all these things together, and tell me what you think, and also what my father thinks.

APPENDIX II.

DURING the preparation of this biography, many of Mr. Robertson's personal friends have sent to me brief accounts of their relations with him, and their several estimates of his character. It has struck me that perhaps the best mode of making use of these letters is to arrange them here in an Appendix, where they can be seen together. They agree and disagree, but their very disagreement will throw light upon some of Robertson's characteristics. They are remarkable, with two exceptions, for their absence of anecdote, or of any description of his external life or peculiarities. Indeed, the great difficulty of making his biography interesting is, that he seems to have impressed himself so strongly on men as the thinker, — as a spiritual essence, — that what he did and said in outward life fell into the shade. Every one writes about his character, — few remember anecdotes in illustration of his character. He seems, if I may so express it, to have been rather *felt* than *seen* by men.

The first letter is written by a college friend, and gives an account of him which is interesting from the prominence in which it sets his youthful idealism; the second pictures vividly the impression he made at Cheltenham; the third is an extract from a letter from one of his congregation at Brighton whom he frequently visited, and gives some idea of his relation to the world of society; the fourth gives an estimate of him from a clerical point of view; the fifth is a recollection of his mode of life in a country-house; the sixth describes him as he appeared to its writer during the last year of his career; and the last, the seventh, interesting not only for the love and earnestness with which it is written, but also for the vivid description which it gives of the service in Trinity Chapel, is especially worth reading for the details which it supplies of some of the last weeks of the life of Mr. Robertson.

LETTER A.

Odiham Vicarage: July 28, 1862.

MY DEAR SIR,—You have assigned me no easy task in asking for recollections of an old college friend, after a lapse of more than twenty years. I became acquainted with F. W. Robertson very soon after his entrance at Brazenose College, Oxford, by meeting him at the rooms of the Rev. H. B. W. Churton, at that time a fellow and tutor in the College. His ardent temperament, his vivid imagination, his earnestness and purity of mind, his lofty aspirations after whatsoever things were true, honest, just, pure, lovely, and of good report,— in short, his eager thirst for moral and intellectual improvement, rendered him a most interesting companion.

His intellect was above the common order; and the deeper tone of thought, the naturally pensive feelings of his soul, made the mere social, festive, light-hearted circle of Oxford companionship uncongenial to his taste, and unsuited to his delicate, refined, and perhaps oversensitive disposition.

His friends were sought among the thinking, the literary, the devout-minded, and intellectual men of his day. Light and trivial or foolish conversation was always most abhorrent to him. His idea and endeavor with respect to social enjoyment were mental gain or spiritual improvement. He was dissatisfied, and even uncomfortable, restless, and unhappy, unless from the company and society of friends he could feel that he had either derived or imparted some solid, lasting gain, either in point of information or of clearer perspicuity on any subject of abiding interest. Progress was his watchword, improvement his aim.

Mere recreation or mere amusement were regarded by him as little better than waste of time. The common every-day talk, the joke, the sharp repartee of men fresh from public schools and elated with youthful spirits, found no sympathy in his breast, and were positively distasteful to him. He would often say, with emphasis, "To think that men should have nothing better to converse about than all this trash!" His turn of mind led him to an almost contemptuous dislike for what he called "the froth, the scum, the vanity of all these things!"

But with all this loftiness of mind, feeling, and aspiration, instead of a halo of brightness there was often a mist of sadness and disappointment hovering over his soul, which damped the ardor of his spirits and checked his joyousness.

On entering on a college life, his glowing imagination had raised an ideal in his mind so high, that it could hardly fail to produce a reaction of feeling after testing the reality of actual experience. He had anticipated a more elevated standard of manners and morals than he afterwards found in existence. His preconceived notion of Oxford lectures and tutors, as well as of the society of the undergraduates and other members of the University, was a high degree of perfection and of intellectual superiority.

Every lecture was to be a concentrated mass of learning, every tutor a paragon of excellence;· every party and every social circle in Oxford were to be redolent with wit, powerful in logical argument, abounding in scientific and philosophical conversation.

His own pure, noble, and lofty wishes were partly parental to the idea; and then his soaring spirit, his fervid imagination, painted up that preconceived idea in colors too bright, too vivid for earth. He had looked for an Italian sky, and for the sunny genial warmth, as it were, of an Italian climate; but he found, amid much that was bright and beautiful, fogs and vapors intermingled, which he had not anticipated. He met with storms as well as sunshine. The lesson was a painful one, but most profitable. While it somewhat damped the glow of his heart, and cast a tinge of melancholy over his soul, it rendered him a more practical man,— it led him to see that here we must be satisfied to fight our way onward through difficulties, darkness, and misunderstandings.

This was the secret, this was the origin of that strain of sorrowful disappointed feeling which runs through his sermons. It was the language of one who had learned by sorrowful experience that all was vanity and vexation of spirit, and this fitted him in a peculiar manner to address with power those who, still absorbed in the world's busy and engaging round of business and pleasures, had not as yet been taught the same lesson. He spake the things which he had seen and heard and felt, and there was consequently a telling influence in what he said. I well remember on one occasion, after gathering around him a breakfast-party of reading and rising men, — men of acknowledged intelligence and information, — the distress and almost disgust with which, subsequent to the breaking-up of the party, he commented upon the tone of the conversation, which had not risen so high, or proved so intellectual and improving, as he had anticipated from the class and character of the men selected for invitation.

He would make little or no allowance for the feeling of desire, in hardworking and reading men, for relief from severe studies in the social enjoyment of free unconstrained intercourse. He could not sympathize with them in the buoyant ebullition of youthful spirits, which must have its fling. But this turn of thought and tone of mind were in another respect a hindrance to the success of his university course, with regard to obtaining the honors to which his talents would undoubtedly have entitled him, if he could only have brought his mind to exercise those powers in the ordinary way necessary for securing academical honors. He could not bring himself to descend to all the minute accuracies of grammar and of philological lore essential to form a finished scholar. It was the same with many of the technicalities and minutiæ of science, without which the knowledge required for the examination-schools could not be mastered. To spend precious hours upon such comparative trifles appeared to him a waste of valuable time and of mental powers as well. He felt disappointed that the examinations should depend, in a manner, upon an accurate acquaintance with all these elements, these little niceties of language, these minute points and distinctions in philological, scientific, and philosophical subjects; instead of depending merely upon enlarged views, original ideas, and exalted sentiments arising out of a comprehensive and intellectual grasp of such matters by a reasoning and powerful mind. In preference, therefore, to fettering the mind, as he considered, by working in the tramway marked out for honors in the wisdom of the university, he allowed others of inferior powers to pass by him, and to attain those rewards of diligence and mental cultivation while he was climbing over the rocks on a path of his own.

I remember on one occasion the great disgust he expressed at a man of very superior mind and of undoubted talent being actually plucked in the public schools at the final examination for lack of technical information and want of accuracy, while he saw the testamur handed to many others of inferior powers of mind, who had earned it by common care, industry, and perseverance. He did not at that time perceive how much of valuable training, disciplining, and strengthening the mind, as well as of increasing its natural endowments, were involved in all this minuteness and accuracy of detail.

Thus the very brilliancy of his talents proved a stumbling-block in the way of his carrying off those rewards which his friends would have desired for him, and which they saw, under ordinary circumstances, might undoubtedly have been made his own. Neither academical honors nor Oxford society came up to the high standard he had preconceived, and his thoughts were then directed onwards to the great work of the ministry, and to preparation for it. His exalted notions of Holy Orders and of the high privileges and blessings in connection with the office of the ministry in the Church, again led him to look forward with zest and pleasurable anticipation to coming spiritual and intellectual enjoyment; and although there was much of this in his after-course, yet even here he experienced in the actual reality that "Hope told a flattering tale."

Upon the subject of religion, his inquiring mind was always in search of truth. With an early education in what is termed the Evangelical school, he brought an unbiassed and unprejudiced spirit to bear upon this all-important matter.

In Oxford he was an attentive and diligent hearer of teachers and of preachers differing considerably in views and sentiments. He attended the ministry on the one hand of Mr. Champneys at St. Ebbe's, and on the other hand of Mr. Newman at St. Mary's. He had as yet marked out for himself no distinctive line of religious sentiments, but the earnest, anxious question of his mind was, "What is truth?"

He saw much that struck him as excellent and desirable in both parties. He felt keenly, moreover, that there were deficiencies in each. He wished to amalgamate what he saw that was good, excellent, and scriptural in one system with what he saw to be devotional and stricter in form and discipline in another. He desired, with an enlarged mind and unprejudiced spirit, to embrace the excellences of both, without becoming addicted to either,—without allowing himself to be a party-man.

Nullius addictus jurare in verba magistri.

But the tendencies of his mind as well as his early training led him to lean more to the tenets and doctrines of the Reformers. He took special delight also in scriptural and Greek Testament readings, and in devotional exercises afforded him and others from time to time in Mr. Churton's rooms. These seasons often proved a solace to his anxious and restless spirit: they refreshed his soul by leading him directly to the fountain of wisdom and consolation.

He derived much advantage, moreover, from the instructions of the senior tutor in the college, — soon after the vice-principal of Brazenose, the Rev. T. T. Churton. From him he frequently received most friendly cautions and warnings with regard to the dangers and erratic tendencies of Tractarianism, as it gradually unfolded and developed itself into its distinctive features. In his rooms he often fell in with kindred spirits to himself, and greatly enjoyed the friendly and social gatherings of dons and undergraduates brought together by Mr. Churton's kindness and hospitality.

He was greatly indebted to the instructions of this valuable tutor for the views and sentiments which he carried with him from Oxford into the ministry, and from which he did not diverge until after the close of his ministry in Cheltenham and the commencement of his labors in Brighton.

Yours very sincerely,
T. G. CLARKE,
Vicar of Odiham.

LETTER B.

Lansdown Lodge, Cheltenham: February 21, 1865.

DEAR SIR, — I have already explained to you that I was not intimately acquainted with the Rev. F. Robertson. My intercourse with him was casual and limited. Occasionally I met him in private society, and entertaining, as I did from the first, the greatest admiration of his character and abilities, never lost an opportunity of conversing with him. But he was so much engaged in the performance of his duties, as the curate of a large district in this town, that these opportunities were few and far between; and thus, I regret to say, I can do little towards the elucidation of the comparatively short period of his life during which I had the privilege of personal communication with him, beyond giving a general description of the main points in his character as they appeared to me.

I always considered that he possessed, in a remarkable and pre-eminent degree, a combination of three qualities, — courage, gentleness, and liberality or tolerance. As regards the first, I believe him to have been, both physically and morally, one of the bravest men that ever lived. Had it been his lot to have followed the military profession (for which I have understood he was originally intended), he would probably, with opportunities, have attained the highest eminence in it. His presence was commanding though his figure was slight, and his dark eye glanced with a mixture of fire and softness which indicated at once that he was no ordinary man. There was nothing which he would have shrunk from saying or doing in the interest of truth or justice, for either of which he would willingly have undergone martyrdom.

At the same time his gentleness was as great as his courage. Even the very tones of his voice bespoke the fact. Conscious of his great and commanding abilities, he must have been conscious too (for he had proof of it in their acts) of the bitter jealousy which his superiority excited in the minds of some of those with whom he had to deal. But notwithstanding his extreme sensitiveness, which must have made him feel deeply the treatment he received, no acrimonious expression, so far as I am aware, ever escaped his lips; and the tone in which he spoke of these things was ever that of one who prayed that his enemies might be forgiven, as not knowing what they did. He was totally devoid of pride or assumption; and though his mind was stored with thoughts on every subject usually discussed by thinking men, he was as ready, perhaps more ready, to listen than to speak. But when he did speak, you felt at once that he was speaking from the heart; what he said was plainly and simply expressed, as might be expected where the speaker was candid and sincere, free from affectation, egotism, or pedantry of any kind.

But perhaps the grandest features of his character were liberality and toleration. He was an ardent seeker after truth, and having found it, would have defended it with his life. But if ever a man was aware of the difficulty of finding truth, it was he; if ever a man was aware of his own and others' fallibility, it was he. It may be doubted whether, in the whole of his writings, a single word, or a single expression, can be found displaying a spirit of dogmatism or denunciation. Possibly the natural liberality of his mind may have been encouraged and increased by the antagonism in which he felt that he was placed to the intense bigotry of which he was not unfrequently a witness. Exemplifications of this spirit of liberality, the more remarkable as being in opposition to the common prejudices of many around him, may be found in those of his sermons which treat of the "Sunday Question," in his remarks on Shelley in the "Lectures on Poetry," and in the fact, which I well remember, that when, many years since, a renegade Roman Catholic priest visited Cheltenham for the purpose of pouring forth loud-tongued and reckless abuse upon the religion he had forsworn, — when he was attended and listened to by admiring and sympathetic crowds, however unable to comprehend the Italian language in which he spoke, — no persuasion would induce Robertson to follow in the wake. With a pleasant smile he would ask what weight could be attached to the ravings of a Protestant priest who had deserted *his* religion, — a question to which I am not aware that he ever received a reply.

When he died, I believe that they who had had the privilege of knowing him even so slightly as I did, felt that a man was gone who had been, and would have continued to be, a light to the world; and who, if not in a worldly, certainly in a spiritual and intellectual sense, would have reached an eminence as high as has been attained by any of the greatest men that England ever saw. For his intellect was ever expanding, and it may be doubted whether, when he was removed, that intellect had attained its full development and possible maturity. Even during the period during which I knew him here, attending the church in which he preached, there was a marked progress in his power of thought, expression, and delivery. I may add, as a very subordinate point, that from specimens which I have seen of his Greek composition, evincing exquisite taste and great grammatical accuracy, there seems little doubt that he might have attained the highest academical distinction. But he felt that he was destined for higher and better things than running in an academical groove, and becoming even a great classical scholar. I mention the fact, not as thinking thereby to add anything to the lustre of his intellectual character, but because I am unwilling to omit anything known to me regarding him.

I should have been glad if I could have made this short and imperfect sketch more adequate to the subject with which I have attempted to deal. But having been requested to contribute something to so grand an object as the elucidation of the character of such a man, I could not, in justice either to the living or the dead, refuse, — even though the contribution were, as it is, but a mite.

His saltem accumulem donis, et fungar inani
Munere.

I am, dear Sir, faithfully yours,

W. DOBSON.

LETTER C (EXTRACT).

Brighton.

HE used to fight continually on the "Woman's Right" question, and I used to delight in rousing his ire by one or two things he detested, — by making a casual use of slang, by dashing my words in writing, and by punning, in which latter delinquency he used himself to indulge at times. I do not think he was ever humorous so much as witty, — not that I attempt to define the much-vexed difference between wit and humor; — but I should say that his fun shone and sparkled rather than warmed and glowed; and ever and anon — and almost always when one got in earnest — there rose up that tinge of bitterness which seemed to underlie all his estimate of human character and events. His own experience, I suppose, was at war with his aspirations. This struggle, I fancy, was what made him so painfully interesting. I used to think, especially when I first knew him, that his conversation was pitched in too high a key for general society, and he certainly wanted that little vulgar social sympathy which harmonizes all by tuning one's self only to the "third" above and not to the "octave."

He read out better than ever man read; he never preached but he always elevated and spiritualized every subject, and I never met any one so deferential and gentle in argument: he never pooh-poohed a remark, but always listened and carried on our remarks, — never forced on us more than we seemed likely to take in comfortably. He had the rare art of giving comfort, advice, and even blame, with such almost humble gentleness, such entire freedom from any assumption of superiority, that it could not wound the sorest heart nor irritate even the most rebellious spirit.

I think a touch of geniality or of sensuousness would have improved his character, but perhaps my materialistic tendency misleads me there, and a tinge of asceticism may be a necessary element in all apostleship.

* * * * *

The following letter of Mr. Robertson's will illustrate some of the points dwelt on in the above extract: his gentleness in refusal, his impatience with fruitless enthusiasm, his stern views of the world, and his feelings on the subject of the "Rights of Women":—

DEAR MADAM,—I regret exceedingly to be unable to take the part you ask me to do in obtaining signatures to Lord Shaftesbury's petition. I should be sorry that my refusal should be construed into want of sympathy in this great cause of charity and right, or into inability to appreciate warmly and admiringly the motives of ladies who like yourself have signed the paper. His would be a cold heart, indeed, who did not acknowledge proudly and gratefully the promptness of his countrywomen to feel rightly on all great questions, and to join in all generous works. But I humbly venture to differ from Lord Shaftesbury as to the expediency of this pressing mode of attempting to meet the evil.

First, it is known to be the result of a burst of feeling produced by a book, "Uncle Tom's Cabin," which by thousands in America is considered an exaggerated statement of the case, and has produced much exasperation of feeling in the Southern States. *I* do not believe it to be exaggerated: it merely exhibits what under such laws is for ever possible, and must be often fact. But the Americans deny it: and in the heated state of feeling produced by the book, I fear that a remonstrance known to be grounded on its allegations, or roused by its pictures of slavery, would produce resentment instead of conviction, and only harden the American ladies in their resolve to maintain the institution. For, strange to say, it is the American ladies — for ladies are conservatives ever of the things that be — who are said to be most vehement in the upholding of the institution: the ladies and the clergy, — for, alas! the appeal on Christian grounds which the address contains has been answered, they say, already a thousand times by the arguments with which the clergy have indoctrinated the slaveholders and their wives and daughters. Of this there are abundant traces in "Uncle Tom's Cabin."

In the first place, I feel convinced that the American reply will be: Look at home, — look at Ireland, — look at the pauperism of England, more frightful than slavery! What are the high-born ladies of England doing who saunter life away in Belgravia and Tyburnia, leaving their own slaves uncared for, stimulated by a novel into a burst of virtuous indignation, which costs them nothing beyond the trouble of signing a paper and the pleasurable excitement of the agitation, and pledges them to nothing beyond the easy task of calling on others to do good? I know that to hundreds who will sign the address this will not apply, but I confess that even *I*, an Englishman, should be forced to acknowledge it to be a fair retort to thousands.

Once more, you will forgive me for saying that while I hope earnestly for an increasing dignity and breadth to be given to the position of woman by the spirit of the Gospel, I am not yet quite American enough to feel quite reconciled to the idea of the public conferences and agitations and excitement which a measure like this involves in the female world. I do not put this forward as a real objection; I admit it to be perhaps an old-fashioned prejudice, and if there were no other objection, it should not stand in the way of my co-operating in a good cause. My only excuse for this long letter is my wish not to appear discourteous or abrupt in declining to comply with your request.

I am, dear Madam, your obedient servant,

F. W. R.

LETTER D.

MY DEAR SIR, — As I understand your letter, you ask me to add something to the materials now being collected for a "Life of Robertson." I wish I could send something worthy of such an object; but my incapability of writing all that I feel about him is my fair excuse for not giving more than what follows. It is right at the same time that I remind you that my friendship with him was, strictly speaking, a clerical friendship, and that he hardly ever spoke to *me* upon any other subject than that which directly or indirectly touched upon a clergyman's duties.

First of all, I will declare that, though he was not faultless any more than other human beings, he was, without exception, the most faultless clergyman I have ever known. It is easy to trace how this comparative clerical faultlessness had its original spring, — in (1) his strict obedience to his father's will that he should take Holy Orders and sacrifice the Army, in which his heart was; and (2) in his exceeding truthfulness of character. These two points ran through his life,— self-sacrifice and truth. "If I am to be a clergyman," was the language of his thoughts, "I will do my best to be a clergyman in reality, even though I have no preference for the profession." With this determination before him, he told me he prepared for ordination, and amongst other studies before he left college he literally learnt by heart the whole of the New Testament, not only in English but in Greek; and so completely did he devote himself to stiff theological study for the examination of the Bishop of Winchester, that he sought relaxation to his mind before the day of ordination by reading Wordsworth's "Excursion" as his orisons. "Some clergymen," he said, "would think it strange to do this. It was my refreshment."

His favorite private prayer-book was Bishop Andrewes's "Devotions," which he used until he found his wants more perfectly expressed by the language of his own copiously flowing thoughts. His love for the Holy Bible was exceedingly remarkable, and especially for those parts which are (as he expressed it himself) full of Christ; and it is worth recording that, upon one occasion, he remarked to me that the longer he lived the more fond he became of turning to the four Gospels by preference,—a fact borne out by the list of his sermons.

But Robertson was pre-eminently the clergyman of thought. He would wring his very brain for the sake of those pure thoughts which abound throughout his writings. And yet it was not for the sake of exalting the intellect above religion that he did this, but in order to make the fullest use of the great faculties which God had blessed him withal. I was curate of Hurstpierpoint in 1851, and having at heart the opening of a parish reading-room, I applied to my friend to assist me with an address. His generosity encouraged the request, but it was with difficulty that I could prevail upon him to sacrifice any time from his congregation. "My congregation must come first," he repeated; and then he rapidly sketched the amount of work which was demanded of him, in order that I might understand his sermons to be the chief object of his work,— not his lectures, because intellect ought to bend to Christianity.

I am not fulsome in my language of him, when I say that the spirit of Christ saturated everything he said and did. For my own part, I have never learnt so much of the mind of Christ, and what is meant by following Christ, as from him. Like his *Master* (as he fearlessly loved to call the Saviour, in whatever company he was), he had two distinct sides to his character. Perfectly conscious of his great mental powers, and very modest about introducing them except where plain duty obliged him, he was ready to acknowledge excellence and rarity of endowments in every one who possessed them, and to judge of others who had them not in a kindly spirit. There was a *daring* in him to speak what he was persuaded was truth, which was quite unsubject to the good or bad opinions of the world. Yet this fearlessness was always governed by a most *generous* charity. If he mentioned the name of any one whose life offended him, he was sure to make me see the good in the person as well as the vice. If he spoke of any one who differed with him in religion, he was bent upon my seeing that he loved the individual while he hated his false faith. To the Church of England he was affectionately attached: he regarded it as the best form of Christianity in the world, but he would never refuse to recognize what was true and good in those outside it. I well remember the substance of his words in conversation with me on this point: — " There is only *one* thing we have to wage a perpetual war with, — sin and wrong, in whomsoever found, — Churchman, Roman Catholic, or Protestant Dissenter. There is only *one* thing we should wish to see either in ourselves or in others, — the love of Christ; and in whomsoever a *spark* merely of this love is found, whether in one whom we have regarded as awfully wicked, or in one whom we have looked on as not enjoying the same superior light with ourselves, — one branded by the hard name of Papist, or a Greek, or a Dissenter, or an Arian; if in any of these the love of Christ is found, showing itself in the adoration and the worship of Him"; — and then, I remember well, he added, with a tone which has fixed these words exactly upon my memory, " O, if I could adore Him and love Him and serve Him as some of these do, I should be a different person to what I am now ! Then, while we hold fast our own opinion and be ready to die for it, we must acknowledge *this good* in those who differ from us, — we must rejoice that Christ is received. We call this person by that name, and that person by this; but God does not regard the names we may give to this one or that, to this form or that, to this faction or that. He only notices the love, the adoration, the service we show to His dear Son."

There was a nobility of disposition about him which ever forbade his meeting any opponent except upon the most open field of controversy or defence. He was too honorable, and his view of a clergyman's course of life was too high in principle, to admit of his countenancing any underground dealings with any one. Yet he was able to accommodate himself to, and deal in a winning way with, all the various tempers and habits of those to whom he ministered, whether in or out of his church. He was able to go into the most varying society of the world, coming out unscathed, and having always held his own. It was his rule never to limit himself to one class or party, but to act before all as one who ought to bear about with him, as a clergyman of the Church, a sort of universal character.

Such was the brave, true, honest, and simple mind which was so misunderstood — almost universally — during life, but which is now as universally acknowledged to be useful far beyond the Church of England.

F. ERNEST TOWER.

LETTER E.

MANY years ago I met F. W. Robertson, and lived in the same house with him for three weeks. I was very young, and his gracious manner and winning courtesy I shall not easily forget. The testimony of his oldest friends is true, — he listened to the crude theories and dogmatic opinions of a young man with a sympathy which awoke thought, and a compassion which did not offend.

No cloud rests upon my memory of him.

I recall the first day I met him as vividly as if it were yesterday, — the serious smile of welcome, the questioning look from his eyes, the frankly offered hand. We walked up a hill commanding a noble view of sea and mountain. His face lit up, — he drank in with a deep breath the wide landscape. The contrast of the white foam dashing on the beach of blue slate pebbles, — the racing of the scattering and fitful breezes upon the sea, — the purple of the distant hills, — were all marked by him with loving observation. He was happy in pointing out the delicacy of the clouds which an upper current was combing out upon the sky. He stooped to gather the wild daffodils which were tossing in the wind. Nothing was lost upon him. He touched all the points of the scene, clearly enough to instruct his listeners how to see them, but with such poetic tact that he did not injure what I may call the sensibility of nature. One thought more, that is, of the loveliness he spoke of than of the speaker. It was the unconscious art of genius.

I saw him again in a country-house. He rose early, and taught for two hours before breakfast some of his young friends. One hour was given to instruction in the Bible. I have seen most suggestive notes on the Epistle to the Romans which were taken down during these morning conversations. The second hour was employed in teaching, sometimes Physical Geography, sometimes English Grammar, sometimes Chemistry. His subjects were mastered perfectly, and taught with happy illustrations and with a crystal lucidity of expression. After breakfast he generally went out shooting. Starting long before the rest of the party, he never relaxed his swift and eager walk till he arrived upon his ground. He went straight as an arrow, heeding no obstacles, and leaping easily ditches which the gamekeepers refused. He followed his birds till night fell, too impatient even to eat luncheon. He shot well, almost never missing his aim; and with all his excitement, there was a business-like method in his work· which showed, in spite of the way his eye flashed, that he could always command himself when success was in question. The breaking of the dogs interested him greatly, and he was angry when the gamekeeper lost his temper with them. He returned worn out, ate his dinner almost in silence, and remained scarcely a quarter of an hour over his wine.

After dinner we generally walked in the grounds till 10 o'clock, and then adjourned to the school-room. By this time he had recovered all his energy and lightness. We played historical games, wrote poetry, capped verses. The freshness, eagerness, and anxiety which he displayed in these were delightful to us all. The humor with which he put down ignorance, the playfulness with which he exposed a mistake by wilfully making another of the same kind twice as bad, the frown with which he pounced upon an offender whose metre was halting, the bright smile with which he welcomed a new thought or a happy expression, the social art with which he brought into relief and elucidated our different characters, made the hours fly, and have left to me pleasant memories.

He often walked with us while we rode through the woods, his active step keeping up easily with the rapid pace of the horses. He talked with delightful yet quiet enthusiasm. If a ray of sunlight came slanting through the trees on the grass, — if a bough hung over the green path with remarkable beauty, — if an orange fungus made a spot of bright color on the way, he was sure to remark them. It was wonderful how much he made us see. A rabbit-burrow, a hare racing in the distance, a bird singing in the wood, brought out anecdote after anecdote of the habits of animals. I shall not easily forget his delight when the woodcocks came and he was the first to see one, nor the way in which he absolutely ran over with stories of their manner of life. He seemed to me to know all the poetry which referred to animals, and quoted Wordsworth till I wondered at his memory.

He himself rode often. He made his horse his friend, talked to it, loved it, I think ; and the horse knew this, and bore him with evident pleasure. His hand upon it was as delicate as a woman's, and he sat it like a knight. He seemed to become more than himself on horseback, and to throw off all the weight of life in the excitement of a gallop.

He dressed during the day in a dark-gray shooting suit, a black cravat, loosely tied, and a black wideawake. His clothes seemed to belong to him. He was exceedingly nice in his dress, without vulgar precision. On Sunday he appeared dressed as a clergyman. I went to church with him with the rest. I remember his quiet words of remonstrance when one of the persons staying in the house said that " he should stay at home because the preacher was not worth hearing," and the gentle determination with which he

T

gained his point. His manner in church was that of sacred and manly reverence, and no word of carping criticism followed on a very poor sermon.

I only heard him read out once, but I have not forgotten it. We had walked up to an old seat beneath an elm, and he suddenly seemed struck with some suggestion from the view. He drew "In Memoriam" from his pocket, and read, "Ring out, wild bells, to the wild sky." At first I did not like it, it seemed too solemnly toned; but the deep voice made its way, and I was so impressed with the consciousness that he felt a hundred meanings in the verses, which were concealed at that time from me, that I was awed and humbled. I never read the stanzas now without hearing his voice, without feeling what he meant when he closed the book, repeating twice over, with solemn hopefulness, "Ring in the Christ that is to be."

He rose when he had finished, and leaned over the wooden fence. Before him there lay in the still evening light a wide expanse of pasture-land dotted with weird thorns, and rolling up to a hill covered with firs. In the distance, sharply defined against a yellow sky, was a peculiar mountain-peak, dark purple. A faint blue mist was slowly rising and had filled the hollows. The wind was singing loudly through the withered bents of grass. He was silent for a few minutes, and then, as if to himself, began slowly to repeat Keble's hymn, "Where is Thy favored haunt, Eternal Voice?"· When he came to those lines, —

"No sounds of worldly toil ascending there,
Mar the full burst of prayer;
Lone Nature feels that she may freely breathe;
And round us and beneath

> Are heard her sacred tones, the fitful sweep
> Of winds across the steep,
> Through withered bents, — romantic note and clear,
> Meet for a hermit's ear," —

his voice seemed to take the tone of the wind, and I cannot describe how well the landscape explained the verses, and the verses the landscape. It was a happy instance of his power of fitting thought to things. He did not spoil the impression by telling us that he meant the poetry to elucidate the scene. He was silent, only saying briefly, "*That* is my favorite hymn."

I left the house shortly afterwards, and never saw him again. I was told that at the harvest-home, which was held during his stay, he spoke with a charm and with a simplicity to the assembled laborers and tenants which touched rude hearts, and stirred the whole mass into enthusiasm.

He struck me as being the possessor of a great oratorical power. Whoever were his listeners, he had his hand upon their pulse the whole time that he was speaking. The prevalent feeling of the audience was felt by him. In sympathy thus with them, he could play upon their hearts as on an instrument. This was the impression which his conversation made upon me, and, from what I have heard, it was this which made him the master of his congregation, and the conqueror of the disaffected workmen in his second address to the Mechanics' Institute at Brighton.

He had a strange, unique character. I do not think he could, under any circumstances, have lived long, or ever have been serenely happy. Too much fire was put into everything he said and did. Nothing ever seemed *common* to him. His senses appeared to me to be as preternaturally sensitive as his feelings. His pleasure and his pain were proportionally intense. To him the every-day joys of humanity were passionate delights; to him its every-day pains were keener than the life-sorrows of ordinary men. His very quietude was like the quietude of the sea, seemingly at rest, but traversed and stirred by a thousand currents. He wanted the rough bark which protects the tree against wounds, enables it to resist sharp winds and to reach old age. But the world should not complain, for it seems to me that it was this very want which made the beauty of his genius and the greatness of his life.

LETTER F.

Brighton.

MY DEAR SIR, — I believe that you agree with me in the opinion that Mr. Robertson's *life*, in the deepest sense of the word, has already been given to the world in his sermons.

In complying with your request that I should furnish you with some personal reminiscences of Mr. Robertson, it is perhaps incumbent on me to state, though I have special reasons for cherishing his memory more than that of any other man whom I ever called a friend, that my acquaintance with him was rather intensive than extensive. It was only during the last year of his life that our intercourse deepened into friendship; nevertheless, that comparatively brief period, with its occasional meetings, sufficed to reveal to me what manner of man he was. I know that in private life, and especially in the society of younger minds, whose sympathies and aspirations were still unchanged by the leaven of worldliness, he would at times discourse with the same clearness, beauty, and indignation which characterized his utterance when he delivered his great defence of the *In Memoriam;* but, speaking for myself, it was not so much what he *said* as what he *was* that struck me. And, with reference especially to his moral character, I noted that in him truth and honor partook more of the quality of passionate attributes than of merely formal principles, and that a righteous indignation against meanness and hypocrisy burned in him like a consuming fire. There seemed nothing within the limits of the lawful and the right which he would not do, or dare, for those whom he honored with his friendship. In the presence of true sorrow, or of penitence, he was tender as a woman; but there was a sternness in his spirit which recalled that of the Hebrew prophets when, in private life, he had to confront those who, to his knowledge, had wronged or slandered another. In such a case it was bootless to talk to him of "extenuating circumstances." Evil had been done, and the evildoer must be humiliated. He himself walked in such a sunlight of integrity, that any deviation in others from the path of righteousness inflicted on him actual pain; and not only so,—he had such a vivid sense of the destructive and deadly power of sin, as seemed quite to have quenched in him the hope that, in certain cases, the restorative influences revealed in Christianity would ever be able to effect any healing. Would to God that all preachers believed, as Robertson did, that the wages of sin — now, and not hereafter only —

is death! But the Gospel surely proclaims that good is mightier than evil; and as I recall Robertson's conversations, which indicated so rooted a despair with regard to the destiny of many for whom Christ died, my old impression is revived, that *that* despair had largely to do with the sorrow of heart which seems to flow as an undercurrent through all his sermons. I seemed to comprehend from his hopelessness of this kind the depth of St. Paul's words:—"If in this life only we have hope in Christ, we are of all men most miserable."

To a mind thus sensitive to the sins and sorrows of our humanity, sadness could not be unfamiliar. His own lofty ideal necessarily entailed on him many griefs and disappointments. And indeed he sometimes thought that all true souls were unhappy. One day, as we were speaking together of the rich endowments of a youth in whom we were mutually interested, he said with emphasis: "How unhappy he will be!"

The impression which the grandeur of Robertson's moral and spiritual character has left within me has almost encroached, so to speak, on that of his intellectual power. But no one who ever even saw him, or listened to his earnest, eloquent talk — his tremulous, clear-ringing, musical voice imparting a richer sense to common words — could doubt for a moment that he was possessed of the rarest mental gifts. Still it was in the pulpit that the whole man came out, and there he was indeed as one inspired.

Robertson's sermons, even as we now possess them, are the "bloom and wonder" of modern pulpit eloquence. Exceptionally lucid in expression, they reveal such a combination of the analytic with the constructive and imaginative faculty; they are charged so abundantly with arrows of lightning, to flash home conviction on the "conscience as she sits within her lonely seat"; they indicate such intense prophetic earnestness; they contain such fearless denunciations of evil, in high places and in low; they manifest such a sympathy on the part of their author with the lonely, the hardworking, the suffering, and the poor; they display such a mastery of the latest European thought, so profound an acquaintance with both the letter and the spirit of the Scriptures, as of the innermost secrets of the life which is "hid in God,"—its sorrows, its battling with doubts, its triumph through clinging to the cross of Christ; they disclose such a creative ability to turn truisms into living truths, or to convert the dry bones of orthodox assertions into vital influences for the daily life; they show such a grasp of great spiritual and historical principles, such a power to sever the essential from the accidental in the discussion of questions of Christian casuistry, such wisdom and liberality in the treatment of subjects like that of the Christian Sabbath — that Robertson must be pronounced, of all later Christian public speakers, *facile princeps*. He was at once philosopher, poet, priest, and prophet.

I fear that I cannot put on paper the image of Robertson's personal appearance which lives in my heart; but the following pen-and-ink sketch may at least dimly represent the great preacher to those who never saw him.

In person he was rather above the average height, and his graceful and well-knit figure indicated the possession of much physical energy and activity. There was a remarkable *springiness*, if I may use the word, in his gait, and I can see him now bounding across the street to grasp the hand of a friend. His face was not striking from any peculiarity, but it was a beautiful one. The nose was straight and finely proportioned. The mouth showed great delicacy, and purity of taste and feeling, and, when the lips, with their rich sweeping curves, were closed, inflexible resolution. Compared with the upper part of the face, the chin seemed lacking somewhat in development; and the dark blue eyes, which left their light with you after he had gone, though set well apart, were smaller than the eyes of our greater poets generally are ; but the noble forehead, so high, so full, so ideally rounded, and shaded by his rich brown hair, imparted, at a glance, the assurance that here was a man of great moral elevation of character, and of large intellectual power.

In addition to what I have already said of my impression, as a whole, of Robertson's various mental and moral attributes, I would now single out for special mention the following characteristics.

And, first, I would speak of the manly simplicity which lighted up his whole life. His very appearance — his look, bearing, and even his dress — seemed to proclaim this quality. His language was always that of a thoroughly true and clear-seeing man. He spoke with a quiet natural intonation. His conversation was that of a man who believed that truth and goodness commend themselves to the hearts which are ready to receive them, and that aught like *cant* springs from a root of unbelief. By the grace of God Robertson's yea was yea, and his nay was nay.

Edward Irving, as you will remember, in an ordination charge, said to a young Scottish minister, "Be the clergyman always, less than the clergyman never." Robertson's words would rather have been, "Be the man always, the Christian man, and less than the man never." The priestly self-consciousness implied in Irving's counsel would have been intolerable to Robertson; and he believed that by simply being a man to his "brother men" he could best by his living "show that glory of the Divine Son" which he "set forth" with such power in his "preaching."

From my connection with the Mechanics' Institution of this town, I had special and frequent opportunities for observing what Robertson had been to the workingmen of Brighton,—what he had done for them. He has built himself a living monument in their hearts, of which the Memorial Column in the Brighton Cemetery over his grave is but the outward and visible sign; and he has given an impulse to many of their lives, which I cannot but believe will endure through all the Future. And what was the secret of his influence? What brought the hardworking men of Brighton to Trinity Chapel, and at last gathered them by hundreds, amid ill-suppressed tears, to his grave? Doubtless his teaching was such as they had not heard in church before. Moreover, as he spoke to them from the platform, his fervid oratory, his practical wisdom, his sympathy with their doubts and struggles, his fearless exposition of their own special weaknesses, temptations, and sins, as well as of their rights and claims, called forth an unwonted response from their heart and conscience. But so far as I could learn from personal intercourse with the working class, it was this manliness, this straightforwardness of which I am writing, that won their affections. They felt that he was not afraid of losing caste by associating with them. He sought to make them truer men, better workmen, worthier Englishmen; to awaken in them the full consciousness of that common high-calling to be sons of God, which we have received through our Lord and Elder Brother, Jesus Christ.

This same manly simplicity characterizes all his sermons. And hence, while eloquent as no other modern sermons are, they have the sweetness and freshness of nature itself; they have nothing artificial about them. They seem to grow directly out of his life, — a life that he lived in this God's world, responsive to all its grandeur, and rejoicing in its manifold beauty and harmony.

But, secondly, closely allied with this reigning simplicity was his love of clearness both in thought and expression. He never dealt in hints or innuendoes. The thing he did not see he never tried to say; but what he saw he said plainly and strongly. One is never at a loss to find out his meaning. He has no *arrière pensée*, no pet doctrine, suited for the few but too precious to be thrown down amidst the multitude. What he had received he freely gave, — believing that truth is not private property, but the heritage of the world.

Thirdly, Robertson was a master in logic. His moral integrity and his intellectual love of clearness led him to a severe self-discipline in logic. His sermons are "music in the bounds of law." The materials of his discourses, to use another figure, were fused as in a furnace seven times heated, but they flowed out into quietly prepared forms. They are as true to the laws of thought as they are faithfully representative of Christian doctrine, feeling, and aspiration. "You do not know a subject thoroughly," says Schiller, "until you can play with it." Few could play so gracefully and yet so logically with his subjects as Robertson could; and hence I am not surprised when I find that each of his sermons — even when we have but fragmentary notes of it — is a logical unity, just as in other respects it is a poetical one.

Fourthly, Robertson was eminently didactic. For popularity, as such, he had a scorn that some might call morbid. But he was ambitious, if I may use the term, to be regarded as a *teacher*. It is in this character that he is now and will be known to the church and the world for years to come. Prophet I have called him; but he was more the teacher than the prophet.

He did not so much enlarge the horizon of our vision, as illuminate what already lay within the field of it. And in this respect, the power of his genius has, since his death, showed itself sublimely victorious over the clamor raised against the tendencies of his preaching. But during his life, those who had not endeavored to translate the familiar terms of Christian doctrine into language more in harmony with the modes of thought and speech which God's Spirit teaches Englishmen in this century, missed the accustomed sounds, were startled by the use of common human words in the pulpit, and were alarmed by illustrations borrowed at will from the daily life and pursuits of the various classes who thronged his church, — " from art, from nature, from the schools." Others, again, who had hitherto failed to apprehend that all ideas of truth, justice, and mercy among men are directly inspired (if they are not mocking shadows) by Him who is absolute truth, absolute justice, absolute mercy, shrunk from doctrinal statements which seemed to commend themselves rather too clearly to the apprehension of the intellect, and too much to the approval of the human heart and conscience. Then, those who leaned more to the dogmas of Unitarianism were ready to fancy that his representations of the Fatherhood of God and the perfect Humanity of Christ, involved admissions incompatible with the honest acceptance of the creeds of the church. But men on both sides confounded the flashes of genius with the aberrations of heresy.

As a teacher, he has done more than almost any of his contemporaries to remove the dust and rust from what I may call the currency of the church. Nay, more; great truths which platitude had done its best to degrade into unmoral shibboleths, he relieved of their dross, and sent forth into the world as pure coinage, bearing the image and superscription of the Heavenly King. By way of illustration, I need only refer — and must indeed do no more than refer — to his teaching on Baptism, Absolution, the Atonement, and Imputed Righteousness.

Finally, a fervid believer in Christ, Robertson was to his heart's core a loyal son of the Church of England. All her rites and ordinances were specially dear to him; and I know well, tolerant as he was, how his tastes and principles imparted to him an antipathy from dissent, and with what freedom of conscience, with what thankfulness of heart, he found himself a minister of the National Church.

But I must bring this letter — I fear too long already — to a close.

In speaking as I have done, I am but giving expression to the love which is cherished by all his surviving friends. He had one mutual friend who will not read these lines, and by whom I stood at Robertson's grave, on the day of his funeral, — Lady Byron. She used to say that from the first day of her acquaintance with Robertson, she "could not but painfully discover that he was *sowing himself* beyond his strength, and that his very calm was a hurricane." It was even so. But we must take great men as we find them; and I for one must here give God thanks for what Robertson was, and for all that He wrought through him.

I am, dear Sir, yours very truly,

A. J. Ross.

LETTER G.

MY DEAR SIR, — During Mr. Robertson's life at Brighton, I saw and spoke with him frequently; but of the many conversations which I had with him, scarcely a trace remains, except the impression, deep and abiding, that he was the truest, purest, and most gifted man I have ever seen.

I never heard talk so luminous as his. When he spoke upon an obscure or difficult subject, it was as if a cloud had been lifted from a landscape, and all its details were soon shining in the full glory of clear sunshine.

To meet him in the street and to see his radiant smile of recognition, was to receive an upward influence. I know that, to many, a casual rencontre with him was a cherished hope in the morning and a delightful thought at night, — that his presence was to such more than that of any other man, — that his words were treasured by them as divinely-given oracles.

The congregation which he gathered round him was a remarkable one. A large portion of it, in strong contrast to the other churches in Brighton, was composed of men. Some of the most thoughtful had been drawn thither from other congregations, and became habitual worshippers at Trinity Chapel; while others, who had never come to church before, found in his preaching the attraction of the Gospel of Christ to be both irresistible and life-long.

I have never heard the liturgy read as Mr. Robertson read it. He carried its own spirit with him; and those prayers, so often degraded by careless reading into mere forms, were from his voice felt to be instinct with a divine life and spirit. The grave earnestness and well-weighed emphasis with which he read the Gospel of the day, were absolutely an exposition of its meaning. A friend turned round and said to me once, "He need not preach a sermon now, that is sufficient."

I have seen no one so free from trick or affectation in manner, voice, or gesture. One of his anonymous critics wrote to him once, to complain of his wearing a ring while he was preaching. Though the ring was endeared to him as the last gift of a friend, he henceforward, from a Christian fear of offence, removed it always on entering the pulpit. He remained long in prayer during the hymn which preceded the sermon, and then stood up with eyes so closed that they seemed sunk into his head. On giving out his text he began with a voice tremulous at first, but which gathered strength forthwith, and had tones and power in it which enthralled our ears and stirred our hearts.

I cannot describe to you in words the strange sensation, during his sermon, of union with him and communion with one another which filled us as he spoke. I used to feel as if every one in the congregation must be thrilling with *my* emotion, and that *his* suppressed excitement was partly due to his consciousness of *our* excitement. Nor can I describe to you the sense we had of a higher Presence with us as he spoke,—the sacred awe which filled our hearts,—the hushed stillness in which the smallest sound was startling,—the calmed eagerness of men who listened as if waiting for a word of revelation to resolve the doubt or to heal the sorrow of a life,—the unexpected light which came upon the faces of some when an expression struck home and made them feel,— in a moment of high relief from pain or doubt,—this man speaks to *me*, and his words are inspired by God. And when the close came, and silence almost awful fell upon the church, even after a sigh of relief from strained attention had ceased to come from all the congregation, I have often seen men so wrapt that they could not move till the sound of the organ aroused them to the certainty that the preacher had ceased to speak. To such utterances, a prayer of Alexander Knox seemed to be the only fitting close, "Deepen these impressions in me, O Lord!".

I have read over what I have written, and I say

again that mere words can never reach to the true height of what this man was in the pulpit. I never understood till I knew him what Inspiration was; and whether in the church or in the street, he always seemed to speak as if under a higher than earthly influence. It is among the greatest blessings as well as responsibilities of my life that for nearly six years I heard, and knew somewhat of Mr. Robertson.

His bearing was always gracious, courteous, patient; his conversation vivid, rapid, translucent, and marvellously gentle. One evening he came in and asked if I had gone to hear A. J. Scott lecture on Dante. I answered "No, —" and asked him how he had been satisfied. In reply, he gave me a swift analysis of the Lecture, touching all the points, and omitting not a single thought of value. I heard afterwards from some of the audience that the Lecture was uninteresting to them; but I can only say that, as it had passed through his mind, and as he rendered it to me, it was not only a wonderful exhibition of his power of memory, but also bright with interest, and as luminous by its clear exposition of principles as it was by its admirable choice of illustrations.

Some little time afterwards I went to tell him that I was going to be married. I shall never forget the deep earnestness of his conversation with me on this occasion, nor the strange beauty of his words as he blessed me, and bade me God speed.

I wish I could recall one conversation which impressed me deeply. He had been visiting ———, whose wife had just died, and we passed on to the subject of recognition and reunion after death. He startled us by saying that he saw no cause, either in Scripture or Reason, for believing that there was any universal law of recognition. Spiritual likenesses, he said, would draw together. The spiritual and intellectual affinities would alone determine the relationships of that state. "I shall know," he continued, "and converse there with men whom I have never seen, yet for whom my spirit has the profoundest reverence, while many with whom I may have been in constant communication on earth I shall never see in that other world."

My wife was pained by this; her thoughts, like mine, were then dwelling on the child who had first awoke the parental feeling in our hearts, and who had passed from us after the briefest stay. We had nothing but the heart's instinct to oppose to an argument which, from his lips, seemed to be irresistible in its cogency.

On another occasion he came with two other friends to a cottage I had in the country. We were to have a day upon the hills. He was in an odd solitary humor, and full of quiet fun. Detaining me to ask some question about the flowers, he looked quaintly after the others who had preceded us by the road, and said, "Can we evade them; is there any backway to the Downs?" I told him he would have to leap a wall. "O, that is nothing!" He sprang lightly over the orchard wall, raced over the turf, and after a rapid walk, during which he seemed to drink the breeze, we reached a grove of beeches, and waited for our friends. We lunched, and for the only time I ever saw him so, he was merry, and full of wild paradox in his talk. Late in the summer evening he left with some flowers

which he had charged his son to take great care of—
"Mamma loves flowers, you know, Charlie."

Once again he came to that house to stay a few days. It was when his life was wellnigh spent. He had been forbidden to preach; he was suffering keenly from bodily pain as well as from the worry and anxiety consequent on the Vicar's refusal to let him have Mr. Tower as his curate. He insisted on seeing all that was said in the papers on this subject; yet when I brought them to him, not one bitter word escaped his lips respecting a matter on which I do not pretend even now — twelve years after — to have mastered my own indignation.

He walked to church with us, for he was come to be sponsor for my boy, and in the evening asked that he might have tea upon the grass. I well remember that evening. We sat on the edge of the lawn in front of a great walnut-tree; all of us clustered round him till twilight deepened into night. We were almost silent listeners, while he talked on for hours unremittingly. It was almost the only time I ever heard one of his wonderful monologues, ranging over many subjects, bringing light into the dark recesses of each, and linking them all, diverse as they were, to one another with a power which could only have arisen out of the possession of great principles arranged in his own mind in harmonious connection with one another. I only remember that one topic was the taste for French light literature, on the evils of which he spoke with fiery energy. In that soft summer air we might have sat there the whole night, — for he held us under his spell, — had not the appearance of the wearied servant reminded us that it was twelve o'clock.

I never saw again this lightning of the intellect. It seemed to be the last effort of his expiring power.

The next morning he began to read family prayers, and broke down, asking me to finish. Then he sat under the trees, or in an easy chair for hours, with eyes closed, — sometimes dozing, more often suffering pain. On the Sunday he prepared to accompany us to church; it was Communion Sunday, and he said he should like much to go. As we walked together on the road, he suddenly stopped and said, "I cannot go; I am in such extreme pain that I cannot answer for myself." My wife wished that we should stay with him; but he would not permit it, saying he should be better by and by.

Now and then during his stay he would speak for a little while with the old interest; but chiefly he was silent, and we forbore talking except when he spoke. He said once that the sense of his being able to talk or be silent, to do exactly what he liked, was very consoling to him.

Before he left he spoke earnestly with my wife of a change I was then contemplating, approved it heartily, and in answer to an expression of sorrow that it must separate us from his public ministry, replied, "My work is done!" and once again he said to me, "If I have been able to do any true work for you, be very sure some one else will come to you to carry it on." On the way to Brighton he was roused up by seeing in a field some birds which he remarked he had never observed in Sussex before. I could not even see them, they were so far away, but his sight, keen even then, distinguished them so clearly as to mark their peculiarities.

Once afterwards I saw him for a few minutes at his own house. He was coming out of the door with me, when his little girl called to him from the top of the stairs, — "O papa, you are going out without kissing me!" "No, my darling, I will not," was his reply, as he stepped back, took her into his arms, and kissed her.

In less than two months that great heart had ceased to beat; and we who had loved him so deeply, yet felt sincerely that we had not honored and loved him as he deserved to have been. A sense of great irreparable loss fell upon us, and at first it seemed as if in the great shock of bereavement his flock were scattered to the winds, and that his work was naught.

But in common with many who shared with me the privilege of that wonderful ministry, I believe he is only now, so to speak, beginning to be appreciated, and his work to bear fruits.

What that work will be in its rich and glorious ultimates, that Soul can best discern which can see farthest into the future of the Church, in virtue of a life of ceaseless prayer that Christ's kingdom may come, and His will be done on Earth as it is done in Heaven.

APPENDIX III.

THE following notes of two lectures on Genesis are inserted here to show the manner in which Mr. Robertson prepared for his afternoon pulpit. They are too broken and unfinished for publication in any other shape, but they give a very fair idea of the close and affluent thought which he brought to bear on Old Testament subjects. The lecture on Abraham's temptation is a fine example of his mode of handling a dangerous and difficult subject.

These notes are dashed down partly in pencil, partly in ink, upon the backs of old letters folded in half. They have been evidently carried in his pocket, and thoughts added here and there as he walked. They were not as they stand here taken into the pulpit. An abstract of them was made, in which merely the heads of the discourse were jotted down and a few of the leading thoughts; and even this, as I have already mentioned, was forgotten and dropped out of his hand when he had fairly got afloat upon the stream of his sermon.

GENESIS XVIII.

A solemn passage, pregnant with subjects for thought. To these thoughts attention shall be directed; not to the framework of history in which they are enclosed. This framework is only the Form.

Concerning that *form* I say nothing and decide nothing. It is easy to exercise ingenuity on the subject. But whether one of the mysterious Three remained as the representative of God, or whether then Abraham drew near to the invisible Jehovah, or whether this was an expostulation with one commissioned to represent the mind of God, I presume not to decide.

Let us confine ourselves to the kernel of the matter, instead of examining the shell which encloses it: —

I. The doom of the cities of the plain.
II. Abraham's intercession.

I. Doom, &c.

1. *Destruction of Sodom, &c., predetermined.*

God's modes of punishment are manifold, — famine, pestilence, war, revolution.

But it does not follow that these are equivalent to destruction. Whether they be or not depends on the character of the nation. Defeat, even slavery, may only develop energies; it *destroyed* Jerusalem and Rome.

Revolution may be only the healthy overthrow of abuses, or the anarchy of a country thoroughly disordered. Never yet did a nation perish from without, but by a decay from within. The moral ruin preceded the violent outward one. Sarmatia never fell "unwept without a crime."

The destiny of a nation is decided by its morals. First purity tainted; then —— Compare the morals of these two nations. Under Abraham's tent were the incipient destinies of Israel: in the palaces of the cities, the decaying glory of a nation past its prime; not ripeness, but decay. One had a past, the other a future.

See Abraham standing in the door of his tent,— simple, primitive, rising up at sight of strangers, the true gentleman, the true nobleman, not high-bred but well-bred. Charity, hospitality, the graces of the simple and the uncorrupted.

Then compare the population of these cities,—feeble, enervated, cowardly,—unable to resist a foreign foe,— serving Chedorlaomer, buying off and deprecating his wrath by tribute, then restless under his yoke,—cankered to the core with vice.

Do we not feel that in the one case there was vigorous young life,—the blood of a thousand years yet to run in Israel's veins? In the other, a nation past its prime, ready to fall at the first blast. Was it not *decreed* that Sodom must fall? the question *how* she fell being a matter of indifference.

A solemn thought for England? Anxious considerations press upon us. It matters not what our ancestry have been; not our wealth nor our dazzling power will save us. Better to have a glorious future than to have had a glorious past.

Simple, austere virtues, these we want. Self-respect, domestic purity of the hearthstone; less love for light, corrupting foreign literature.

2. *Rectitude of Divine justice.*—"God came down to see," &c. This is the *form* of the truth. Remember it is but form. Revelation is poetry; make it prose, and it becomes insipid. It addresses the heart and the imagination, not the logical understanding. Say, that this must be taken literally, and that because the Bible says "God *came down*," He did come down, and we are guilty of an absurdity.

Disengage the truth. There is no haste in Divine judgments. Deliberate, slow examination. This is not fury. Observe, however, for this reason the inexorable character of justice, — long-suffering; but when the hour has come, no voice can save.

We speak in soft ways of God, — "love," and as if love and justice had to be reconciled. Whereas love is justice applied to different objects; just as the electric spark is different to different senses; to the ear a sound, to the tongue a sulphurous taste, to the eye a blinding flash. So God, speaking by one apostle of his character as a whole, says, "God is love"; by another, also as a whole, "God is a consuming fire."

Was not this *love?* Could love save Sodom? Would it have been love to let such a city go on seeding earth with iniquity? No! God is just; not to be bought off, coaxed off, reasoned off, prayed off. He is immutable.

3. *Prophetic anticipation by Abraham of this doom. Form* in which this anticipation appears, — "Shall I hide from Abraham this thing which I do?" *Spirit,* — It was not hidden from Abraham.

Now, what gave him this foresight? Of course, the Rationalist replies, political sagacity, experience, intellectual acumen. No such thing. "I know Abraham, that he will command his children," &c., verse 19.

Strong convictions of the sanctity of the moral *law*, Reverence to law. Justice, judgment — to do them, not to talk about them. Such was Abraham's character; and from such men few things are hidden. "If any man will do His will, he shall know," &c. Close connection between doing and knowing, between acting truly and seeing clearly.

Such men see into the life of things; something of the seer is in them; something prophetic. They live with God; doing God's will, they understand God's ways. Abraham looked at Sodom, and felt, i. e. the voice within him said, "That city is doomed."

II. Abraham's intercession.

1. His perplexity.

A suspicion of the Divine justice, — "That be far from Thee, Lord, to slay the righteous with the wicked. Shall not the Judge of all the earth do right?"

The most horrible with which the mind of man can be tempted. Dreadful to doubt one's own salvation, and feel suspended over the gulf! But a more terrible gulf when we doubt whether all is right here. "O, to see the misery of this bleeding world!"

Consider for a moment the misconception of these words, "Shall not the Judge," &c. They have been used to prove the sovereignty of God. God is judge, therefore what he does is right. He has a right, and therefore it is right. But Abraham does not say *that*. So far from acquiescing in the predestinarian feeling, — it is to be, and therefore it is right; God is a Sovereign, and may do what He pleases, — he is precisely doubting this, whether, though God be Judge, His deeds are right, taking the moral sense of Abraham as a test, and considering it horrible if God's acts do not agree with it.

It is a perilous way of speaking, "God has a right to decree what He will; my salvation, your damnation." It is not so the Bible speaks. It appeals to the sense of justice, "Are not My ways equal," &c. God never says, "I create a thing right, therefore I do it."

God's will does not make a thing right. It is God's character which determines His will.

For else, if the devil had created this world, wrong would be right, because his will, and we should have the terrible doctrine, Might makes Right.

2. Christian right to lay open our feelings respecting the great events of life in prayer.

A child may express his foolish wishes to his father. The father will not grant them. Yet is the privilege worth nothing?

Do not say, I must not go into that august Presence with a turbid, excited heart, with feelings all in disorder. You may and *must*. Abraham did, his heart tossed with wild suspicions of God. Suppose he had waited till he saw things in their right light before he prayed!

Christ in unrest, — rare to Him, — when his soul was troubled unto death, took these very means of calming it; left disciples, and all that was human, and turned to prayer.

3. False view of prayer as a talisman or a wishing-cap, by which we can have whatever we want; a charm by which we can bend the will of God to ours; whereas it is rather that whereby we get our hearts into harmony with God, see as He sees, and feel that His will is right.

A disappointing view, perhaps! a privilege destroyed. Yet think, my Christian brother——

4. Messianic intercession. "He ever liveth to make intercession for us."

Do not materialize this text as if the prayer of Christ changed the will of God, as if God relented at His intercession. Christ is the mind of God expressing itself. Christ's intercession is the human mind of God declaring itself in words. Do not think of Him as interceding with an unwilling father, and prevailing. Think that God has already resolved love; and that Christ is the *Word* by which the mighty heart of God finds utterance.

GENESIS XXII.

The temptation of Abraham's trial. "Tempted by God." It was *the* trial of his life; and it is this — *the* trial — which fixes character.

1. It was *not the only trial*.

In truth, all his life had been trial. Outward prosperity, — inward suffering. For many years, while his life was waning away, he had had no heir. Then came the parting with Lot, then the banishment of Hagar, and the final severance from Ishmael. Again, he had incurred the risk of losing Sarah and his own life twice. The danger of Lot, public calamities, famine, — all added their sum to the account. Now this is the inner life of a life comparatively calm outwardly.

Life is temptation; yes, and temptation from God. Christ was led by the Spirit into the wilderness to be tempted of the devil.

It is sad to think it so. Yet if it were otherwise! Cloistered virtue! Of what value is it? In some of these trials Abraham fell; in others he came off conquering.

He was by no means a perfect man; no specimen out of romance. His was a real life. What matter slips and failures, so that the heart be right at core?

Experience, profited by, that is the grand thing. Not that a man has been faultless, but that out of fault he has organized strength.

2. Trials do not become lighter as we go on. "*After these things?*" What! no repose? Is there no place of honorable quiet for the Emeritus? No. Harder and yet harder trials. For the Christian soldier there is no rest except in the grave.

Let a man conquer, and fresh trials will open, and fresh victories will ensue.

Nay, even *that* victory did not guarantee the future for Abraham.

Trials will assail us where we are most vulnerable. Everywhere. Head and heart, and heel. We must dismiss, therfore, the thought that we can ever put off our armor.

    I. Difficulty.
    II. Nature of the trial.
    III. How sustained.

I. *Difficulty.*

God seemed to require what was wrong, — to sanction human sacrifice.

1. Reply. God did *not* require it. You must take the history as a whole; the conclusion as well as the commencement. Had it ended in Abraham's accomplishing the sacrifice, I know not what could have been said. A dark and painful spot in Scripture. Plainly, the doctrine of God's sovereignty would have been inadequate as an explanation.

But "lay not thine hand on the lad." This is the final decree.

Here we must distinguish. Human sacrifices were forbidden.

God really required surrender of will, although He *seemed* to demand sacrifice of life. But further still,—

It did not *seem* wrong to Abraham. It is not enough defence to say, God did not command wrong. Had God seemed to command wrong, the difficulty would be as great. Abraham's faith would have consisted then in doing wrong for the sake of God.

Now it did not. Abraham lived in a country where human sacrifices were common. He was familiar with the idea.

Just as familiarity with slavery makes it seem less horrible, so familiarity with this as an established and conscientious mode of worshipping God removed from Abraham much of the horror we should feel. Else Abraham did not show faith in obeying, but—

For, only consider. A voice orders him to transgress the first rule of conscience. Ought he not to reckon it a horrible temptation of the devil?

Could any miracle prove to *us* that such a sacrifice was right? Faith would have been shown in disobeying the voice, and saying, This voice within is God's,—*that is not*.

This is of primary importance, that Abraham's moral conscience was not outraged by the command.

No conflict more horrible than when two duties clash; as, for example, Jephtha's vow. Herod's vow.

But it is more hideous still, if God's commandments, backed by miracles, command that which His voice within forbids. I can see no escape but insanity.

I dwell on this because there is a possible delusion, when the idea presents itself, of sacrificing conscience as a duty.

Some argue thus: — If it be noble to sacrifice life for God or man, how much more to sacrifice the soul: to tell a lie to save a life! or to speak falsely in order to establish a doctrine; to sacrifice virtue for the sake of one loved; to surrender political principle to save one's party. Such arguments are felt often by the weakly good. Observe; had Abraham outraged his conscience, it were not faith, but sin: and I say, reject such arguments as Satanic temptations. He who sacrifices his sense of right, his conscience for another, sacrifices the Godlike within him. He is not sacrificing self.

II. The Nature of the Trial. .

1. *With circumstances of accumulated keenness; with aggravations.* " My Son — my only Son — whom I love — with whom all the future is connected — long waited for — the heir, full of promise and so dear, anything else, not that."

God seems to take malignant pleasure in dwelling on the suffering he was about to cause.

Now the dread trial of this is to think " God requires that! *His* name love? Father? Nay, insatiate tyrant, this is the very tyranny of strength."

Forgive this blasphemy. I only put into words the rebellious feelings of many a heart here, if it had dared in its trial-hour to say out all. You who have so suffered can appreciate Abraham's manly resignation. To subdue the father in the heart, — that a Roman has done; but to subdue it, and still say — not Fate, but Love requires this, — that was the trial: and to do it without petulance, with a fierce steeling of the heart; in fine, to *trust* God.

2. *With his own hand.*

Not by a delegate. Not as Moses' parents did in their obedience to the king's command, leaving matters to take their chance, — hoping for some accident at last. Abraham was to preclude escape.

We do our sacrifices in a cowardly way; we leave loopholes for escape. We do not with own hand at His call cut asunder the dearest ties. We do not irrevocably take the path, but wait for some accident which may make it impossible. But when we are true to ourselves, conscience says with a terrible voice, No, with your own hand. The knife must be sharp, and the blow true. Your own heart must be the sacrifice, and your own hand the priest; it must not be a sacrifice made for you by circumstances.

III. How met.

1. *Without ostentation.*

He left the servants and went on alone. Had the sacrifice taken place, there was none to tell *how;* how the father's lips trembled while the Hebrew hand was firm. It had been done in secret, God alone seeing.

Here was no boast, — no analysis of feeling, — no self-consciousness. Men who make sacrifices do not talk of them. Here was no love of theatrical display, so common and so bad. Those are true sacrifices which have been done alone, and hidden. The world knows too much of what we feel and of what we lose.

2. *In earnest.* Two particulars.

(1.) Abraham did not tell Sarah. The mother's heart would have pleaded, marred the sacrifice. Do we not know how men tell some weaker being — a mother or a wife — of the risk that is to be run, hoping that they will do that which it would be a shame for us to do, — give notice or hinder it; or, perhaps, with entreaties and tears, excuse us to ourselves for not making the sacrifice.

Abraham did not tell Sarah, nor did he tell Isaac. He was in earnest. He *meant* to take his son's life.

Consider when you plan a generous deed which is afterwards hindered. Did you *mean* to do it?

(2.) In not expecting Isaac back. Had Abraham expected what took place it had been no sacrifice.

Some persons make sacrifices expecting to be repaid. They say and teach, — " Do right, and you will not be the worse. Give up, and somehow or other, God will make it up to you."

True, my brother. " No man hath left house and parents," &c., &c., " who shall not receive manifold more in this present world," &c.; but if you do it with that feeling, it is not religion, but traffic, barter. If you make sacrifices, expecting that God will return you your Isaac, that is a *sham* sacrifice, not a real one.

There is infinite gain in sacrifice. Yes, but not always in kind. Isaac is not always restored. You will be taken at your word. Do good, then, hoping for nothing in return.

Application.

1. The Christian sacrifice is the surrender of the will, the surrender of ourselves. When all the will has been submitted, then God says, " Now I know that thou fearest God, seeing thou hast not withheld thy son, thine only son, from me."

So the great sacrifice of Christ was pleasing, not because of the shedding of blood, but by reason of the surrender of will. It was not Isaac's blood which pleased, but Abraham's will. It was not Christ's blood that pleased, but —— "now I know."

2. Real love. "Whom thou lovest." Had Abraham not been willing to part with Isaac into the hand of God, his love even to Isaac would have been feeble.

> I could not love thee, dear, so much,
> Loved I not honor more.

He who prefers his dearest friend to the call of duty, will soon show that he prefers himself to his dearest friend.

3. We need not seek for sacrifices. We need not be anxious to find a cross. There is in some a wild, romantic wish to find occasions.

Whereas plenty will occur every hour and moment, by God's appointment better than any devised by you.

God will provide Himself a lamb for a burnt-offering.

As a supplement to these notes of lectures, I add a letter written in answer to a request that he would permit a short-hand writer to take down his sermons. He has been often accused of rash and unconsidered statements in the pulpit. The following will plead his cause, and afford a better reply than I can give to an accusation which those who are extempore preachers themselves should be slow to make:—

MY DEAR ——: — Many thanks for your kind note, in which you ask me respecting my feelings on the subject of the short-hand reports of my sermons. I will try to reply in a few words.

I need scarcely say that it is gratifying — more than gratifying — to know that any of my congregation value my attempts sufficiently to think them worthy of preservation. I am most grateful for it, and for the kindly feeling towards myself of which I am not, perhaps, vain in saying that I accept it as the proof.

Some time ago you showed me some sermons taken down by a relation of your own, and were kind enough to ask if I disapproved of the continuance of this. Of course, I replied, no. I regretted that any expense should have been incurred, but the thing being private, I could no more object than I could to the practice which many members of the congregation have of taking down the discourses every Sunday, some in ordinary hand, some in short-hand. Mr. —— put the case to me as one in which several kind friends united — and at great expense — to pay a regular reporter, and to preserve the sermons for their common, may I say, edification? and, I understood, my future use, if needed.

I saw one or two of these, and thought them, from a cursory glance, very accurate. But if you ask me to state candidly what I feel upon the subject, I should say that I think the plan very undesirable. I will not lay much stress on my *great* regret that so large an expense should be incurred for that which is not worth it, — for tastes are unaccountable, and fortunes have been given for a tulip-root, streaked in a particular way, or with eight petals instead of seven, — I should only say, *I* think you paid dear for your funnily-striped tulip. The Dutchman would say, I think not; it is my fancy.

But I will only say that there are a great many things said in extempore preaching which pass with the occasion, which are meant so to pass, which have not been deeply examined, and which will, therefore, not bear to be coldly scrutinized in manuscript. A printed or written sermon is always scrutinized as if it claimed infallibility, and positive injury might be done to influence if such a hasty expression were stereotyped, as it were. I could not undertake to correct such sermons weekly; I am glad to forget all I say as soon as possible, and, consequently, I should not like to be answerable for such.

Add to this, that often one at least of the Sunday discourses is insufficiently prepared, the *expressions* utterly unstudied beforehand, the thing itself poor and jejune and worthless. I should not *like* to own it, though, as all but the general *impression* dies with the half-hour of its delivery, it may be well enough as a collection of hints and germs of thought. I think the knowledge, too, that what I said was being taken down in this way would hamper entirely the freeness of expression. As it is, I try to speak unshackled by any attempts to please, to form sentences, and to deprecate disapproval, — I do not think I *could* be free were this done. For myself, I would far rather that all should perish except, as I said, the impression the moment after delivery. I preserve few records myself, except on a few occasions, — I can scarcely bear to read over anything I have said. It would be a relief to me to know that no trace subsisted, except a few hints for my own use, and for future development of the thoughts touched upon.

I do earnestly trust that this may not seem discourteous. Of course I do not pretend to express strong disapproval if any one should still be determined to proceed. But in reply to your kind question, I have no hesitation in saying that it would give me real pain if the plan were adopted.

    Believe me,
      Most sincerely yours,
        F. W. R.

APPENDIX IV.

AS a specimen of Mr. Robertson's teaching of his class of candidates for Confirmation, and of his explanation of the doctrines of the Church of England, the following may be interesting. The notes on the Commandments are too broken to be of use; and of those on the Sacraments, the few which remain have been so largely embodied in his sermons that they are here omitted. The same might be said of the questions and answers here given on Baptism, were it not that the subject is considered in a new light, and that the opinions form so radical a portion of his teaching, that, wherever he expresses them, I am inclined to insert them:—

Q. What is Baptism?
A. The authoritative declaration of a fact.
Q. What fact?
A. That I am God's child.
Q. Why then do you say that I am so *made*, in baptism?
A. Being *made*, I mean — *declared to be.*
Q. Explain what you mean.
A. As soon as a king dies, his successor is king. Coronation *declares the fact* but does not *make* him king. He was one before, but it corroborates, declares,

affirms, seals the fact by a recognized form used for that purpose.

Q. Illustrate further.

A. At midday, at sea, after the observation of the sun's altitude has been taken, the following form takes place:—The commander asks what is the hour? The reply is, 12 o'clock. He then rejoins, *make it so!* No act of his can literally determine midday; that is one of the facts of the universe; but that authoritative declaration in a most important sense does *make* it 12 o'clock; it makes it 12 o'clock *to them;* it regulates their hours, their views, the arrangement of their daily life, their whole course. So Baptism by authoritative revelation declares a fact, which it cannot *make* to be a fact, but to all practical purposes, makes it a fact to us; for, without such a declaration, it would be as if it were not.

Again, in the ceremony of marriage,—marriage is a spiritual fact; the mutual consent of two persons in holy wedlock. Based upon the precedent fact, the Church pronounces the marriage to be completed. *Forasmuch as M. and N. have consented, &c., I pronounce, &c. &c.*

The Church does not pretend to *create* the union. She only notifies it in her own language; but observe how that notification, being authoritative, in a very important sense, *makes it!* Suppose a ceremony, which was not authoritative, performed by a mock priest; or ratified only by the breaking of a coin between the parties. No one would venture to say that a *fact* had not taken place, recognized by the eyes of God: which the parties themselves could not without sin undo, yet, because destitute of authority, the marriage is invalid as à social contract.

(In Scotland, however, its true validity is maintained.) Could we say that the giving of the ring was nothing? That the words of the priest are nothing? Are they not *everything* to realize and give sanction to the union?

So does baptism,—pronouncing the fact in God's name to exist, *make* that real on earth, which in itself real before, was unreal to those to whom the ratification had not been shown.

Q. Tell me some of the prevailing opinions on this subject.

A. The Roman Catholics, and those who hold their views on this subject, believe that at baptism a magical change takes place in the infant; that he is changed from a child of wrath into a child of grace.

For instance, as in the "Arabian Nights," on the pronunciation of certain words, human beings were changed by magicians into the forms of beasts and birds, &c.

Q. What is one of the evils of this, besides its falseness?

A. That on the commission of sin in after life, we are taught to believe that we are fallen from the grace of baptism, and that every step must be retraced in penitence and tears.

It puts a drag upon life and hope, quenches energy, and prevents the looking onwards and upwards.

Q. In what other way is this right regarded?

A. Dissenters, Evangelicals, &c., hold that grace may, or may not, be given at baptism; it is a *perhaps*.

Q. What results from this?

A. Uncertainty,—self-consciousness,—education on

a wrong basis. Uncertainty! The child does not know whether *it is*, or whether it is not, God's child. Parents do not know whether to regard it as the child of God, or of the devil. It is taught to look *to itself*, and not to God, for the attestation of the fact; hence come morbid feeling, egotism, self-retrospection, uncertainty. One day a child happens to feel well and cheerful; consequently the sun is bright to him, he has good thoughts, is happy in God. The next day the sky is overcast, — he feels languid, — he cannot use the cant terms of the professions, else he would call himself "a castaway," a child of wrath.

Q. Does this view involve falsehood and contradiction?

A. Yes; we are taught that we become God's children by believing that we are his children!

Q. How can you believe a thing that is not true, until you believe it?

A. This is reasoning in a circle. I see no way out of the difficulty in which this view involves us.

Q. So, according to them, baptism may be *nothing*, *may be* a falsehood?

A. Evidently: and I now understand the evils that must result in education, from this false view.

Q. How should a child be brought up?

A. It should be educated as God's child; not on *a perhaps*. You *are* "a child of God, a member of Christ, an inheritor of the kingdom of heaven." It should be brought to enter into the full meaning of the glorious privileges it was put into possession of at its baptism.

Q. Why are god-parents necessary?

A. In the baptism of an adult two things are necessary, — 1st. He must be accepted by God. 2nd. He must declare his belief in that; but, in the case of an infant, only one thing is necessary, — God's acceptation of him.

Q. Are sponsors *absolutely* necessary?

A. No; but most desirable. Take, for instance, a club, or a society. A man wishes to enter; he cannot do so until he is proposed and seconded by two of the members, who answer for him that he is fit to become a member.

In the same way it is necessary, for the sake of order, that the Church should require a guarantee, to guard itself against the introduction of improper persons; it is an ecclesiastical institution to keep it from confusion.

In adult baptism the person is required to declare his faith; but as the *infant* cannot express faith, repentance, love, charity (having, as yet, none of these feelings), in infant baptism sponsors are appointed to speak for them, and at Confirmation the children take these vows upon themselves.

Q. Why are we bound by their promise?

A. Because those obligations were on us from our *birth*. If they had promised I should be brought up as a nun, or a sailor, or bound to any particular trade, of course such promises would not be obligatory upon me; but my god-parents only *declare* that to which I am bound by an eternal obligation; they impose on me no *new* obligation.

Q. If they had not promised, would you not be bound to keep God's commandments?

A. Of course; though not done for him by the child's consent, sponsors make promise of what, by eternal laws, he is *bound* to do hereafter.

Q. Is this essential to the validity of baptism?

A. Not *essential*, but *desirable*, as I have shown before.

Q. Why is it desirable?

A. As an ecclesiastical act.

Q. What is the earthly use of baptism?

A. To mark Christians from those who are not Christians. Without *god-parents*, the Church would have no guarantee that its members would be brought up as Christians; just in the same manner, those men in a club who propose a new member promise that he shall not disgrace a society. The promise in either case is made *implicitly*, if not *explicitly*.

Q. Suppose if, hereafter, the child turns out badly, how far are the sponsors guilty?

A. If they had every reason to believe that his parents would bring him up well, they need scarcely inquire further; but if they did not know enough of them, and if the parents were careless, then the sponsors are to blame. Sponsorship was evidently instituted to serve very different purposes from what it does at present; the titled and rich are chosen, instead of Christian people, who would do their duty.

Q. What does the Church show?

A. The Church is a society of people existing on earth, to destroy evil, and keep its members in God's ways. This great society is continually replenished by fresh members, — an ecclesiastical necessity essential for the existence of a church.

Q. What is a state of salvation?

A. Saved already! you. *are* God's child. Born so, naturally, you may be ignorant of great principles, you may live below them, and refuse to avail youself of that which is yours. This is a revelation from God that you are such. The inheritance is yours! If you will not claim it, you may forfeit your rights, you may live as children of the world, of the flesh, and of the devil.

Q. What is to be said to such an one, who is living forgetful that he is "God's child?"

A. You are baptized. St. Paul looked on all such as Christians. Heb. iii. 14, "We are made partakers." 2 Cor. xiii. 5, "Know ye not that Jesus Christ is in you, if ye be not reprobates?" "Know ye not that your bodies are temples of the Holy Ghost?"

Q. What is the meaning here of the word reprobate?

A. Castaway.

Q. What does this great and beautiful doctrine of God prevent our doing with regard to others? What distinction does it forbid us to make?

A. It forbids us to say *we* are God's children, and *you* are of the world. No! erring, ignorant, if you will, but God's child, nevertheless, and our brother, though living below his privileges.

2dly. It destroys the possibility of vanity and exclusiveness; there is an end of all spiritual pride, for there is no merit of our own.

Q. How is this truth taught by Christ?

A. The beginning of His prayer represents it, — "*Our* Father." The universal Father. This simple, small word contains the essence of Christian faith.

Q. We talk of resisting "the world, the flesh, and the devil"; what do we mean by the *flesh?*

A. The flesh means all the desires that come through the channel of the senses, such as gluttony, idleness, love of ease, &c. In a desert island, we should be subject to the desires of the flesh.

Q. Are we to destroy, crush, crucify those desires?

A. Not to destroy, to ennoble them.

Q. When we say "we are fallen," what do we mean?

A. We mean that our will is disordered, that it does not take its proper place. There is within us a *mob* (as Plato has described it), a host, a crowd of smaller passions all striving for the mastery. Take for instance a watch with the regulator broken; all the wheels must go in disorder.

Q. Why is this view of our nature an important one?

A. Because if we look upon the desires as to be *extirpated*, we shall go out of the world with monks and hermits. This produces asceticism. Monks and hermits taught that the powers of the body were to be destroyed in order to ensure the destruction of the lusts; or, rather, the way in which they set about it effected the ruin of the physical energies, — such as starvation, loss of sleep, constant flagellation, &c.

There is no *goodness* in the extirpation of feeling.

Q. When are the baser parts of our nature ennobled?

A. When they are under the rule and guidance of our higher nature, — "This I say, then, walk in the Spirit, and ye shall not fulfil the lusts of the flesh."

Let Christ rule in you, and then these "baser parts" will be sanctified. Take, for instance, woman and her sphere: —

She ministers to the grosser wants of our nature,

preparing food, keeping the house clean, and many such offices, which, if they were done to gratify mere brutal appetites, would be mean and low, but if done in *love*, the services are transformed by the higher spirit into something *divine*.

The cup of cold water given in Christ's name, is the spirit of love and tenderness and pity.

Think of all these minor services as ruled and directed by love, by self-denial. Beasts, when ruled by the higher mind of man, become noble; they remain bestial if not ruled.

We are commanded, "Glorify God in your body." This was a root-thought of St. Paul's; you will find it almost everywhere in his writings; he has seized that great idea, "Let the baser and the meaner feelings be ennobled by the higher."

Let us understand this thoroughly, otherwise we shall take false views of human nature. Eating and drinking are not wrong. "Whether ye eat or drink, do all to the glory of God." The lusts of the flesh are not to be crushed, otherwise we shall form wrong conceptions of our nature.

Q. What is the *world* as distinguished from the flesh?

*A.**

Q. What are the dangers of the world?

A. Its spirit, tone, and temper working on us to do that which is *contrary* to the spirit of Christ.

Q. Are the world's maxims always the same?

A. In the days of chivalry, the world had a peculiar code of honor, and they made offences against that

* No answer, — but see Sermon XIII., Second Series.

code all in all. Pride was thought nothing of,—not reckoned as sin,—but if a man was a coward he was disgraced.

Q. How in this instance would the Christian and the man of the world be at issue?

A. If a man, for the sake of conscience, refused to fight, he would be condemned by the *world*, and pointed at.

Q. In our day, what is the worldly spirit, *par excellence?*

A. The love of money, the wish to get on in the world; the result of this is, in trade, false maxims, worldly ways of advancing, which are opposed to the Christian spirit of justice and fair-dealing.

Q. Again, what is the spirit of the world in the London season?

A. The love of pleasure,—frivolity,—money,—love of waste of time, &c. Whatever is opposed to the spirit of Christ is the spirit of the world. To render homage to rank and wealth, when in connection with what is false and unworthy and mean. Making these worldly distinctions the chief ends of our being, instead of renouncing the world, when it is opposed to the spirit of Christ.

Q. We have now seen what the lusts of the flesh and the world are; what is it to renounce the *devil?*

A. His works are the sins of our higher nature, spiritual offences,—such as envy, pride, anger, malice. The *solitary* sins are those of the *flesh*, and of the *devil.* The world's spirit does not recommend envy, or intemperance, or sloth. All the sins which attack our higher nature, which might come to us as *spirits*, if we had no bodies at all, and which assail us as *solitary* spirits, are sins of the *devil*.

Q. Distinguish them from sins of the flesh, and of the world.

A. To rebel against God; to bow down to wrong. They appeal to our pride, to our ambition. Our Saviour's answer was, — " Get thee behind me, Satan ! "

In the estimation of the world these are not condemned. Pride is admired. We are most ashamed of confessing our meaner sensual sins, — gluttony, &c., &c., the slavery to our lower passions. When we yield to them, we sink to a level with the brute; but when we yield to the sins of our *higher* nature, we are then on our way to become *devils*, — vitiating that which should lead to the highest in us.

Q. Let us consider now " all the articles of our Christian faith." How many creeds are there in the Church of England?

A. Three, — the Apostles', the Nicene, and the St. Athanasian.

Q. Why is a correct faith necessary to salvation?

A. Because what we believe becomes our character, forms part of us, and character *is* salvation or damnation; what we *are*, that is our *heaven* or our *hell*. Every sin bears its own punishment.

Q. If I doubt the doctrine of immortality, for instance, what effect will that have on my character?

A. It will narrow all our infinite desires to a span, and, almost inevitably, the passion or the temptation of the moment will conquer. It is true it did not affect the *Stoics* thus, for they held that right was better than wrong, and the sacrifice of evil inclinations was nobler than the indulgence of them, though they did not believe in the immortality of the soul. The noblest creed ever made out by human beings was that of the Stoics.

Q. From our creed, what sort of a religion is Christianity?

A. An historical religion; it deals with facts, not feelings; it *stands* upon facts. These things *have* been. Jesus *did* live. He suffered, died, rose again!

Q. What do you learn from your belief?

A. &c., &c., &c.

Q. What notion is here attached to the name of God?

A. That He is "*our Father.*" Homer calls Jupiter the *father* of gods and men, — *he* meant merely creator.

Q. What do we imply in the word *Father?*

A. ———

Q. What is there between the father and the child?

A. A likeness between them.

Q. In what respect? Not in form?

A. No; in character. Our *spiritual* relationship to God is a relation of likeness. Anger, love, &c. are not *different* in Him and in us. They are the same in kind in Him as in us, but in Him they are pure. These are words not perfectly correct, but they express the affinity between us and God, — that He feels *like us*, and *with us*. If He be only a cold abstraction, there can be no love, devotion, trust.

Q. What more is implied besides community of likeness?

A. That His love extends to *all*.

Q. Are any shut out?

A. Not any.

Q. Whom did *Christ* select as a brother?

A. A Samaritan, a heretic, an alien, a foreigner.

Q. What startled the Jews most in the teaching of Jesus?

A. His proving to them, by their own Scriptures, that the God of their fathers was not the God of the *Jews* only.

Instances brought forward: —

Elijah was sent to the widow of Sarepta, she being a Gentile; Elisha to Naaman the Syrian.

All were put on an equality with the Jews. Christ says, "In long-past times, your own history teaches you what I have come to proclaim, that *they* are God's children."

The parental character so manifested to the Jews was hateful to them. We, too, are as far as ever from the reception of that great truth. We too often treat servants, the poor, people of a different creed, as if they were not of the same flesh and blood, had not the same *Father.* Realize that *thoroughly,* — God our *Father!* "I believe in God the Father!"

I have said previously that Robertson's care of his Confirmation candidates was an individual care. The following letter, brief and ephemeral as it is, will yet show how that watchfulness was supported to the last, and with what wise thoughtfulness he endeavored to seize the moment of quietude in a girl's existence, that he might make it a moment of heavenly quietude, and a starting-place from whence a devoted life of sacred peace in Christ might spring: —

w

My dear ——:

I wish to write one line which will reach you the day before the Confirmation, partly to remind you that I shall be with you all, generally and individually, on the 27th at the appointed hour, and partly to advise you to be as much alone as possible the evening before. It is a valuable opportunity for pausing in the career of life, for taking breath as it were before you begin again, reviewing the past and considering the future. A few years ago and you were not:—a few more, and on this stage of life you will be no more. Much has been done, much is yet to be done in the interval. You are now at the outset of womanhood. Woman's duties, woman's strange and mixed destiny of suffering, feeling, and deep life is beginning. I pray that it may end as wisely and beautifully as it is now, I trust, beginning purely and gently. May God give you earnestness when you breathe your promise on Tuesday next! May He strengthen you to keep it through all life with unfaltering fidelity! May He bless you now, my dear young friend, and always!

APPENDIX V.

IT may interest some to read the inscriptions placed on Mr. Robertson's Tomb; on the Window in Brasenose College Chapel; and on the Bust in the Bodleian.
On his Tomb, by his Congregation and Friends:—

M. S.
The Reverend
FREDERICK WILLIAM ROBERTSON, M. A.,
Perpetual Curate of Trinity Chapel, Brighton,
Born 3rd of February, 1816;
Died 15th of August, 1853.

Honored as a Minister,
Beloved as a Man,
He awakened the holiest feelings
In poor and rich, in ignorant and learned;
Therefore is he lamented,
As their guide and comforter,
By many who, in the bond of brotherhood,
And in grateful remembrance,
Have erected this monument.
Glory to the Saviour, who was his all!

By the Working-men:—

TO THE REV. F. W. ROBERTSON, M. A.,
In grateful remembrance of his sympathy,
And in deep sorrow for their loss,
The members of the Mechanics' Institution,
And the working-men of Brighton,
Have placed this medallion
On their benefactor's tomb.
A.D. 1855.

APPENDIX V.

On the Memorial Window in Brasenose College Chapel:—

FREDERICO GULIELMO ROBERTSON,
ACADEMICI ET AMICI A. D. 1861.

Above, on a Scroll:—

TE DEUM LAUDAT PROPHETARUM LAUDABILIS NUMERUS.

On the Bust in the Bodleian Gallery:—

IN MEMORIAM FREDERICI GULIELMI ROBERTSON,
AMICI POSUERE.

NATUS 1816.
OBIIT 1853.

The following is a list of Subscribers to the Memorial Window in Brasenose College:—

The late Earl of Carlisle, K. G.
The Bishop of Winchester, D. D.
The Bishop of Oxford, D. D.
The Bishop of St. David's, D. D.
The Bishop of Lichfield, D. D.
The Bishop of Chester (Dr. Jacobson), D. D.
The Bishop of Tasmania, D. D.
The Bishop of Argyle and the Isles, D. D.
The Dean of St. Paul's, D. D., Brasenose College.
The Dean of Westminster, D. D.
The Dean of Christ Church, D. D.
The Dean of Ely, D. D.
The Principal of Brasenose, D. D.
Rev. B. H. Kennedy, D. D.
Rev. E. M. Goulburn, D. D.
Rev. H. M. Butler, D. D.
Rev. J. Caird, D. D.
Rev. J. Mitchinson, D. C. L.
Rev. Professor Thompson (Cambridge), M. A.
Rev. Professor Jowett, M. A.
Rev. Professor Price, M. A.
Rev. Professor Wall, M. A.
Rev. Professor Plumtre, M. A., Brasenose College.
Rev. Canon Smith, M. A.

APPENDIX V. 357

Rev. Canon Thicknesse, M. A., Brasenose College.
Rev. R. P. Graves, M. A.
Rev. J. Martineau, M. A.
Rev. F. D. Maurice, M. A.
Rev. H. Lewis, M. A.
Rev. J. Ll. Davies, M. A.
Rev. G. G. Bradley, M. A.
Rev. H. B. Wilson, M. A.
Rev. W. Berkley, M. A., late of Brasenose College.
Rev. H. Highton, M. A.
Rev. G. Butler, M. A.
Rev. G. S. Drew, M. A.
Rev. G. H. Ray, M. A.
Rev. L. Campbell, M. A.
Rev. J. B. Mayor, M. A.
Rev. C. W. Sandford, M. A.
Rev. H. Sandford, M. A.
Rev. A. S. Farrar, M. A.
Rev. W. Ince, M. A.
Rev. T. H. Sheppard, M. A.
Rev. W. Merry, M. A.
Rev. T. R. Halcomb, M. A., late of Brasenose College.
Rev. T. Fowler, M. A.
Rev. W. M. Wollaston, M. A.
Rev. F. Tozer, M. A.
Rev. C. Wickham, M. A.
Rev. E. Moore, M. A.
Rev. L. J. Harrison, M. A.
Rev. T. W. Norwood, M. A.
Rev. H. Ffolkes, M. A.
Rev. C. S. Overton, M. A.
The late Rev. E. C. Boyle, M. A.
Rev. T. W. Dowding, M. A.
Rev. A. T. Bonner, M. A.
Rev. H. Pearson, M. A.
Rev. C. L. Coldwell, M. A.
Rev. H. Fearon, M. A.
Rev. S. Clarke, M. A.
Rev. R. S. Cobbett, M. A.
Rev. J. Macnaught, M. A.
Rev. H. G. De Bunsen, M. A.
Rev. J. T. Barker, M. A.
Rev. Stopford A. Brooke, M. A.

Rev. W. Yates, M.A., Brasenose College.
Rev. T. H. R. Shand, M. A., Brasenose College.
Rev. A. Watson, M. A., Brasenose College.
Rev. B. Lambert, M. A., Brasenose College.
Rev. R. Stanley, M. A., Brasenose College.
Rev. W. K. Macrorie, M. A., Brasenose College.
Rev. G. H. Squire, M. A., Brasenose College.
Rev. C. B. Jackson, M. A., Brasenose College.
Rev. J. R. Rawdon, M. A., Brasenose College.
Rev. R. B. Leach, M. A., Brasenose College.
Rev. G. H. Barlow, M. A., Brasenose College.
Rev. J. T. Ryves, M. A., Brasenose College.
Rev. Charles Coldwell, B. A., Brasenose College.
Rev. W. M. Myers, B. A., Brasenose College.
Rev. F. G. Blackburne, B. A., Brasenose College.
Rev. H. J. Carpenter, B. A., Brasenose College.
Rev. T. G. Davies, B. A., Brasenose College.
Rev. C. J. Parkin, B. A., Brasenose College.
Rev. H. Syers, B. A., Brasenose College.
Rev. F. Bradshaw, B. A., Brasenose College.
Rev. G. A. How, B. A., Brasenose College.
Rev. S. C. Austen, B. A., Brasenose College.
Rev. B. Jackson, B. A., Brasenose College.
Rev. A. H. Blunt, B. A., Brasenose College.

APPENDIX V.

Rev. H. Allen, B. A.
Sir John Maxwell, Bart.
The late E. S. Cayley, Esq., M.P.
Alfred Tennyson, D. C. L.
John Ruskin, M. A.
Professor Goldwin Smith, M. A.
Professor Conington, M. A.
Professor Acland, M. A.
Professor Rolleston, M. A.
Herbert Fisher, Esq., M. A.
J. S. Philpotts, Esq., M. A.
A. Vansittart, Esq., M. A.
W. L. Newman, Esq., M. A.
H. E. Oakley, Esq., M. A.
G. Griffith, Esq., M. A.
J. R. Magrath, Esq., M. A.
Kenelm Digby, Esq., M. A.
F. Daubeny, Esq., M. A., Brasenose College.
A. Holt-White, Esq., M. A., Brasenose College.
W. Harrison, Esq., M. A., Brasenose College.
W. E. Gumbleton, Esq., B. A., Brasenose College.
E. J. Townley, Esq., B. A., Brasenose College.
F. Barker, Esq., B. A., Brasenose College.
F. Brandt, Esq., B. A., Brasenose College.
W. L. Stonehouse, Esq., B. A., Brasenose College.
A. Playne, Esq., B. A., Brasenose College.
J. C. Danbury, Esq., B. A., Brasenose College.
J. R. Waddelow, Esq., B. A., Brasenose College.
R. Shepherd, Esq., B. A., Brasenose College.
A. M. Lipscombe, Esq., B. A., Brasenose College.
R. J. Crosthwaite, Esq., B. A., Brasenose College.
H. T. Allen, Esq., B. A., Brasenose College.
C. A. Houghton, Esq., B. A.

A. E. Dobbs, Esq., B. A.
C. S. Hannington, Esq.
W. B. Dawkins, Esq., B. A., F. G. S.
Dr. Hall.
Dr. Allen.
Dr. Acworth.
H. Crabb Robinson, Esq.
A. Macmillan, Esq.
F. Symonds, Esq.
T. R. Jefferson, Esq.
A. Lockyer, Esq., Melbourne.
W. Mansell, Esq.
G. W. King, Esq.
C. G. Blackadder, Esq.
H. L. Newman, Esq.
Henry Willett, Esq.
J. Ray, Esq.
Reginald E. Lewin, Esq.
F. Monro, Esq.
H. A. James, Esq.
M. Ricardo, Esq.
Henry S. King, Esq.
R. Mushet, Esq.
R. H. Fielden, Esq.
E. B. Ray, Esq.
F. Robertson, Esq.
A. Rimington, Esq.
Lady Henly.
Hon. Mrs. Vansittart.
Mrs. Norris.
Mrs. Grahame.
Mrs. Hinton.
Mrs. Burgess.
Mrs. Ridley.
Mrs. J. Pocock.
Mrs. Wrench.
Mrs. Myers.
Mrs. Dalzell.
Mrs. Huish.
Miss Russell.
Miss Howard.
Miss Napier.
Miss Downes.
Miss Hutchinson.
Miss Ellis.
Miss Wolfe.
Miss K. Skinner.

Hon. Secretaries.

Rev. CHARLES COLDWELL, B. A., Hulmian Exhibitioner, of Brasenose College, Oxford.
THOMAS ALLEN, Esq., M.D., 23 Regency Square, Brighton.
HENRY S. KING, Esq., 65 Cornhill, London, E. C.
ALEXANDER MACMILLAN, Esq., Trinity Street, Cambridge.
Rev. A. H. BLUNT, B. A., Brasenose College.

THE END.

Cambridge : Stereotyped and Printed by Welch, Bigelow, & Co.

www.ingramcontent.com/pod-product-compliance
Lightning Source LLC
Chambersburg PA
CBHW020316240426
43673CB00039B/820